Practice*Planners*®

Homework Planners feature dozens of behaviorally based, ready-to-use assignments that are designed for use between sessions, as well as a disk or CD-ROM (Microsoft Word) containing all of the assignments—allowing you to customize them to suit your unique client needs

❑ Brief Couples Therapy Homework Planner ....978-0-471-29511-2 / $55.00
❑ Child Psychotherapy Homework Planner, Second Edition........................978-0-471-78534-7 / $55.00
❑ Child Therapy Activity and Homework Planner ....978-0-471-25684-7 / $55.00
❑ Adolescent Psychotherapy Homework Planner, Second Edition ....978-0-471-78537-8 / $55.00
❑ Addiction Treatment Homework Planner, Third Edition............................978-0-471-77461-7 / $55.00
❑ Brief Employee Assistance Homework Planner ....978-0-471-38088-7 / $55.00
❑ Brief Family Therapy Homework Planner...978-0-471-38512-7 / $55.00
❑ Grief Counseling Homework Planner ....978-0-471-43318-7 / $55.00
❑ Divorce Counseling Homework Planner ....978-0-471-43319-4 / $55.00
❑ Group Therapy Homework Planner ....978-0-471-41822-1 / $55.00
❑ School Counseling and School Social Work Homework Planner ....978-0-471-09114-1 / $55.00
❑ Adolescent Psychotherapy Homework Planner II ....978-0-471-27493-3 / $55.00
❑ Adult Psychotherapy Homework Planner, Second Edition ....978-0-471-76343-7 / $55.00
❑ Parenting Skills Homework Planner...978-0-471-48182-9 / $55.00

Progress Notes Planners contain complete prewritten progress notes for each presenting problem in the companion Treatment Planners.

❑ The Adult Psychotherapy Progress Notes Planner....................................978-0-471-76344-4 / $55.00
❑ The Adolescent Psychotherapy Progress Notes Planner ....978-0-471-78538-5 / $55.00
❑ The Severe and Persistent Mental Illness Progress Notes Planner..........978-0-471-21986-6 / $55.00
❑ The Child Psychotherapy Progress Notes Planner....................................978-0-471-78536-1 / $55.00
❑ The Addiction Progress Notes Planner..978-0-471-73253-2 / $55.00
❑ The Couples Psychotherapy Progress Notes Planner ....978-0-471-27460-5 / $55.00
❑ The Family Therapy Progress Notes Planner..978-0-471-48443-1 / $55.00

Client Education Handout Planners contain elegantly designed handouts that can be printed out from the enclosed CD-ROM and provide information on a wide range of psychological and emotional disorders and life skills issues. Use as patient literature, handouts at presentations, and aids for promoting your mental health practice.

❑ Adult Client Education Handout Planner ....978-0-471-20232-5 / $55.00
❑ Child and Adolescent Client Education Handout Planner.........................978-0-471-20233-2 / $55.00
❑ Couples and Family Client Education Handout Planner............................978-0-471-20234-9 / $55.00

Name_____
Affiliation_____
Address_____
City/State/Zip_____
Phone/Fax_____
E-mail_____
❑ Check enclosed   ❑ Visa   ❑ MasterCard   ❑ American Express
Card #_____
Expiration Date _____
Signature _____

Add $5 shipping for first book, $3 for each additional book. Please add your local sales tax to all orders. Prices subject to change without notice.

To order by phone in the US:
Call toll free 1-877-762-2974

Online: www.practiceplanners.wiley.com

Mail this order form to:
John Wiley & Sons, Attn: J. Knott,
111 River Street, Hoboken, NJ 07030

TheraScribe®

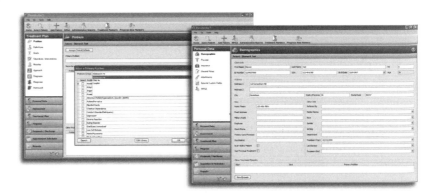

WILEY CONTINUING EDUCATION
FOR BEHAVIORAL HEALTH PROFESSIONALS
BOOK-BASED ONLINE LEARNING

Earn Accredited Continuing Education Online and On Time

NOW YOU CAN EARN CONTINUING EDUCATION CREDITS THROUGH OUR NEW BOOK-BASED, ONLINE EDUCATION PARTNERSHIP.

Our publications provide high quality continuing education to meet the licensing renewal needs of busy professionals like yourself. Best of all, you can complete this continuing education when and where you choose! Simply read the book, take the online test associated with the book and as soon as you have passed the test and completed the evaluation, you can print out your CE credit certificate— a valuable benefit for those facing imminent license renewal deadlines.

Clinical book content and the associated assessments meet the requirements of many state licensing boards and national accreditation bodies such as:

- American Psychological Association
- Association of Social Work Boards
- National Board of Certified Counselors
- National Association of Alcohol and Drug Abuse Counselors
- American Nurses Credentialing Center

Topics covered include:

- Addiction and Recovery
- Forensic Psychology
- Psychological Assessment
- School Psychology
- Therapy and Counseling

Each available book has a companion online cou that consists of the Learning Objectives, post-test course evaluation, so you can take them from anywh you have Internet access. Likewise, you can take th courses at your own pace, any time of the day night—whenever you have the time.

IT'S EASY TO GET STARTED!
Visit us online today at
www.wiley.com/go/ceuLearn
to find out how.

WILEY
Now you know.
wiley.com

*Wiley CE is provided through our partnership with Essential Learning.

The Suicide and Homicide Risk Assessment & Prevention Treatment Planner

Practice*Planners*® Series

Treatment Planners

The Complete Adult Psychotherapy Treatment Planner, Third Edition
The Child Psychotherapy Treatment Planner, Third Edition
The Adolescent Psychotherapy Treatment Planner, Third Edition
The Addiction Treatment Planner, Second Edition
The Continuum of Care Treatment Planner
The Couples Psychotherapy Treatment Planner
The Employee Assistance Treatment Planner
The Pastoral Counseling Treatment Planner
The Older Adult Psychotherapy Treatment Planner
The Behavioral Medicine Treatment Planner
The Group Therapy Treatment Planner
The Gay and Lesbian Psychotherapy Treatment Planner
The Family Therapy Treatment Planner
The Severe and Persistent Mental Illness Treatment Planner
The Mental Retardation and Developmental Disability Treatment Planner
The Social Work and Human Services Treatment Planner
The Crisis Counseling and Traumatic Events Treatment Planner
The Personality Disorders Treatment Planner
The Rehabilitation Psychology Treatment Planner
The Special Education Treatment Planner
The Juvenile Justice and Residential Care Treatment Planner
The School Counseling and School Social Work Treatment Planner
The Sexual Abuse Victim and Sexual Offender Treatment Planner
The Probation and Parole Treatment Planner
The Psychopharmacology Treatment Planner
The Speech-Language Pathology Treatment Planner
The Suicide and Homicide Risk Assessment & Prevention Treatment Planner
The College Student Counseling Treatment Planner

Progress Note Planners

The Child Psychotherapy Progress Notes Planner, Second Edition
The Adolescent Psychotherapy Progress Notes Planner, Second Edition
The Adult Psychotherapy Progress Notes Planner, Second Edition
The Addiction Progress Notes Planner
The Severe and Persistent Mental Illness Progress Notes Planner
The Couples Psychotherapy Progress Notes Planner

Homework Planners

Brief Therapy Homework Planner
Brief Couples Therapy Homework Planner
Brief Adolescent Therapy Homework Planner
Brief Child Therapy Homework Planner
Brief Employee Assistance Homework Planner
Brief Family Therapy Homework Planner
Grief Counseling Homework Planner
Group Therapy Homework Planner
Divorce Counseling Homework Planner
School Counseling and School Social Work Homework Planner
Child Therapy Activity and Homework Planner
Addiction Treatment Homework Planner, Second Edition
Adolescent Psychotherapy Homework Planner II
Adult Psychotherapy Homework Planner

Client Education Handout Planners

Adult Client Education Handout Planner
Child and Adolescent Client Education Handout Planner
Couples and Family Client Education Handout Planner

Documentation Sourcebooks

The Clinical Documentation Sourcebook, Second Edition
The Forensic Documentation Sourcebook
The Psychotherapy Documentation Primer
The Chemical Dependence Treatment Documentation Sourcebook
The Clinical Child Documentation Sourcebook
The Couple and Family Clinical Documentation Sourcebook
The Continuum of Care Clinical Documentation Sourcebook

Complete Planners

The Complete Depression Treatment and Homework Planner
The Complete Anxiety Treatment and Homework Planner

PracticePlanners®

Arthur E. Jongsma, Jr., Series Editor

The Suicide and Homicide Risk Assessment & Prevention Treatment Planner

Jack Klott

Arthur E. Jongsma, Jr.

WILEY

JOHN WILEY & SONS, INC.

Library of Congress Cataloging-in-Publication Data:

ISBN 0-471-46631-X

Printed in the United States of America.

10   9   8   7   6   5   4

CONTENTS

PRACTICE*PLANNERS*® SERIES PREFACE

The practice of psychotherapy has a dimension that did not exist 30, 20, or even 15 years ago—accountability. Treatment programs, public agencies, clinics, and even group and solo practitioners must now justify the treatment of patients to outside review entities that control the payment of fees. This development has resulted in an explosion of paperwork. Clinicians must now document what has been done in treatment, what is planned for the future, and what the anticipated outcomes of the interventions are. The books and software in this Practice*Planners* series are designed to help practitioners fulfill these documentation requirements efficiently and professionally.

The Practice*Planners* series is growing rapidly. It now includes not only the original *The Complete Adult Psychotherapy Treatment Planner,* Third Edition, *The Child Psychotherapy Treatment Planner,* Third Edition, and *The Adolescent Psychotherapy Treatment Planner,* Third Edition, but also Treatment Planners targeted to specialty areas of practice, including: addictions, juvenile justice/residential care, couples therapy, employee assistance, behavioral medicine, therapy with older adults, pastoral counseling, family therapy, group therapy, psychopharmacology, neuropsychology, therapy with gays and lesbians, special education, school counseling, probation and parole, therapy with sexual abuse victims and offenders, and more.

Several of the Treatment Planner books now have companion Progress Notes Planners (e.g., Adult, Adolescent, Child, Addictions, Severe and Persistent Mental Illness, Couples). More of these planners that provide a menu of progress statements that elaborate on the client's symptom presentation and the provider's therapeutic intervention are in production. Each Progress Notes Planner statement is directly integrated with "Behavioral Definitions" and "Therapeutic Interventions" items from the companion Treatment Planner.

The list of therapeutic Homework Planners is also growing from the original Brief Therapy Homework for Adults to Adolescent, Child, Couples, Group, Family, Addictions, Divorce, Grief, Employee Assistance, and School Counseling/School Social Work Homework Planners. Each of these books can be used alone or in conjunction with their companion Treatment Planner. Homework assignments are designed around each presenting problem (e.g., Anxiety, Depression, Chemical Dependence, Anger

Management, Panic, Eating Disorders) that is the focus of a chapter in its corresponding Treatment Planner.

Client Education Handout Planners, a new branch in the series, provide brochures and handouts to help educate and inform adult, child, adolescent, couples, and family clients on a myriad of mental health issues, as well as life skills techniques. The list of presenting problems for which information is provided mirrors the list of presenting problems in the Treatment Planner of the title similar to that of the Handout Planner. Thus, the problems for which educational material is provided in the *Child and Adolescent Client Education Handout Planner* reflect the presenting problems listed in *The Child* and *The Adolescent Psychotherapy Treatment Planner* books. Handouts are included on CD-ROMs for easy printing and are ideal for use in waiting rooms, at presentations, as newsletters, or as information for clients struggling with mental illness issues.

In addition, the series also includes Thera*Scribe*®, the latest version of the popular treatment planning, clinical record-keeping software. Thera*Scribe* allows the user to import the data from any of the Treatment Planner, Progress Notes Planner, or Homework Planner books into the software's expandable database. Then the point-and-click method can create a detailed, neatly organized, individualized, and customized treatment plan along with optional integrated progress notes and homework assignments.

Adjunctive books, such as *The Psychotherapy Documentation Primer*, and *Clinical, Forensic, Child, Couples and Family, Continuum of Care*, and *Chemical Dependence Documentation Sourcebook* contain forms and resources to aid the mental health practice management. The goal of the series is to provide practitioners with the resources they need to provide high-quality care in the era of accountability—or, to put it simply, we seek to help you spend more time on patients, and less time on paperwork.

ARTHUR E. JONGSMA, JR.
Series Editor

ACKNOWLEDGMENTS

When Dr. Art Jongsma and I first met to discuss the concept of the *Suicide and Homicide Risk Assessment & Prevention Treatment Planner*, I felt a significant fear about my ability to complete the task. It has only been with his guidance that I was able to complete this work. I remain deeply indebted to him for not only the opportunity, but also the patient support he has provided during this effort. Our manuscript manager, Jennifer Byrne, also has been a major contributor to this final product; and to her I give a sincere thank you!

I began my study of the complexity of suicide in 1976, when I was assigned the duty of developing a Suicide Prevention Program for the Veteran's Administration Hospital in Battle Creek, Michigan. With the support of that facility, I was exposed to an abundance of trainings and seminars to develop and broaden my knowledge base of this most significant of human tragedies. During that process I have met many of the leaders in the study of suicide in our society, and to all of them I want to express my most sincere thanks. Although I have met many of them, I am sure they hardly know me. They all made those moment-in-time, cameo appearances that shaped my thinking on the nature of the suicide and homicide act. Dr. Edwin Shneidman spoke to me about the complexity of suicide and encouraged me always to be searching for the real issue of pain. Dr. David Clark impressed on me the value of specific, labor-intensive epidemiology to distinguish certain cultural, psychological, and gender issues that individualize the suicide populations. Dr. John McIntosh gave me insight into the suicidal crisis of the elderly. And, finally, Dr. Ron Maris greeted me with personal warmth as a fellow student in the pursuit of the truth about violent behavior. To all of these men I feel a sincere sense of gratitude for their insights.

Finally, I thank the untold numbers of men and women I have had the privilege of meeting over the past 30 years; those men, women, teens, and children who have led me to where they hurt and gently have guided me as to how to help them.

J.K.

INTRODUCTION

PLANNER FOCUS

The Suicide and Homicide Risk Assessment & Prevention Treatment Planner acknowledges and respects the challenging complexity of these tragic human behaviors. Edwin Shneidman (*Definition of Suicide,* 1985 and *The Suicidal Mind,* 1996), icon of the study of suicide in our society, claimed years ago that there are only two questions the therapist need ask the suicidal or homicidal client: "Where do you hurt" and "How can I help you?" The structure of this *Treatment Planner* is based on that simple and profound approach. In the 27 chapters of *The Suicide and Homicide Risk Assessment & Prevention Treatment Planner,* the reader will find a focus not on a diagnosis or condition but on the person. Each individual will come to the therapist's table with his or her own stressors that result in unbearable psychological agony. The tragic suicides of the 19-year-old college student and the 52-year-old homeless alcohol abuser need separate examination and treatment focus. While their outcomes were similar, the pathways were dramatically different. It is common today to abandon the exploration of the client's unique personal experiences of pain. Clinicians rely, instead, on standardized and boilerplate risk-assessments and treatment plans that put all suicidal or homicidal clients into one category. The complexity of each suicidal client fails to be respected.

Therefore, the first task for the therapist is to know the client and discover the unique nature of his or her hurt. With that in mind, the initial section of each chapter of this *Treatment Planner* is the risk-assessment phase. The examiner must pursue a thorough examination of the individual variables that put a client in harms way for suicidal or homicidal activity. The reader will find that in each of the 27 chapters the assessment section will note idiosyncratic factors, consistent with current research, that contribute to the suicide or homicide intent in each population.

Men and women who seek the help of counselors and therapists do so because the pain they are experiencing has escalated to an unbearable level and, therefore, they feel out of control. Ironically, suicide, and in some circumstances assaultive and homicidal behaviors becomes a problem-solving strategy for those seemingly unbearable psychological agonies. The initial stage of the therapy alliance is designed to provide hope. That hope will be nurtured by allowing the client to sense, with the therapist's help, alternatives to suicide or homicide as methods of managing their pain. The key issue in that process is the term *management.* The elimination of pain is the ultimate goal of the suicide or homicide intent. The therapist is encouraged to facilitate the client's insight that psychological turmoil is an unavoidable human experience. Increased feelings of self-worth and self-confidence serve to enhance the capacity to safely cope with the painful experiences that life has to offer. This is the goal of therapy.

Edwin Shneidman urges that the priority in treatment is to identify and reduce the level of turmoil, or "perturbation," that the suicidal or homicidal client feels as unbearable. This can be done in a variety of ways. One common approach is to evaluate the client for an underlying mental illness and introduce a medication program. However, there are traps here. The current environment appears too eager to reduce all maladaptive human behaviors to biochemical mayhem. An example is depression. Sadly, we are treating suicidal and homicidal intents by introducing the clients to medication. The problem is that we stop there. We fail to respect that, while any medication program has an important place in a treatment plan, it cannot be the *only* focus. Depression and other mental illnesses play an important role in the multidimensional malaise correlated to suicidal and homicidal behaviors, but we cannot accept a suicide or violence treatment plan that is nothing more than an effort to diminish the symptoms of mental illness through a prescription. We also need to examine the client's coping skill deficits and historical pattern of maladaptive problem solving. More often than not, the therapist will find the client to be deficient in this area. Therefore, we teach. We develop a plan that identifies the most hurtful conditions currently felt by the client and we help them to learn individually formulated coping strategies. We give them alternatives to implementing suicide and homicide as problem-solving techniques; therefore, we provide hope.

An important piece in this teaching effort is to respect that our clients come to us with historical *baggage.* These are personality traits that are basically developed in early childhood but, later in life, become personal vulnerabilities and hinder the client's efforts to effectively cope with life's tragedies. An example is the role of perfectionism in the client's personality. With this trait comes the inability to cope with self-identified failures. Perfectionism is usually developed through early childhood experiences in which the child attempts to meet the needs of a demanding love object. In adulthood, however, perfection can become a vulnerability and a significant impediment to healthy coping. Our teaching efforts with this client, therefore, may be significantly challenged if we don't spend some effort revealing this issue to the client and working toward a resolution.

Finally, *The Suicide and Homicide Risk Assessment & Prevention Treatment Planner* addresses special issues for healing. Encouraging such issues as acculturation efforts, social cohesion, and spiritual enhancement can play a vital role in the overall strategy of allowing the client to live a full, if not challenging, life.

Our goal in the development of *The Suicide and Homicide Risk Assessment & Prevention Treatment Planner* is to discourage boilerplate treatment plans for suicidal and homicidal populations. Therefore, we encourage the development of treatment strategies that respect the individual client and the special cultural, environmental, medical, actuarial, gender, and psychiatric issues he or she presents, which contributes to the wish to die or to kill. The *Treatment Planner* was developed with a focus on current research and studies on each of the 27 populations noted. The reader will note many commonalities among those populations. However, their differences are more important. This *Treatment Planner* is designed to help you focus on, assess, and treat the idiosyncrasies that the client presents that have precipitated a crisis.

HISTORICAL BACKGROUND

Since the early 1960s, formalized treatment planning has gradually become a vital aspect of the entire health-care delivery system, whether it is treatment related to physical health, mental health, child welfare, or substance abuse. What started in the medical sector in the 1960s spread into the mental health sector in the 1970s as clinics, psychiatric hospitals, agencies, and so on, began to seek accreditation from bodies such as the Joint Commission on Accreditation of Healthcare Organizations (JCAHO) to qualify for third-party reimbursements. For most treatment providers to achieve accreditation, they had to begin developing and strengthening their documentation skills. Previously, most mental health and substance abuse treatment providers had, at best, a bare-bones plan that looked similar for most of the individuals they treated. Clients were uncertain about what they were trying to attain in mental health treatment. Goals were vague, objectives were nonexistent, and interventions were applied equally to all clients. Outcome data were not measurable, and neither the treatment provider nor the client knew exactly when treatment was complete. The initial development of rudimentary treatment plans made inroads toward addressing some of these issues.

With the advent of managed care in the 1980s, treatment planning has taken on even more importance. Managed care systems *insist* that clinicians move rapidly from assessment of the problem to the formulation and implementation of the treatment plan. The goal of most managed care companies is to expedite the treatment process by prompting the client and treatment provider to focus on identifying and changing behavioral problems as quickly as possible. Treatment plans must be specific as to the problems and interventions, individualized to meet the client's needs and goals, with measurable milestones that can be used to chart the client's progress. Pressure from third-party payors, accrediting agencies, and other outside parties has therefore increased the need for clinicians to produce effective, high-quality treatment plans in a short time frame. However, many mental health providers have little experience in treatment plan development. Our purpose in writing this book is to clarify, simplify, and accelerate the treatment planning process for clients who are in danger of suicidal or homicidal activity.

TREATMENT PLAN UTILITY

Detailed written treatment plans can benefit not only the client, therapist, treatment team, insurance community, and treatment agency but also the overall psychotherapy profession. A written plan stipulates the issues that are the focus of the treatment process. It is very easy for both provider and client to lose sight of what the issues were that brought the client into therapy. The treatment plan is a guide that structures the focus of the therapeutic contract. Since issues can change as therapy progresses, the treatment plan must be viewed as a dynamic document that can and must be updated to reflect any major change of problem, definition, goal, objective, or intervention.

Clients and therapists benefit from the treatment plan that focuses on outcomes. Behaviorally stated, measurable objectives clearly focus the treatment endeavor. Clients no longer have to wonder what therapy is trying to accomplish. Clear objectives also allow the client to channel effort into specific changes that will lead to the long-term goal of problem resolution. Therapy is no longer a vague contract to just talk honestly and openly about emotions and cognitions until the client feels better. Both client and therapist are concentrating on specifically stated objectives using specific interventions.

Treatment plans aid providers by forcing them to think analytically and critically about therapeutic interventions that are best suited for objective attainment for the client. Therapists were traditionally trained to "follow the client," but now a formalized plan is the guide to the treatment process. The therapist must give advance attention to the technique, approach, assignment, or cathartic target that will form the basis for interventions.

Clinicians benefit when clear documentation of treatment provides a measure of added protection from possible client litigation. Malpractice suits are increasing in frequency, and insurance premiums are soaring. The first line of defense against allegations is a complete clinical record detailing the treatment process. A written, individualized, formal treatment plan that is the guideline for the therapeutic process, that has been reviewed and signed by the client, and that is coupled with problem-oriented progress notes is a powerful defense against exaggerated or false claims.

A well-crafted treatment plan that clearly stipulates presenting problems and intervention strategies facilitates the treatment process carried out by team members in inpatient, residential, or intensive outpatient settings. Good communication between team members about what approach is being implemented and who is responsible for which intervention is critical. Team meetings to discuss client treatment used to be the only source of interaction between providers; often, therapeutic conclusions or assignments were not recorded. Now, a thorough treatment plan stipulates in writing the details of objectives and the varied interventions (pharmacologic, milieu, group therapy, didactic, recreational, individual therapy, etc.) and who will implement them.

Treatment agencies or institutions are looking for ways to increase the quality and uniformity of the documentation in the clinical record. A standardized, written treatment plan with problem definitions, goals, objectives, and interventions in every client's file enhances that uniformity of documentation, easing the task of record reviewers inside and outside the agency. Outside reviewers, such as JCAHO, insist on documentation that clearly outlines assessment, treatment, progress, and termination status.

The demand for accountability from third-party payors and health maintenance organizations (HMOs) is partially satisfied by a written treatment plan and complete progress notes. More and more managed care systems are demanding a structured therapeutic contract that has measurable objectives and explicit interventions. Clinicians cannot avoid this move toward being accountable to those outside the treatment process.

The psychotherapy profession stands to benefit from the use of more precise, measurable objectives to evaluate success in mental health treatment. With the advent of detailed treatment plans, outcome data can be more easily collected for interventions that are effective in achieving specific goals.

DEVELOPING A TREATMENT PLAN

The process of developing a treatment plan involves a logical series of steps that build on each other much like constructing a house. The foundation of any effective treatment plan is the data gathered in a thorough biopsychosocial assessment. As the client presents himself or herself for treatment, the clinician must sensitively listen to and understand what the client struggles with in terms of family of origin issues, current stressors, emotional status, social network, physical health, coping skills, interpersonal conflicts, self-esteem, and so on. Assessment data may be gathered from a social history, physical exam, clinical interview, psychological testing, or contact with a client's guardian, social service worker, and school personnel. The integration of the data by the clinician or the multidisciplinary treatment team members is critical for understanding the client, as is an awareness of the basis of the client's struggle. We have identified six specific steps for developing an effective treatment plan based on the assessment data.

Step One: Population Selection

Although the client may initially present as belonging to a specifically designated population, the clinician may have to explore special issues that pertain to other populations. This will reveal other problems on which to focus the treatment process. As an example, an Adolescent Male presents with suicidal impulse. It may be discovered, however, that some of the contributing issues of his intent are gender identity concerns that may be included in the Gay/Lesbian/Bisexual chapter. Therefore, the clinician will establish a *primary* focus that will attend to those concerns established in the assessment process that appear to have the highest correlation to a specific population. However, that same youth may be also well served by creating flexibility in the treatment plan to include problems from other populations.

At all times, it is essential to include opinions from the client on his or her prioritization of treatment issues which appear to be at the core of the suicide or homicide intent. A client's motivation to participate in and cooperate with the treatment process depends on the degree to which treatment addresses his or her greatest needs.

Step Two: Problem Definition

Each client presents with unique nuances as to how a problem behaviorally reveals itself in his or her life. Therefore, each population that is selected for treatment focus requires a specific definition about how it is evidenced in the particular client. The symptom pattern should be associated with diagnostic criteria and codes such as those found in the *Diagnostic and Statistical Manual* or the *International Classification of Diseases (DSM-IV)*. The *Planner*, following the pattern established by

DSM-IV, offers such behaviorally specific definition statements to choose from or to serve as a model for your own personally crafted statements. You will find several behavior symptoms or syndromes listed that may characterize one of the 27 presenting populations.

Step Three: Goal Development

The next step in treatment plan development is that of setting broad goals for the resolution of the target population. These statements need not be crafted in measurable terms but can be global, long-term goals that indicate a desired positive outcome to the treatment procedures. The *Planner* suggests several possible goal statements for each population, but one statement is all that is required in a treatment plan.

Step Four: Objective Construction

In contrast to long-term goals, objectives must be stated in behaviorally measurable language. It must be clear when the client has achieved the established objectives; therefore, vague, subjective objectives are not acceptable. Review agencies (e.g., JCAHO), HMOs, and managed care organizations insist that psychological treatment outcomes be measurable. The objectives presented in this *Planner* are designed to meet this demand for accountability. Numerous alternatives are presented to allow construction of a variety of treatment plan possibilities for the same presenting problem. The clinician must exercise professional judgment as to which objectives are most appropriate for a given client.

Each objective should be developed as a step toward attaining the broad treatment goal. In essence, objectives can be thought of as a series of steps that, when completed, will result in the achievement of the long-term goal. There should be at least two objectives for each problem, but the clinician may construct as many as are necessary for goal achievement. Target attainment dates should be listed for each objective. New objectives should be added to the plan as the individual's treatment progresses. When all the necessary objectives have been achieved, the client should have resolved the target problem successfully.

Step Five: Intervention Creation

Interventions are the actions of the clinician designed to help the client complete the objectives. There should be at least one intervention for every objective. If the client does not accomplish the objective after the initial intervention, new interventions should be added to the plan.

Interventions should be selected on the basis of the client's needs and the treatment provider's full therapeutic repertoire. *The Suicide and Homicide Risk Assessment & Prevention Treatment Planner* contains interventions from a broad range of therapeutic approaches, including cognitive, dynamic, behavioral, multisystemic, pharmacologic, family-oriented, and patient-centered therapy. Other interventions may be written by the provider to reflect his or her own training and experience. The addition of new problems, definitions, goals, objectives, and interventions to those found in the *Planner* is encouraged because doing so adds to the database for future reference and use.

Some suggested interventions listed in the *Planner* refer to specific books that can be assigned to the client for adjunctive bibliotherapy. Appendix A contains a full bibliotherapy reference list. When a book is used as part of an intervention plan, it should be reviewed with the client after it is read, enhancing the application of the content of the book to the specific client's circumstances. For further information about self-help books, mental health professionals may wish to consult *The Authoritative Guide to Self-Help Books* (2003) by Santrock, Minnett, and Campbell (The Guilford Press, New York, NY).

A list of resources is also provided for the professional provider in Appendix B. These references are meant to elaborate on the methods suggested in some of the chapters.

Assigning an intervention to a specific provider is most relevant if a client is being treated by a team in an inpatient, residential, or intensive outpatient setting. Within these settings, personnel other than the primary clinician may be responsible for implementing a specific intervention. Review agencies require that the responsible provider's name be stipulated for every intervention.

Step Six: Diagnosis Determination

The determination of an appropriate diagnosis is based on an evaluation of the client's complete clinical presentation. The clinician must compare the behavioral, cognitive, emotional, and interpersonal symptoms that the client presents to the criteria for diagnosis of a mental illness condition as described in *DSM-IV.* The issue of differential diagnosis is admittedly a difficult one that research has shown to have rather low interrater reliability. Mental health professionals have also been trained to think more in terms of maladaptive behavior than disease labels. In spite of these factors, diagnosis is a reality that exists in the world of mental health care and it is a necessity for third party reimbursement. (However, recently, managed care agencies are more interested in behavioral indices that are exhibited by the client than the actual diagnosis.) It is the clinician's thorough knowledge of *DSM-IV* criteria and a complete understanding of the client assessment data that contribute to the most reliable, valid diagnosis. An accurate assessment of behavioral indicators will also contribute to more effective treatment planning.

HOW TO USE THIS PLANNER

Our experience has taught us that learning the skills of effective treatment plan writing can be a tedious and difficult process for many clinicians. It is more stressful to try to develop this expertise when under the pressure of increased client load and short time frames placed on clinicians today by managed care systems. The documentation demands can be overwhelming when we must move quickly from assessment to treatment plan to progress notes. In the process, we must be very specific about how and when objectives can be achieved, and how progress is exhibited in each client. *The Suicide and Homicide Risk Assessment & Prevention Treatment Planner* was developed as a tool to aid clinicians in writing a treatment plan in a rapid manner that is clear, specific, and highly individualized according to the following progression:

1. Choose one presenting population (Step One) you have identified through your assessment process. Locate the corresponding page number for that problem in the *Planner*'s table of contents.
2. Select two or more of the listed behavioral definitions (Step Two) and record them in the appropriate section on your treatment plan form. Feel free to add your own defining statement if you determine that your client's behavioral manifestation of the identified problem is not listed. (Note that while our design for treatment planning is vertical, it will work equally well on plan forms formatted horizontally.)
3. Select a single long-term goal (Step Three) and again write the selection, exactly as it is written in the *Planner* or in some appropriately modified form, in the corresponding area of your own form.
4. Review the listed objectives for this population and select the ones that you judge to be clinically indicated for your client (Step Four). Remember, it is recommended that you select at least two objectives for each problem. Add a target date or the number of sessions allocated for the attainment of each objective.
5. Choose relevant interventions (Step Five). The *Planner* offers suggested interventions related to each objective in the parentheses following the objective statement. But do not limit yourself to those interventions. The entire list is eclectic and may offer options that are more tailored to your theoretical approach or preferred way of working with clients. Also, just as with definitions, goals, and

objectives, there is space allowed for you to enter your own interventions into the *Planner.* This allows you to refer to these entries when you create a plan around this problem in the future. You will have to assign responsibility to a specific person for implementation of each intervention if a multidisciplinary team is carrying out the treatment.

6. Several *DSM-IV* diagnoses are listed at the end of each chapter that are commonly associated with a client who has this problem. These diagnoses are meant to be suggestions for clinical consideration. Select a diagnosis listed or assign a more appropriate choice from the *DSM-IV* (Step Six).

To accommodate those practitioners that tend to plan treatment in terms of diagnostic labels rather than presenting populations, Appendix C lists all of the *DSM-IV* diagnoses that have been presented in the various presenting populations chapters as suggestions for consideration. Each diagnosis is followed by the presenting population that has been associated with that diagnosis. The provider may look up the presenting populations for a selected diagnosis to review definitions, goals, objectives, and interventions that may be appropriate for their clients with that diagnosis.

Congratulations! You should now have a complete, individualized treatment plan that is ready for immediate implementation and presentation to the client. It should resemble the format of the "Sample Treatment Plan" presented on page 11.

A FINAL NOTE

One important aspect of effective treatment planning is that each plan should be tailored to the individual client's specific population needs. Treatment plans should not be mass-produced, even if clients have similar problems. The individual's strengths and weaknesses, unique stressors, social network, family circumstances, and symptom patterns *must* be considered in developing a treatment strategy. Drawing on our own years of clinical experience, we have put together a variety of treatment choices. These statements can be combined in thousands of permutations to develop detailed treatment plans. Relying on their own good judgment, clinicians can easily select the statements that are appropriate for the individuals they are treating. In addition, we encourage readers to add their own definitions, goals, objectives, and interventions to the existing samples. It is our hope that *The Suicide and Homicide Risk Assessment & Prevention Treatment Planner* will promote effective, creative treatment planning—a process that will ultimately benefit the client, clinician, and mental health community.

SAMPLE TREATMENT PLAN

CLIENT: COLLEGE STUDENT

Definitions: Communicates to someone (e.g., friend, counselor, resident assistant, help line, teacher) a wish to die (e.g., "Life just isn't worth living," "I feel like giving up," "I wish my life would end," "There is no solution to my problems other than taking my own life").

Expresses feelings of social isolation because of large geographic distance from home (e.g., foreign or out-of-state students).

Expresses feelings of being under severe pressure to perform academically or athletically to gain a measure of acceptance and self-worth.

Expresses a need to win parental love and/or approval through academic and/or athletic excellence.

Goals: Report a wish to live.

Develop an integrated self-concept and reject the belief that love, affirmation, and value are gained only through performance.

Develop a balanced self-concept that can accept temporary failures and integrate them into the growth experience.

OBJECTIVES	INTERVENTIONS
1. Identify general feelings of satisfaction with the college experience.	1. Explore the motivations for choosing the current college (e.g., proximity to home, distance from home, academic standards, athletic opportunities, elitist reputation, parental pressure, desire to be with close friend) with the client and note any motivations that could be considered problematic for a healthy adjustment.

2. In general terms, explore the client's current feelings toward the college experience (e.g., very satisfied, a balanced view, dissatisfied, very unhappy) and isolate current emotional reactions that could be problematic for a healthy adjustment (e.g., homesick, absence from a significant relationship, feeling lost, missing high school identity).

2. Provide information on personal experiences with high-risk *behavioral* markers for suicide in the college student.

1. Assess the client for the high-risk, college-student suicide marker of escape and/or avoidance behaviors (e.g., missing classes, isolative substance abuse patterns, attitudes of passivity, or social isolation by choice where he/she makes a conscious effort to avoid drawing attention to himself/herself).

2. Assess the client for the high-risk, college-student suicide marker of fascination with issues of death and suicide (e.g., demonstrated in a subtle fashion in study groups, dormitory discussions, or class assigned writing projects).

3. Assess the client for the high-risk, college-student suicide marker of excessive medical consultations (e.g., complaints of fatigue, tiredness, lack of energy but denying or not discussing issues of depression or suicide ideation and/or intent).

3. Provide information on personal experiences with high-risk *emotional* markers for suicide in the college student.

1. Assess the client for the high-risk, college student suicide marker of hopelessness and helplessness (e.g., significant despair that renders current coping strategies inadequate).

2. Assess the client for the high-risk, college student suicide marker of depression (e.g., sadness, self-directed anger, reduced appetite, sleep disturbances, low self-esteem, family history of depression and psychiatric illnesses).

3. Assess the client for the high-risk, college student suicide marker of emerging schizophrenia (e.g., social withdrawal, feelings of persecution, intrusive thoughts, inability to concentrate, thought disorganization).

4. Assess the client for the high-risk, college student suicide marker of socially prescribed perfectionism (e.g., examine closely its linkage to depression and hopelessness, inquire about the object of the need to please, examine the history of the socially prescribed perfectionism, and examine its linkage to the suicide intent).

4. Provide information on personal experiences with high-risk *social* markers for suicide in the college student.

1. Assess the client for the high-risk, college student suicide marker of termination of a romantic relationship or social network disruption because of college bound status.

2. Assess the client for the high-risk, college student suicide marker of rigid family

expectations (e.g., school was chosen by parents because of family tradition or prestige, course of study was influenced by parents because of family tradition or prestige, or parental expectations are seen as exceedingly high and beyond the student's capacity).

5. Identify solutions and coping strategies that do not include suicide or the wish to die.

1. Assist the client in noting in his/her treatment journal a detailed plan (e.g., self-calming techniques, focus on the positive aspects of efforts to accomplish tasks, cognitive restructuring leading the client to replace his/her focus on failure to a sense of "I did good enough," "I did the best I could") with specific instructions responding to and managing the perturbation associated with his/her immediate, priority symptoms; these responses should be detailed and structured to assist the client during extreme emotional upset (e.g., safe and simple skills).

2. Use role-play, modeling, and behavior rehearsal to teach the client to implement the symptom-management skills noted in his/her treatment journal.

6. Increase the frequency of verbalizing statements indicating improved comfort with the college experience, appropriate anxiety with academic demands, and smoother transition to autonomy.

1. Assist the client in finding and utilizing enjoyable aspects of campus life (e.g., creating a life balance between fun and work); encourage a sense of autonomy by emphasizing decisions made that reflect self-determination.

2. Encourage the client to see himself/herself in a social context by emphasizing the benefits of

participation in friendships and group activities; assign participation in selected campus activities or community volunteer activities; reinforce success and redirect experiences of failure.

Diagnosis: 296.22 Major Depressive Disorder, Single Episode, Moderate

I. SUICIDAL POPULATIONS

AFRICAN AMERICAN MALE

BEHAVIORAL DEFINITIONS

1. Verbalizes a wish to die.
2. Reacts to the homicidal death (especially by stabbing) of a friend with a diminished fear of death and a lowered value of life.
3. Is involved in serious patterns of drug dependence (especially cocaine and injectable drugs) to escape reality or cope with life.
4. Reacts to community violence with an attitude of a diminished value of life.
5. Reacts to community poverty or lowered socioeconomic condition with an attitude of hopelessness and helplessness.
6. Demonstrates behaviors positively correlated with the diagnosis of depression (e.g., agitation, sleep disorder, anhedonia, or dysphoria).
7. Distances himself from cultural, family, social, and religious support systems because of negative and hopeless attitudes about their value.
8. Has a history of serious, near-lethal suicide attempts and gestures needing medical attention.
9. Has established a pattern of behavior best described as self-destructive (e.g., joins violent peer groups, is involved in criminal and combative behavior).
10. Has possession of and/or quick and easy access to firearms coupled with a verbalized attitude of "I am ready to die."
11. Exhibits an undiagnosed and untreated paranoid psychosis (either schizophrenia or substance related) coupled with carrying a firearm.

__. _____
   _____

__. _____
   _____

__. _____
   _____

LONG-TERM GOALS

1. Embrace the wish to live and establish futuristic, hopeful thinking.
2. Reestablish involvement with nurturing, supportive community, social, religious, and family systems.
3. Manage community and socioeconomic stressors with positive, healthy coping skills.
4. Have personal pride in cultural history.
5. Integrate traditional African American value system with an increased sense of ethnic identification and social cohesion.
6. Manage perturbation caused by thought or mood disorder.
7. Manage rage caused by acts of racism or discrimination in a resilient, validating fashion.

—. _____

_____

—. _____

_____

—. _____

_____

SHORT-TERM OBJECTIVES	THERAPEUTIC INTERVENTIONS
1. Identify any high-risk characteristics associated with previous suicide activity. (1)	1. Assess for high-risk characteristics inherent in any of the client's previous suicide activities (e.g., did the activity result in medical attention; was it performed with a firearm; was the client under the influence of alcohol or drugs at the time of the incident; was the client motivated at the time by feelings of hopelessness and helplessness connected to current social, economic, or neighborhood stressors; was the activity calculated for rescue, self-interrupted, or was it accidentally stopped against the client's wishes).

2. Identify specifics of current suicide ideation and/or intent. (2, 3, 4)

2. Explore the motivation or goal for the current suicide intent with the client (e.g., escape from hopeless economic, social, or environmental stressors; a passivity toward life because of consistent experiences with poverty, violence, or death; an expressed method of curing rampant chemical dependence).

3. Explore whether the client has any formalized plan for the suicide intent (e.g., will a firearm be used and is it currently or readily available, has a time or place been chosen, has he written a suicide note).

4. Explore whether the client has shared his intent with anyone in his social environment (e.g., wife, minister, or friend) or if he has no identified resource and currently is in social isolation.

3. Provide information on personal experiences with high-risk *behavioral* markers for suicide in African American males. (5, 6, 7)

5. Assess the client for the high-risk African American male suicide marker of cocaine/crack, heroin, and injectable drug abuse; examine for age of onset, current usage, readiness to change, supportive environment, losses because of dependency, or concurrent disorders.

6. Assess the client for the high-risk African American male suicide marker of firearm possession; examine for consistency of possession, motivational factors (e.g., unrealistically high levels of distrust, suspiciousness, or realistic fears of neighborhood

violence), and whether the weapon has been used in violent activity.

7. Assess the client for the high-risk African American male suicide marker of adopting a self-destructive lifestyle in a deprived living environment (e.g., carries an attitude of "I am ready to die"; has witnessed death by homicide; lives in an environment marked by underemployment, non-nurturing social institutions, impoverished and/or segregated conditions; easily engages in fatalistic behaviors, which may include acts of victim-provoked suicide).

4. Provide information on personal experiences with high-risk *emotional* markers for suicide in African American males. (8)

8. Assess the client for the high-risk African American male suicide marker of depression (e.g., low self-esteem, social withdrawal, anhedonia, sleep disturbance, increase in anger/hostility, or low energy levels).

5. Provide information on personal experiences with high-risk *social* markers for suicide in African American males. (9, 10, 11)

9. Assess the client for the high-risk African American male suicide marker of isolation from traditional community institutions (e.g., no sense of family cohesion or nurturing from religious organizations or a demonstrated sense of "being out on the streets").

10. Assess the client for the high-risk African American male suicide marker of low occupational and economic hopes and realities; evaluate current occupational status, educational level and socioeconomic environment, and hopes and aspirations

to improve current socio-economic status.

11. Assess the client for the high-risk African American male suicide marker of being raised in a highly dysfunctional family; examine for a history of physical abuse, incest, extrafamilial sexual abuse, or marital conflicts within the current family or the family of origin.

6. Cooperate with psychological testing designed to evaluate conditions correlated to elevated suicide risk in African American males. (12)

12. Assess the client's risk factors for completed suicide by administering psychological tests most commonly used for this purpose (e.g., MMPI-2, Suicide Probability Scale, Beck Hopelessness Inventory, Reasons for Living Inventory).

7. Designated community resource individuals agree to support the client in his recovery from hopelessness. (13, 14)

13. Develop a list of citizens with knowledge of the current crisis and with whom the client may agree to involve in the treatment plan (e.g., minister, personal physician, community outreach professional, or concerned persons from community-based African American institutions).

14. Integrate the concerned citizens identified by the client into his treatment plan by meeting with them and gathering information.

8. Provide complete information on current mood, affect, and thought process in a psychiatric evaluation, while taking psychotropic medication as prescribed. (15, 16)

15. Refer the client for a psychiatric evaluation to determine the need for psychotropic medication and to validate any at-risk diagnoses (e.g., major depression, generalized anxiety disorder, or antisocial personality disorder).

16. Monitor the client's compliance with the psychotropic medication prescription; chart his side

effects, subjective and objective behavioral changes, and his abuse of alcohol and drugs.

9. Accept feedback on the assessment of the presence of high-risk markers for suicide. (17)

17. Summarize and give feedback to the client and, if possible and available, his caregivers on the presence of high-risk markers found in the evaluation process and outline the treatment plan.

10. Comply with placement in a more protective and restrictive environment. (18)

18. If at any time in the therapy process the client demonstrates an increase in symptoms associated with high-risk for suicide, arrange for immediate placement in a protective therapeutic setting that will provide all necessary super-vision to guard him from suicide impulse, decrease perturbation and isolation, remove environ-mental stress, and result in a close monitoring of medical and psychological treatment effectiveness.

11. Affirm a safety plan that allows a return to the care-givers or the community. (19, 20)

19. In consultation with the inpatient treatment team, discharge planning must include monitoring the client's medication and enhancing the role of social, religious, and family supports.

20. Obtain the client's agreement to a treatment plan that will address chemical dependency and relapse prevention, anger and shame, and improved coping with daily stress.

12. Agree to a written plan for dealing with situations when suicidal urges become strong. (21, 22)

21. Develop a crisis intervention plan to be implemented by the client during trigger stressors and symptoms that includes the following: contacting a

responsible individual in his social and religious support system, contacting the therapist, or using a local help line; provide telephone numbers in writing to the client.

22. Ask the client to agree, as a verbal contract of the therapy relationship, to call someone on the emergency phone list when he experiences strong suicide urges.

13. Identify the stressors and symptoms that contribute to the wish to die by suicide. (23, 24)

23. Assist the client in making a list of his most prominent stressors (e.g., being isolated from supportive family, social, or religious institutions; living in an underemployed urban area; being exposed to frequent violent crime; or struggling with drug dependency); explore his emotional reactions or symptoms (e.g., rage, hopelessness, helplessness, or self-hate) produced by those stressors.

24. Assist the client in identifying symptoms that most seriously affect his functioning, as well as the current symptom-management strategies used (e.g., substance abuse or dependence, acts of violence toward others, suicide gestures, or withdrawal from social supports); highlight the negative consequences created by these maladaptive strategies (e.g., involvement in the justice system, missing educational opportunities, or missing occupational opportunities).

14. Identify coping skills and management strategies for symptoms that do not include suicide or the wish to die. (25, 26, 27, 28)

25. Formulate an appropriate view of the function of suicide with the client: It stems from a need to solve a seemingly unsolvable problem; it is fueled by a sense of hopelessness and helplessness or of self-hate, which creates thoughts such as "The world would be better off without me"; and the antidote is to develop healthy coping strategies for these seemingly unsolvable problems.

26. Establish a therapeutic contract that will decrease the client's feelings of helplessness by ensuring the therapist's help in teaching symptom management, stress reduction, and problem-solving skills, targeting the most serious symptoms for immediate attention (e.g., residential chemical dependence treatment, outpatient treatment for concurrent psychiatric disorders, anger/rage management, reentering educational system, and solution-oriented therapies).

27. Assign the client to begin the use of a treatment journal to track daily stressors, the resulting symptoms, maladaptive coping patterns, and experiences with newly acquired coping strategies.

28. Use role-play, modeling, and behavior rehearsal to teach the client symptom-management skills (e.g., walking away during incidents of rage, breathing and relaxation exercises during high anxiety, and constructive activities during times of

helplessness); have him note in the treatment journal a detailed plan with specific instructions on responding to and managing the perturbation associated with the hierarchy of symptoms.

15. Increase verbalized statements of hope that symptoms can be managed in ways other than suicide. (29)

29. Monitor the client's suicide risk at appropriate intervals by evaluating his high-risk markers (e.g., levels of depression, relapse into substance abuse, or engaging in self-destructive behaviors) and by administering standardized suicide risk assessment (e.g., Suicide Probability Scale); reinforce the client when verbalizing statements of hope for the future.

16. Identify own biological, social, and emotional vulnerabilities that contribute to the risk for suicide. (30, 31, 32)

30. Explore the client's personal vulnerabilities that contribute to the suicidal crisis (e.g., extreme self-hate and self-devaluation, lack of empathy, lack of internal regulation of anger/rage, inability to assume personal responsibility for behaviors, or admiration of high-risk and antisocial behaviors).

31. Assist the client in acknowledging the existence of these traits and the influence they have on decision making (e.g., avoiding emotional reactions to violence with drug abuse, manipulating extreme self-harm or death by high-risk confrontations with law enforcement or opposing gangs, presenting a confrontational personality to defend against feelings of fear and hopelessness).

32. Examine the origins of these traits and vulnerabilities with the client by reviewing his history (e.g., receiving derogatory messages from adults, engaging in social settings where emotions were not permitted, bonding with peer groups through violence and drug abuse); encourage the client to engage in behaviors affirming responsibility for himself (e.g., taking responsibility for behavior, expressing emotions in positive fashion, deciding against firearms possession).

17. Increase statements indicating improved confidence in the future of managing the stressors specific for the African American male population. (33, 34)

33. Examine the client's success at attaining a balanced view of himself as coping with stressors and symptoms improve (e.g., demonstrating better anger management, successfully completing substance abuse treatment with a profound knowledge of personal triggers, or remaining on medication for depression).

34. Encourage the client's confidence and hope that his learned coping skills can greatly reduced self-destructive acts and the wish to die, periodically adjusting certain management strategies that are not effective.

18. Increase behaviors of inclusion in traditional African American community supports that provide an identity in a social, caring, and safe context. (35, 36)

35. Encourage and teach the client to see himself in a social context by emphasizing the benefits of participation in friendships and group activities (e.g., African American community organizations or African American religious groups); give a homework assignment to attend a

group activity and record the experience in his journal.

36. Teach the client the value of verbalizing emotions in the context of personal and intimate relationships (e.g., sharing feelings promotes empathy from others, sharing of the burden reduces its intensity, sharing breaks down a sense of isolation); give a homework assignment to share feelings with a trusted person and record the experience in his journal.

19. Develop a suicide prevention plan that incorporates a treatment journal and all completed homework assignments. (37, 38, 39)

37. Educate client on issues of empowerment (e.g., joining community groups that concentrate on overcoming problems of poverty, underemployment, or crime).

38. Educate the client on preventing relapse into suicidal behavior (e.g., rely on the treatment journal for reminders of strategies for managing stressors and symptoms, implement empowering techniques, avoid isolation and maintain a social network, remain on medications, maintain a clean and sober lifestyle with continued involvement with Alcoholics Anonymous/Narcotics Anonymous (AA/NA), maintain futuristic thinking).

39. Assist the client in writing a personal suicide prevention plan that lists individualized actions learned in therapy that will be taken in the future to manage suicidal urges and continue the newly adopted philosophy of life.

—. _____ —. _____
_____   _____
—. _____ —. _____
_____   _____
—. _____ —. _____
_____   _____

DIAGNOSTIC SUGGESTIONS:

Axis I:
296.3x   Major Depressive Disorder, Recurrent
300.00   Anxiety Disorder NOS
303.90   Alcohol Dependence
305.00   Alcohol Abuse
304.20   Cocaine Dependence
305.60   Cocaine Abuse
292.84   Cocaine-Induced Mood Disorder
292.89   Cocaine-Induced Anxiety Disorder
291.89   Alcohol-Induced Mood Disorder
304.80   Polysubstance Dependence

_____   _____
_____   _____

Axis II:
301.7   Antisocial Personality Disorder
301.9   Personality Disorder NOS

_____   _____
_____   _____

ASIAN AMERICAN MALE

BEHAVIORAL DEFINITIONS

1. Expresses a generalized fatalism about life and an absence of hope for the future.
2. Displays symptoms of depressive disorder (e.g., lack of energy, anhedonia, or social withdrawal).
3. Has a history and current practice of substance abuse.
4. Extremely invested in pleasing others to gain affirmation.
5. Demonstrates a life-long pattern of an inability to access or process emotions.
6. Expresses despair over the inability to meet the expectations of the extended family, which results in losing family support, affirmation, and a sense of belonging.
7. Life-long pattern of impulsive behaviors and poor problem-solving ability.
8. Verbalizes extreme feelings of self-devaluation, isolation, aloneness, and self-hate.
9. Experiences a chronic pattern of suicide ideation with or without a plan.

—. _____
   _____

—. _____
   _____

—. _____
   _____

LONG-TERM GOALS

1. Embrace life with hope for the future.
2. Enhance the development of coping strategies and problem-solving skills.
3. Resolve feelings of worthlessness, self-hate, and isolation that contribute to depressive reactions and the impulse to suicide.
4. Respect vulnerability to depression and remain on physician-monitored prescription medication.
5. Resolve feelings of perfectionism and develop an intrinsic sense of self-worth.
6. Enhance access to emotions that allow involvement in intimate relationships.

__. _____

_____

__. _____

_____

__. _____

_____

SHORT-TERM OBJECTIVES

1. Identify specifics of the current suicide ideation and/or intent. (1, 2, 3, 4)

THERAPEUTIC INTERVENTIONS

1. Explore the client's goal for the intended suicide act (e.g., cessation of severe emotional pain, actions motivated by self-hate and/or self-devaluation, or a solution to a seemingly unsolvable problem).

2. Explore the amount of time and energy the client spent in planning the suicide event (e.g., has a lethal means been considered and/or obtained, has a date or place been assigned, has the suicide intent been communicated to anyone and, if so, what was the reaction).

3. Explore whether any sense of peace, calm, or a renewed

energy level has been experienced by the client since planning for the suicide has started; examine how much time is spent contemplating death and its aftermath.

4. Explore the client's barriers to the plan to die (e.g., personal religious beliefs, fear of emotional impact on survivors, or fear of accidentally surviving); note whether there is any ambivalence displayed about his completed suicide.

2. Identify specifics of any historic pattern of suicide ideation, gestures, or attempts. (5)

5. Explore the client's previous experiences with suicide activity (e.g., chronic experiences of thinking about suicide as a way to solve a problem, deliberate nonfatal self-harm activities designed to fulfill needs other than death, or acts of self-harm where the intent was to die but the activity was accidentally interrupted).

3. Provide information on personal experiences with high-risk *behavioral* markers for Asian American male suicide. (6, 7)

6. Assess the client for the high-risk Asian American male suicide marker of substance abuse (e.g., using drugs to cope with psychological pain or during previous suicide activity, age of onset, or readiness to change).

7. Assess the client for the high-risk Asian American male suicide marker of life-long pattern of impulsivity and poor problem-solving ability (e.g., patterns of dangerous behaviors, escape, denial, and/or projection of blame to manage critical incidents).

4. Provide information on personal experiences with high-risk *emotional* markers for Asian American male suicide. (8, 9, 10)

5. Provide information on personal experiences with high-risk *social* markers for Asian American male suicide. (11)

6. Cooperate with psychological testing designed to evaluate suicide ideation/intent levels. (12)

7. Provide complete information on current mood, affect, and thought process in a psychiat-

8. Assess the client for the high-risk Asian American male suicide marker of depression (e.g., linkage to feelings of melancholic despair, self-devaluation, self-hate, helplessness).

9. Assess the client for the high-risk Asian American male suicide marker of perfectionism (e.g., extreme need to meet the expectations of the extended family, extreme defensiveness when confronted with failure experiences, intense self-criticism traits, or any tendency to define himself based on performance criteria).

10. Assess the client for the high-risk Asian American male suicide marker of emotional constriction (e.g., familial pattern of denying emotional expression, inability to identify specifically felt emotions, or the tendency to define all emotions as painful).

11. Assess the client for the high-risk Asian American male suicide marker of rejection from the extended family (e.g., linkage to fear of failing to meet expectations; feelings of aloneness, isolation, or despair).

12. Administer testing to the client that is most commonly used to reveal and evaluate suicide ideation and/or intent levels (e.g., Beck Hopelessness Scale, Reasons for Living Inventory, or Suicide Risk Measure).

13. Refer the client for a psychiatric evaluation to determine his need for psychotropic medication and

ric evaluation and take psychotropic medication as prescribed. (13, 14)

8. Medical personnel provide relevant, current information on general health issues. (15)

9. If appropriate, school personnel provide relevant, current information on social and academic adjustment in the school setting. (16)

10. Accept feedback gathered from all sources as well as the treatment plan developed from the evaluation process. (17)

11. Comply with placement in a more protective and, possibly, restrictive environment. (18)

to validate any at-risk diagnosis (e.g., major depressive disorder).

14. Monitor the client's compliance with the psychotropic medication prescription; chart the effectiveness of the medication and monitor the side effects.

15. After obtaining appropriate confidentiality and privacy releases, contact the client's primary care physician for a report on his general health issues.

16. After obtaining appropriate confidentiality and privacy releases, contact the client's school personnel for a report on his academic, social, and emotional adjustment.

17. Summarize and give feedback to the client and, if available and appropriate, his caregivers on high-risk markers found in the evaluation process and outline the treatment plan; if available and appropriate, engage supportive caregivers in the treatment strategy (e.g., providing safety during high-risk times, assist in monitoring any prescribed medications, and/or involvement in family therapy).

18. If the assessments reveal the presence of high-risk suicide markers that significantly challenge the client's coping capacity (e.g., increase in symptoms of depression, an increase in statements of self-hate and despair), place him in a structured, supervised therapeutic setting that will protect him from suicide impulse,

decrease perturbation, remove him from environmental stress, and monitor treatment effectiveness.

12. Affirm a plan that allows for a safe return to the community. (19)

19. Review the inpatient treatment team's discharge plan with the client and, if possible and appropriate, the caregivers including placement, support systems, individual and family psychotherapy, activities of daily living, knowledge of helping services, and monitoring of his medication program.

13. Agree to a crisis response plan for dealing with situations when the suicide risk is strong. (20)

20. Develop a crisis intervention plan to be implemented during trigger events and feelings (e.g., failing at a task linked to family expectations, or feelings of isolation and rejection) that includes contacting the therapist, a trusted friend, or a local suicide prevention center or mental health center help line; ask the client to agree, as a verbal contract of therapy, to call someone on the phone list to process these emotions.

14. Identify current stressors and resultant symptoms that trigger the wish to die by suicide. (21, 22, 23)

21. Assist the client in listing his most prominent stressors (e.g., failure to meet expectations, inability to manage substance abuse patterns, or inability to access and articulate emotional reactions); explore his emotional reactions or symptoms (e.g., feelings of despair, isolation, or rejection) produced by those stressors.

22. Assist the client in developing a complete symptom inventory that includes identifying the most disruptive symptoms (e.g.,

feelings of rejection and isolation), how these symptoms are currently managed (e.g., substance abuse, suicidal ideation, outbursts of rage, or impulsive at-risk behaviors), and whether these symptoms create other reactions (e.g., social isolation, self-harm behaviors, or risk of alcohol dependency).

23. Establish a therapeutic alliance with the client that ensures the therapist's help in targeting the most serious symptoms for immediate help (e.g., medications or solution-oriented therapy).

15. Increase verbalized statements of hope that stressors and symptoms can be managed continuously in ways other than suicide. (24, 25, 26)

24. Formulate an appropriate view of the function of suicide with the client: It stems from a need to solve a seemingly unsolvable problem (e.g., despair about meeting extended family's expectations), it is fueled by a sense of hopelessness and helplessness, and the antidote is to develop adaptive problem-solving skills for these stressors and symptoms.

25. Assign the client a treatment journal to track daily stressors, resulting symptoms, maladaptive coping behaviors, and experiences with newly acquired coping strategies (e.g., coping with failure through substance abuse is replaced by an intrinsic sense of self-worth); assign homework targeting symptom management.

26. Use role-play, modeling, and behavior rehearsal to teach the client to use adaptive problem-solving skills to replace

maladaptive coping strategies (e.g., define the problem, seek alternative solutions, list the positives and negatives of each solution, select and implement a plan of action, evaluate the outcome, and adjust the solution as necessary).

16. Identify and diminish the influence of personality vulnerabilities and traits that contribute to suicide ideation and/or intent. (27, 28, 29)

27. Explore the client's personal vulnerabilities that hinder healthy coping strategies and contribute to the suicidal crisis (e.g., perfectionism, the need to please others to gain affirmation, extreme self-devaluation and self-criticism, or the inability to access and articulate emotions).

28. Assist the client in acknowledging his suicide fostering traits and vulnerabilities, understanding how they were acquired (e.g., the need to be perfect acquired from parental expectations that are linked to parental affirmation or emotional constriction acquired from childhood experiences where emotions were not permitted) and their influence in maladaptive coping (e.g., inability to cope with or manage failure).

29. Explore methods and exercises with the client that will diminish the influence of his suicide fostering personality traits on problem-solving efforts (e.g., the inability to cope with failure is replaced by an intrinsic sense of self-worth; the inability to express emotions is replaced by an empathic sense of self-acceptance and the ability to share emotions in the therapy session).

17. Verbalize feelings of intrinsic self-worth. (30, 31)

30. Assist the client in enhancing his self-image by encouraging him to provide self-reports from the treatment journal and the homework assignments on recent incidents of his improved coping, symptom management, and problem-solving skills (e.g., talking to a friend about a difficult emotion or refraining from substance abuse when feeling anxious).

31. Challenge the client to trust the value of himself during times of temporary failure; provide him with examples of others who have risen from failure to enjoy success (e.g., provide titles and/ or readings on examples from culturally relevant articles).

18. Increase the expression of emotions within a social network. (32, 33)

32. Model empathic active listening styles that will set an atmosphere of allowance and permission for the client to access and articulate his emotions; teach him the value of emotional expression (e.g., helps others gain a better understanding of your problems and assists in gaining a sense of being understood).

33. Teach the client the value of social networks for alleviating a sense of isolation, participation in noncompetitive activities, sharing of feelings and ideas; encourage his affiliation with social outlets specifically focused on his need to belong and express feelings (e.g., noncompetitive social activities, culturally relevant groups, or therapy groups for specific populations).

19. Develop a suicide prevention plan that incorporates the treatment journal's homework assignments. (34)

34. Assist the client in writing a personal suicide prevention plan that lists actions he will take in the future to manage the impulse to suicide (e.g., remain aware of strategies for coping with trigger stressors and symptoms, avoid isolation and maintain culturally relevant social network, remain respectful of an intrinsic sense of self-worth, and stay on medications, if prescribed).

__. _____   __. _____
    _____   _____

__. _____   __. _____
    _____   _____

__. _____   __. _____
    _____   _____

DIAGNOSTIC SUGGESTIONS:

Axis I:	296.xx	Major Depressive Disorder
	309.0	Adjustment Disorder with Depressed Mood
	305.00	Alcohol Abuse
	300.02	Generalized Anxiety Disorder
	309.81	Posttraumatic Stress Disorder
	312.8	Conduct Disorder
	_____	_____
	_____	_____

BIPOLAR

BEHAVIORAL DEFINITIONS

1. Expresses a desire to die.
2. Demonstrates a course of bipolar disorder where the depressive phase is of significant severity causing extreme levels of pain.
3. Demonstrates symptoms that correlate with the diagnosis of bipolar II disorder (e.g., a history of major depressive episodes with only hypomanic phases).
4. Demonstrates a pattern of noncompliance with prescribed medications that have been shown to be effective in the treatment of the illness.
5. Verbalizes hopelessness about the future during a severe depressive phase or in the early stages of the illness.
6. Has experienced multiple social disruptions (e.g., divorce, job loss, financial bankruptcy, loss of social network, or significant health issues) that are directly related to bipolar illness.
7. Has a history of multiple inpatient episodes because of severe manic phases that included psychotic conditions.
8. Has a positive family history of suicide and/or bipolar illness.
9. Is currently in a period of recovery just following a period of psychiatric hospitalization.
10. Is currently experiencing a mixed states episode where the depressive condition is combined with agitated, mental alertness.
11. Has demonstrated a pattern of co-occurring alcohol abuse/dependence.

—. _____

_____

—. _____

_____

—. _____

_____

LONG-TERM GOALS

1. Express a desire to live and begin to view self in a futuristic context.
2. Integrate an acceptance of bipolar disorder into the self-concept as a life-long medical condition.
3. Remain compliant with all prescribed medications.
4. Enhance the capacity to manage stressors in the social-occupational milieu associated with bipolar disorder.
5. Engage in a positive, supportive social network and utilize the protective effects of the family.

—. _____

   _____

   _____

—. _____

   _____

   _____

—. _____

   _____

   _____

SHORT-TERM OBJECTIVES	THERAPEUTIC INTERVENTIONS
1. Cooperate with an evaluation of conditions related to bipolar suicide risk. (1)	1. Explore the diagnostic markers of mania, major depression, and hypomania with the client and, if available, caregivers to classify his/her condition as either bipolar I, bipolar II, cyclothymia, mixed episode, or unipolar depression. (Be sensitive to the diagnosis of bipolar II and mixed episode as they are positively correlated to completed suicide.)
2. Provide complete information on current mood, affect, and thought process in a psychiatric evaluation, taking psychotropic medication as prescribed. (2, 3)	2. Refer the client for a psychiatric evaluation to determine his/her need for psychotropic medication and/or a medically managed electroconvulsive therapy series (ECT) and to validate all at-risk diagnoses (e.g., bipolar II, mixed episode, rapid cycling).

3. Medical personnel provide relevant, current information on general health issues. (4)

4. Identify the nature of previous suicide activity and any history of suicide activity in the family of origin. (5, 6)

5. Provide information on personal experiences with high-risk *behavioral* markers for suicide in people with bipolar illness. (7, 8, 9)

3. Aggressively monitor the client's compliance with the prescribed medical interventions (e.g., ECT and/or medications) throughout the course of therapy; any period of noncompliance could be life threatening and should be dealt with quickly through consultation with the treating psychiatrist.

4. After obtaining appropriate confidentiality releases, contact the client's primary care physician for a medical report and evaluation; pay special attention to stress related medical disorders, including cardiovascular and pulmonary diseases because of their high correlation with suicide intent.

5. Explore the client's previous suicide activity (e.g., ideation, gesturing that was self-interrupted or calculated for rescue, or attempts where the activity was accidentally interrupted against the client's wishes) and examine the intended goal; examine his/her psychosocial stressors at the time of the activity.

6. Examine the nature of familial suicide patterns (e.g., did the client witness the death or find the victim, under what psychosocial conditions did the death occur, did the family member have a psychiatric diagnosis).

7. Assess the client for the high-risk bipolar suicide marker of alcohol abuse (e.g., age of onset, abuse/dependency patterns, linkage to depressive and/or

manic symptoms or any previous suicide activity or other acts of violence, calming or agitating effects, use as self-medication, or use in isolation or in a social context).

8. Assess the client for the high-risk bipolar suicide marker of patterns of noncompliance with prescribed medication (e.g., history of hospitalizations because of noncompliance, reluctance to give up the highs or manic experiences, history of unused or hoarded pills used for suicide overdoses, intolerance of side effects, or unwillingness to accept chronic pattern of disease).

9. Assess the client for the high-risk bipolar suicide marker of loss (e.g., partner, friend, financial security, social cohesion, or health) because of poor judgments made in a manic state.

6. Provide information on personal experiences with high-risk *emotional* markers for suicide in people with bipolar illness. (10, 11, 12, 13, 14)

10. Assess the client for the high-risk bipolar suicide marker of experiencing the severe depressive phases with hypo-manic episodes (bipolar II disorder); assess for comorbidity conditions (e.g., alcoholism, personality disorders, inadequate and unpredictable support systems, medication compliance problems, or chaotic lifestyles).

11. Assess the client for the high-risk bipolar suicide marker of experiencing a combination of depressive symptoms; mental alertness; and tense, apprehensive, and restless behaviors are

seen as particularly vulnerable to completed suicide (mixed episodes).

12. Assess the client for the high-risk bipolar suicide marker of experiencing the depressive stage of bipolar disorder; attend to the severity of his/her depression and its remarkable paralyzing features.

13. Assess the client for the high-risk bipolar suicide marker of being in a recovery period, which usually follows a period of inpatient hospitalization (e.g., a problematic combination of a return to normalcy yet feeling hopelessness about the course of the illness).

14. Assess the client for the high-risk bipolar suicide marker of the presence of an underlying personality disorder, especially borderline or antisocial personality.

7. Provide information on personal experiences with high-risk *social* markers for suicide in people with bipolar illness. (15)

15. Assess the client for the high-risk bipolar suicide marker of a positive family history of psychiatric disorders (e.g., identify specific disorders of thought or mood and educate the client on the genetic predisposition for severe psychiatric illnesses).

8. Identify the nature of current suicidal ideation, planning, and/or intent. (16, 17, 18)

16. Explore the goal of the intended suicide act with the client (e.g., hopelessness for the future, cessation of intense psychic pain, embarrassment/guilt because of the manic course of the illness and the resultant behaviors).

17. Examine and assess the level of energy and animation displayed by the client as he/she discusses suicide and, if possible, the planning for the event (special attention should be paid to this level of energy in the context of a recent discharge from an inpatient episode and expressions of hopelessness); attempt to calm the client and, if necessary, arrange for 24-hour supervision or rehospitalization if agitation is severe.

18. Explore whether any impediments to the plan exist with the client (e.g., fear of emotional impact on survivors or religious beliefs).

9. The client and, if available, the caregivers accept feedback on the assessments and treatment plan developed from the evaluation process. (19)

19. Summarize and give feedback to the client and, if available, the caregivers on the high-risk bipolar suicide markers found in the evaluation process; formulate his/her treatment plan and engage, if possible, the caregivers in support of the client (e.g., monitor the client's medication compliance, mood swings, or social/occupational functioning).

10. Comply with placement in a more protective and, possibly, a more restrictive environment. (20)

20. If assessments reveal the presence of high-risk bipolar suicide markers that significantly challenge coping capacity (e.g., severe depression, experiencing a mixed states episode, severe agitation, or bipolar II features) at any time during the therapy process, place the client in a therapeutic setting (e.g., inpatient hospitalization) that will protect him/her from the suicide impulse.

11. Affirm a plan that allows for a safe return to the community. (21, 22)

21. Refer the client to a community-based, clinical case management program that has the capacity to monitor and coordinate his/her medication management, respite services, crisis intervention, and social and occupational functioning as he/she returns to the community from an inpatient stay; obtain his/her affirmation of this plan.

22. Monitor the client's suicide risk at appropriate intervals during the therapy process through interview assessment of high-risk bipolar suicide markers and by administering standardized suicide risk assessments (e.g., Suicide Probability Scale).

12. Agree to a written plan for dealing with situations when suicidal urges become strong. (23)

23. Develop a written crisis intervention plan to be implemented when the client experiences trigger events and feelings (e.g., hopelessness during a depressive phase) that includes contacting the case manager, family member, or supportive friend to discuss emotional reactions to the event; ask him/her to agree, as a verbal contract in the therapeutic relationship, to call someone on the emergency phone list.

13. Identify current stressors and resultant symptoms that trigger the wish to die. (24, 25, 26)

24. Assist the client in making a list of his/her most prominent stressors (e.g., episodes of severe depression, thoughts of being on medication for life, side effects of medication, having to reconcile behaviors performed while in a manic state, or chaotic social network) and emotional reactions or

symptoms (e.g., hopelessness, confusion, distrust, or self-hate) produced by those stressors.

25. Assist the client in producing a complete symptom inventory that includes identifying the most disruptive symptoms (e.g., hopelessness, distrust, or confusion), how these symptoms are currently dysfunctionally managed (e.g., noncompliance with medication, refusing medication while hoping for a return of the euphoria of the manic state) and the results of these choices (e.g., loss of job or chaotic social network).

26. Establish a therapeutic alliance with the client that ensures the therapist's help in targeting the most serious symptoms for immediate attention (e.g., medication, ECT, family therapy, phase specific therapy, solution-oriented behavioral cognitive therapy, or periodic hospitalization for protection and rapid tranquilization).

14. Verbalize statements of hope that symptoms can be managed in ways other than suicide. (27, 28, 29, 30)

27. Formulate an appropriate view of suicide for the client: It stems from a desire to solve a temporarily unsolvable problem (e.g., the bipolar illness and its depressive phase, problematic behaviors because of untreated mania); it is fueled by elements of hopelessness and helplessness; and the antidote is to acquire safe, simple coping and problem solving skills for identified stressors and symptoms.

28. Assign the client to a treatment journal to track daily stressors, the resulting symptoms, maladaptive coping patterns, and experiences with newly acquired coping strategies; assign homework targeting symptom management.

29. Assist the client in noting in his/her treatment journal a detailed plan with specific instructions on managing perturbation associated with his/her immediate, priority symptoms (e.g., when feeling hopeless remember the therapist's promise of working together on goals or when in denial of illness remember to stay on medication); these detailed responses should assist the client during extreme emotional upset.

30. Use role-play, modeling, and behavior rehearsal to teach the client to implement the symptom-management skills noted in his/her treatment journal.

15. Identify own traits and vulnerabilities that hinder coping strategies and contribute to the suicide intent. (31, 32)

31. Explore the client's personal vulnerabilities that impede problem-solving and contribute to the suicidal crisis (e.g., extreme levels of self-directed anger, an overpowering need to please other people, a dysfunctional inability to access emotions, or confusion about self-identity).

32. Assist the client in acknowledging the existence of his/her personal vulnerabilities and their influence on maladaptive

16. Identify strategies that resolve personal traits and vulnerabilities that contribute to suicide potential to enhance coping skills and diminish the suicide intent. (33, 34, 35)

coping (e.g., being manipulated by peers to stop taking medications, alcohol abuse as self-medication, or self-destructive behaviors); help him/her chart the events where personal vulnerabilities and their influence are evident in maladaptive decision making.

33. Examine the source of the client's personal vulnerabilities (e.g., the need to please originating from a performance-oriented family system, self-hate originating from a emotionally and/or physically abusive family system, or emotional constriction originating from a family system that was intolerant of emotional displays) for a better understanding of these personality traits and how they influence coping.

34. Engage the client in a process to replace these vulnerabilities with more adaptive personality traits that will enhance coping strategies (e.g., self-hate and self-devaluation is replaced by a core identity of self-acceptance, emotional constriction is replaced by a willingness to feel emotions, and performance anxiety is replaced by a calm and patient acceptance of failures and personal limitations); use cognitive restructuring techniques to reach these objectives.

35. Maintain the therapeutic relationship (e.g., being with the client throughout the chaotic course of his/her illness,

showing patience during times of medication noncompliance and denial of illness, or consistent focus on the need to keep him/her safe) as a means of bringing stability and affirmation to his/her life.

17. Enhance compliance with medical interventions. (36, 37)

36. Examine the client's personal issues that hinder adherence to his/her medication program (e.g., denial of illness, hopelessness because of life-long course of the illness, side effects, peer pressure to discontinue medication, desire to experience the energy and euphoria of the manic state, fear that the medication might not be effective, resistance to being controlled by medical dictates, or the desire to be in control of one's body).

37. Avoid entering into a debate or power struggle with the client over medication issues, showing empathy for his/her concerns and patience with relapse but a respectful conviction that his/her life is worth living to its fullest potential; formulate a written plan that will integrate the medication program into his/her activities of daily living.

18. Identify the nature of the trauma associated with bipolar disorder and encourage an acceptance of the disorder as a life-long medical condition. (38, 39)

38. Examine the client's expectations of what life will be like since he/she is afflicted with bipolar disorder; educate him/her and, if possible, members of the support system about the expected chronic course of the disease and its management through therapy, hospitalization, and medication.

39. Drawing from the client's history, help him/her develop a positive perspective of himself/herself as a person with bipolar disorder; assist him/her in the development of a future life plan based on his/her revealed strengths.

19. Verbalize a sense of confidence in social and occupational functioning. (40, 41)

40. Encourage the client to see himself/herself in a social context by emphasizing the benefits of participation in friendships and group activities (e.g., especially encourage involvement in support groups for the bipolar population).

41. Assist the client in identifying individual stressors that accompany social and/or occupational functions (e.g., fear of acting inappropriately, embarrassment over the side effects of the medications, or feeling the stigma of having a mental illness); provide supportive techniques for managing these stressors in such functions (e.g., relaxation training, positive self-talk, or a support group).

20. Develop a suicide prevention plan that incorporates the treatment journal and all completed homework assignments. (42)

42. Educate the client about preventing relapse into suicidal behavior (e.g., rely on the treatment journal for reminders of strategies for coping with trigger events, feelings, and symptoms; remain on medication; maintain social network; continue to respect the mental illness; and maintain futuristic thinking).

_____. _____   _____. _____
        _____   _____
_____. _____   _____. _____
        _____   _____
_____. _____   _____. _____
        _____   _____

DIAGNOSTIC SUGGESTIONS:

Axis I: 296.xx   Bipolar I Disorder
              296.89   Bipolar II Disorder
              301.13   Cyclothymic Disorder
              296.80   Bipolar Disorder NOS
              305.00   Alcohol Abuse

              _____   _____
              _____   _____

Axis II: 301.7   Antisocial Personality Disorder
              301.83   Borderline Personality Disorder

              _____   _____
              _____   _____

BORDERLINE PERSONALITY DISORDER

BEHAVIORAL DEFINITIONS

1. Demonstrates a chronic pattern of suicide threats, gestures, and deliberate self-harm activity.
2. Verbalizes repeatedly experiencing suicide ideation.
3. Intolerant of feelings of loneliness and/or being socially isolated or rejected.
4. Uses suicide threats, gestures, and deliberate self-harm activity to coerce others into meeting social and psychological needs.
5. Has difficulty forming mutually reciprocal relationships.
6. Is extremely vulnerable to impulsive decision making.
7. Demonstrates chronic inability to regulate emotions internally.
8. Demonstrates chronic states of confusion about body integrity.
9. Lacks adaptive coping and problem-solving skills.
10. Has a history of being victimized by childhood sexual and/or physical abuse.
11. Has a history of early childhood abandonment and inconsistent nurturing patterns.

—. _____

_____

—. _____

_____

—. _____

_____

LONG-TERM GOALS

1. Develop a healthy concept of self-acceptance that includes termination of self-harm threats and behaviors.
2. Develop appropriate impulse control skills and the ability to delay gratification.
3. Develop reciprocal social skills to enhance interpersonal relationships.
4. Develop adaptive problem-solving skills and strategies.

—. _____

   _____

   _____

—. _____

   _____

   _____

—. _____

   _____

SHORT-TERM OBJECTIVES	THERAPEUTIC INTERVENTIONS
1. Describe experiences of childhood trauma or abandonment. (1, 2, 3)	1. Explore the client's history for experiences of childhood physical and/or sexual abuse.
	2. Examine the client's adoptive status, early childhood abandonment experiences, and inconsistent patterns of nurturing from the primary caregiver.
	3. Explore whether there were issues of narcissism in the primary caregiver and/or the family system that established self-serving expectations for the client (e.g., achievement in sports, academics, social status, occupational endeavors, or financial worth) that he/she could not meet.
2. Describe the details of previous suicide activity. (4, 5)	4. Examine specifics of the client's previous suicide attempts (e.g., intended goal is death with no sense of ambivalence, marked

intensity of planning, lethal means used, no communication of intent before the activity, unintended rescue, note the role of severe hopelessness and despair, note the motivation by intense self-directed rage).

5. Examine specifics of the client's previous parasuicidal behaviors (e.g., suicide communication or clues given before the event, intended goal was not death but a desired change in a relationship, activity was self-interrupted or calculated for rescue, used nonlethal means, was the result of an impulsive decision with no prior planning).

3. Provide information on personal experiences with high-risk *behavioral* markers for suicide in people with borderline personality disorder. (6, 7, 8, 9)

6. Assess the client for the high-risk borderline personality disorder suicide marker of alcohol abuse (e.g., linkage to increase in impulsivity, self-mutilation behaviors, depressive feelings, and suicidal ideation).

7. Assess the client for the high-risk borderline personality disorder suicide marker of chronic impulsivity (e.g., linkage to increase in self-mutilation behaviors, poor decision making, or suicidal ideation).

8. Assess the client for the high-risk borderline personality disorder suicide marker of faulty anger management (e.g., self-directed rage, violent acts toward others, destruction of property, or legal involvement because of violent crimes).

BORDERLINE PERSONALITY DISORDER 55

9. Assess the client for the high-risk borderline personality disorder suicide marker of abrupt cessation of self-harm behaviors; explore the purpose of his/her nonlethal, self-harm behaviors (e.g., possibly provides an outlet, however pathological, for discharging stress and, therefore, may reduce the inclination toward suicide).

4. Provide information on personal experiences with high-risk *emotional* markers for suicide in people with borderline personality disorder. (10, 11, 12, 13, 14)

10. Assess the client for the high-risk borderline personality disorder suicide marker of comorbid, antisocial personality traits (e.g., minimal capacity for empathic reaction to the feelings of others, aggressive behavior patterns, conflict with legal authorities, or blaming others).

11. Assess the client for the high-risk borderline personality disorder suicide marker of comorbid, narcissistic personality traits (e.g., inability to delay gratification or total preoccupation with need fulfillment).

12. Assess the client for the high-risk borderline personality disorder suicide marker of comorbid major depressive disorder, single episode, severe, with psychosis (e.g., elements of significant hopelessness, helplessness, or melancholic despair).

13. Assess the client for the high-risk borderline personality disorder suicide marker of severe and extensive borderline personality disorder symptomatology (e.g., meets all nine

of the *DSM-IV* diagnostic criteria).

14. Assess the client for the high-risk borderline personality disorder suicide marker of comorbid posttraumatic stress disorder (PTSD; e.g., linkage to early childhood trauma, sense of reliving the experience, traumatic dreams, intrusive thoughts, or avoidance of social experiences for fear of stimulating memories of trauma).

5. Provide information on personal experiences with high-risk *social* markers for suicide in people with borderline personality disorder. (15)

15. Assess the client for the high-risk borderline personality disorder suicide marker of unstable interpersonal relationships (e.g., divorce, multiple relationship terminations, sporadic employment history, or living alone).

6. Provide information on personal experiences with high-risk markers for parasuicide activity in people with borderline personality disorder. (16, 17, 18)

16. Assess the client for the high-risk borderline personality disorder parasuicide marker (e.g., nonlethal, chronic, repetitious patterns of self-harm behaviors where the intent is not death but the realization of unmet social, environmental, or psychological needs; and the activity is often communicated to others, calculated for rescue, or self-interrupted) of intolerance of being isolated or lonely (e.g., uses nonlethal, self-harm behaviors to prevent rejection, manage social network, or elicit nurturing from others).

17. Assess the client for the high-risk borderline personality disorder parasuicide marker of maladaptive coping strategies and problem-solving skills

(e.g., uses nonlethal, self-harm behaviors to coercively obtain environmental, social, and psychological needs).

18. Assess the client for the high-risk borderline personality disorder parasuicide marker of the inability to find relief from stressful emotions (e.g., uses nonlethal, self-harm behaviors to regulate overwhelming affect, manage intolerable emotional states, and sooth unstable self-concept).

7. Provide complete information on current mood, affect, and thought process in a psychiatric evaluation, while taking psychotropic medication as prescribed. (19)

19. Refer the client for a psychiatric evaluation to validate any at-risk comorbid Axis I or Axis II diagnostic features (e.g., major depressive disorder, PTSD, other personality disorders); the following guidelines should be used to determine the use of medication: (a) Involve the client, (b) treat only comorbid Axis I conditions, and (c) evaluate risks of overdose.

8. The client and, if available and appropriate, the caregivers accept feedback on the assessments and treatment plan developed from the evaluation process. (20)

20. Summarize and give feedback to the client and, if available and appropriate, the caregivers on high-risk markers found in the evaluation; formulate the treatment plan and, if possible, engage the caregivers.

9. Agree to a written plan for dealing with situations when the suicide intent or the urge to activate parasuicide behaviors becomes strong. (21)

21. Develop a written crisis intervention contract to implement during times when the client experiences trigger events and unbearable emotions (e.g., isolation, rage, anxiety, or confusion) that includes preestablished, well-defined guidelines for the use of inpatient hospitalization

(e.g., displaying behaviors correlated to the high-risk behavioral, emotional, and social markers for suicide).

10. Identify current stressors and resultant symptoms that trigger the suicide intent or the need to engage in parasuicide behaviors. (22, 23)

22. Assist the client in making a list of his/her most prominent stressors (e.g., disruptions in relationships, interactions with abusive caregivers, or functioning at the work place) and the reactions or symptoms (e.g., fear, isolation, panic, or a dissociative state) produced by those stressors.

23. Assist the client in producing a complete symptom inventory that includes identifying the most disruptive symptoms (e.g., self-hate, dissociative states, isolation, or panic), how these symptoms are currently dysfunctionally managed (e.g., self-mutilation, medication overdose, alcohol abuse), and other results created by these behaviors (e.g., alienation of social network or body disfigurement).

11. Verbalize statements of hope that symptoms can be managed in ways other than suicide or parasuicide behaviors. (24, 25, 26, 27, 28)

24. Formulate an appropriate view of suicide for the client: It stems from a desire to solve a temporarily unsolvable problem; it is fueled by elements of hopelessness and helplessness; and the antidote is to acquire safe, simple coping and problem-solving skills to manage identified stressors and symptoms.

25. Formulate an appropriate view of parasuicidal behaviors for the client: It stems from an inability to meet environmental, social,

and psychological needs; it is fueled by an intolerance of aloneness, an inability to regulate powerful emotions, and an inadequate sense of self; it is acted out through coercive self-harm behaviors; and the antidote is to acquire safe, simple strategies to meet needs.

26. Assign the client a treatment journal to track daily stressors, the resulting symptoms, maladaptive coping patterns, and experiences with newly acquired coping strategies; assign homework targeting symptom management; stress to him/her that the goal of therapy is healthy symptom management and *not* symptom elimination.

27. Assist the client in noting in his/her treatment journal a detailed plan with specific instructions to respond to and manage the perturbation associated with his/her immediate, priority symptoms (e.g., in response to the panic associated with isolation, formulate a self-calming program; in response to the shame and guilt associated with sexual abuse, formulate adaptive strategies of self-nurturing).

28. Use role-play, modeling, and behavior rehearsal to teach the client to implement the symptom-management skills noted in his/her treatment journal. These skills should be safe, simple, and easy to access during times of extreme

emotional turmoil (e.g., relaxation training, positive self-talk, or getting a reality check from a trusted source).

12. Identify own biological, social, and psychological traits and vulnerabilities that contribute to the suicide intent and para-suicide behaviors. (29)

29. Explore the client's personal vulnerabilities that impede problem solving and contribute to the suicidal/parasuicidal crisis (e.g., an overpowering need to please others, the inability to access or regulate emotions, extreme levels of shame and guilt, or confusion about self-identity).

13. Identify strategies that will diminish the influence of the personal, biological, social, and psychological traits and vulnerabilities on the suicide intent and parasuicide behaviors. (30, 31, 32, 33)

30. Assist the client in acknowledging the existence of his/her personal vulnerabilities and their influence on maladaptive coping (e.g., using self-mutilation during times of extreme shame or to access an emotional experience); assist him/her in charting the events when these personal vulnerabilities and their influence are evident in the course of suicide intent and parasuicidal behaviors.

31. Examine the source of the personal vulnerabilities with the client (e.g., guilt and shame originating from childhood sexual abuse experiences or the need to please originating from patterns of early childhood abandonment) for a better understanding of these personality dynamics and how they influence coping and problem-solving strategies.

32. Engage the client in a process to replace vulnerabilities with more adaptive personality traits that will enhance coping

strategies (e.g., shame and guilt is replaced by an understanding of his/her victimization with a gentle sense of self-acceptance or the need to please replaced by examining and practicing mutuality and reciprocal skills in relationships).

33. Engage the client in the therapeutic relationship to accomplish replacement of personal vulnerabilities (e.g., being with him/her during the chaotic course of treatment, teaching empathic self-regard, formulating the well-boundaried and caring therapy alliance, and teaching the acceptance of pain and trust in the consistency of the relationship).

14. Develop strategies that will enable engagement in mutual, reciprocal relationships. (34, 35)

34. Educate the client's significant others about the extreme sensitivity of the client to feelings of rejection and the challenge this presents in relationships; teach him/her and significant others specific relational skills (e.g., conflict resolution; or empathic listening skills, boundaries, and roles).

35. Assist the client in developing skills of mutuality and reciprocal strategies (e.g., practicing conflict-resolution skills); ask him/her to note in the treatment journal the diminished function of coercive self-harm behaviors to manage relational issues (e.g., threatening suicide or slashing) and the enhanced role of reciprocal skills (e.g., verbalizing fears of abandonment to therapist).

15. Verbalize the development of a core image of self-acceptance. (36, 37)

36. Ask the client to include an autobiography in his/her treatment journal; review the material together, encouraging a balanced view of his/her history, recognizing failures and accomplishments, reframing unjustified self-criticism, recognizing guilt where it is appropriate, pride where it is justified, and praise when due.

37. Drawing from the client's history, help him/her develop an accepting perspective of himself/herself; assist him/her in the development of a future life plan based on his/her revealed strengths.

16. Implement strategies that will enhance the capacity for internal regulation of emotions. (38)

38. Assist the client in identifying emotions that cause the most turmoil and lead to self-harm acts; target those emotions for self-calming strategies and verbalize them in the context of personal and intimate relationships.

17. Develop a prevention plan for suicide intent and parasuicidal behaviors. (39, 40)

39. Educate the client to prevent relapse into suicidal and/or parasuicidal behaviors (e.g., rely on the treatment journal for reminders of strategies for coping with trigger events, feelings, and symptoms; respect himself/ herself and the challenges of the borderline personality disorder; and maintain futuristic thinking).

40. Assist the client in writing a personal suicide/parasuicide prevention plan that lists individualized actions that will be taken in the future to manage suicidal urges.

18. Develop strategies for the appropriate termination of the therapeutic relationship. (41)

41. Anticipate and plan for termination at the beginning of therapy: as therapy nears an end expect an increase in transference issues; make the termination a collaborative effort with the client; empathize with the client's emotions on termination and consistently review his/her growth; challenge him/her to trust the value of self and his/her wisdom gained from the therapy experience.

__. _____   __. _____

     _____   _____

__. _____   __. _____

     _____   _____

__. _____   __. _____

     _____   _____

DIAGNOSTIC SUGGESTIONS:

Axis I:	296.xx	Major Depressive Disorder
	308.3	Acute Stress Disorder
	300.02	Generalized Anxiety Disorder
	305.00	Alcohol Abuse
	300.14	Dissociative Identity Disorder
	300.15	Dissociative Disorder NOS
	309.81	Posttraumatic Stress Disorder
	298.9	Psychotic Disorder NOS
	_____	_____
	_____	_____
Axis II:	301.83	Borderline Personality Disorder
	301.7	Antisocial Personality Disorder
	301.50	Histrionic Personality Disorder
	301.81	Narcissistic Personality Disorder
	301.6	Dependent Personality Disorder
	_____	_____
	_____	_____

CAUCASIAN FEMALE—ADOLESCENT

BEHAVIORAL DEFINITIONS

1. Verbalizes an attraction to death and a repulsion of life.
2. Demonstrates dangerous at-risk behaviors (e.g., reckless driving, high risk promiscuity, or drug abuse), which is ascribed to a passive attitude about life (e.g., "I don't care if I live or die).
3. Verbalizes a wish to escape from an intolerable situation and/or a painful psychological state that is focused on family/relationship turmoil.
4. Verbalizes a sense of hopelessness that a current painful life event will never get better.
5. Verbalizes a sense of helplessness about the management of a painful life event.
6. Demonstrates behaviors positively correlated to a diagnosis of depression (e.g., anhedonia, dysphoria, irritability, sleep problems).
7. Frequently verbalizes feelings of worthlessness, self-hate, intense guilt, self-criticism, failure, rejection, or isolation.
8. Has experienced a recent loss of a loved one or significant acquaintance to suicide resulting in a reduction in the fear of death.
9. Engages in self-mutilation behavior.
10. Has a history of eating disorders.
11. Demonstrates a chronic pattern of suicide ideation with or without a plan.
12. Demonstrates consistently distorted and negative body image.
13. Demonstrates a chronic pattern of nonlethal suicide gestures.

—. _____
_____
_____
—. _____
_____
_____
—. _____
_____

LONG-TERM GOALS

1. Report a wish to live.
2. Develop an engaging attitude toward life.
3. Develop a sense of hope for the future and an ability to define self in a futuristic context.
4. Enhance and strengthen a sense of competence in managing the daily stress related to family/relationship turmoil.
5. Resolve feelings of worthlessness, self-hate, or isolation that contribute to the suicide impulse.
6. Manage the perturbation caused by a mood disorder.
7. Develop a concern for body integrity and body protection.

—. _____
    _____
—. _____
    _____
—. _____
    _____

SHORT-TERM OBJECTIVES	THERAPEUTIC INTERVENTIONS
1. Identify facts and feelings associated with childhood abuse experiences. (1, 2)	1. Explore the client's early childhood experiences of self-defined emotional, physical, or sexual abuse.
	2. Assist the client in identifying any maladaptive behavioral and emotional and/or cognitive reactions to her abusive childhood experiences (e.g., self-directed anger as expressed in self-mutilation, changes in eating behavior, feelings of worthlessness, rejection, or isolation).
2. Identify academic and social conflicts, frustrations, and struggles related to school experiences. (3, 4)	3. Assist the client in identifying areas of concern in her school setting, focusing on truancy, isolation patterns, numerous

school site changes, and failing academic patterns.

4. Explore the client's emotional and/or cognitive reactions to school-setting problems (e.g., feelings of rejection, isolation, failure, worthlessness, and/or humiliation); be alert for a feigned stance of apathy toward the problems.

3. The client and caregivers provide information on facts and feelings surrounding family history and relationships. (5, 6)

5. Explore the client's family dynamics (e.g., perceived quality of support system, attachment issues with father, incest, communication patterns, stability of home environment, consistency of caregivers, early childhood abandonment issues, family member substance abuse patterns, family suicide history, or family members with diagnosed mental illness).

6. Meet with caregivers to explore the client's history and current functioning from their perspective, focusing on issues of sexual, physical, or emotional abuse; school performance; social network; communication patterns; substance abuse; depression signs; recent relationship turmoil; self-mutilation, or eating disorders.

4. Cooperate with psychological testing designed to evaluate suicidal ideation. (7)

7. Administer an objective assessment inventory to reveal and evaluate suicidal ideation and intent levels (e.g., Suicidal Ideation Questionnaire, Beck Depression Inventory, Beck Scale for Suicide Ideation, or Suicide Probability Scale); provide feedback to caregivers

and client on test results and treatment implications.

5. The client and caregivers provide information on the client's personal experiences with high-risk *behavioral* markers for adolescent female suicide. (8, 9)

8. Assess the client for the high-risk adolescent Caucasian female suicide marker of substance abuse by administering a thorough evaluation (e.g., inquire about mood-altering drug use: history, frequency, age of onset, variety and types of drugs used, excessive alcohol abuse, peer use patterns, perceived benefits gained, psychological dependency signs, parental reaction).

9. Assess the client for high-risk adolescent Caucasian female suicide markers of runaway behavior, eating disorder behaviors, self-mutilation, sexualized self-image, and promiscuity.

6. The client and caregivers provide information on the client's experience with high-risk *emotional* markers for adolescent female suicide. (10, 11, 12)

10. Assess the client for the high-risk adolescent Caucasian female suicide marker of depression (e.g., inquire about depth of sadness, hopelessness, low energy, lack of interest or pleasure in activities, social withdrawal, low self-esteem, or sleep disturbance).

11. Assess the client for the high-risk adolescent Caucasian female suicide marker of panic and anxiety (e.g., level and pervasiveness of worry, motor tension and restlessness, rapid heartbeat, shortness of breath, dry mouth, concentration difficulties, sleep disturbance, or irritability).

7. The client and caregivers provide information on the client's personal experience with high-risk *social* markers for adolescent female suicide. (13, 14)

8. School personnel provide information on the client's behavior and academic issues. (15)

9. Medical personnel provide relevant, current information on the client's general health issues. (16)

12. Assess the client for the high-risk adolescent Caucasian female suicide marker of posttraumatic stress symptoms, especially distinctly dissociative experiences.

13. Assess the client for the high-risk adolescent Caucasian female suicide marker of relationship turmoil (e.g., romantic relationship termination, abuse patterns in romantic relationships, peer group rejection, amount of time spent alone, family communication patterns, loss of autonomy to gain acceptance, sexual orientation issues, or college bound status).

14. Assess the client for the high-risk adolescent Caucasian female suicide marker of contagion related to recent media reports of suicide or death of a significant other that diminishes her fear of death and increases her repulsion to life.

15. After obtaining the appropriate confidentiality releases, contact the client's school officials for a report on her attendance, behavioral, and academic patterns; continue consultation with school officials throughout the therapy process.

16. After obtaining appropriate confidentiality releases, contact the client's medical providers for a report on her health history (e.g., diseases, bodily injuries, psychosomatic complaint pattern, STD history, pregnancy history, or abortions); continue

consultation with the primary care provider throughout the therapy process.

10. Provide complete information on current mood, affect, and thought process in a psychiatric evaluation, taking psychotropic medication as prescribed. (17, 18)

17. Refer the client for a psychiatric evaluation to determine her need for psychotropic medication and to validate any at-risk diagnoses (e.g., posttraumatic stress disorder, depression, or generalized anxiety disorder).

18. Monitor the client's compliance with her psychotropic medication prescription, chart her subjective and objective behavioral changes, and monitor side effects.

11. The client and caregivers accept feedback on the assessment for high-risk markers for suicide. (19)

19. Summarize and give feedback to the client and her caregivers on high-risk markers found in her presentation; outline the treatment plan and, if possible, engage the caregivers.

12. Comply with placement in a more protective and restrictive environment if the assessments reveal high-risk suicide markers. (20, 21)

20. Monitor the client's suicide risk at appropriate intervals through interview and by administering standardized suicide risk assessment instruments (e.g., Beck Depression Inventory, Beck Scale for Suicide Ideation, or the Suicide Probability Scale).

21. Place the client in a supervised and structured therapeutic setting that will protect her from suicidal impulse, decrease perturbation, remove her from environmental stress, decrease her isolation, and allow monitoring of treatment effectiveness; this action should be taken any time the client begins to experience or demonstrate an

increase in high-risk markers that appear to exceed her capacity to cope.

13. Affirm the safety of a plan that allows for a return to the home and family environment. (22, 23)

22. Note changes in the client's family equilibrium and hold a session with caregivers to focus on effecting system change to accommodate her return to the home environment (e.g., improving communication patterns, resolving issues of autonomy, providing safety from abuse patterns, and removing predatory members).

23. Develop a discharge plan with the client, her caregivers, and the inpatient treatment team that includes consideration of placement issues, school responsibilities, support system, individual and family psychotherapy treatment, activities of daily living, and local support services.

14. Agree to a written plan for dealing with situations when suicidal urges become strong. (24)

24. Develop a written crisis intervention plan to be implemented during trigger events and emotions (e.g., arguments, failures, or rejections) that includes contacting therapist, trusted friend, or local help line (provide all these telephone numbers to the client written on a card) to discuss emotional reactions to events when she is experiencing strong suicidal urges.

15. Identify any history of suicide activity and specifics of the current suicide ideation or intent. (25, 26, 27, 28)

25. Explore the intended goal of the current suicide urge (e.g., cessation of emotional pain, revenge against an offending person, an urge to self-murder, or an empathy-seeking act) with the client.

26. Examine any previous suicide activity (e.g., ideation, gestures, or lethal attempts) and detail the motivation and outcome with the client. Pay close attention to those activities that were self-interrupted or calculated for rescue (suicide gestures) and those activities that were accidentally interrupted against the client's wishes (suicide attempts).

27. Explore the amount of time and energy spent in planning and beginning implementation of the suicide event (has a lethal method been chosen and obtained, has a date and place been assigned, have symbolic good-byes been said, has anyone been told of the plan and, if so, what was the reaction) with the client.

28. Explore whether client's feelings of anxiety or depression have been eased or calmed since a decision to plan death began and explore any barriers to the plan to die (e.g., fear of pain or emotional impact on survivors or religious beliefs) with the client.

16. List current stressful situations that produce symptoms that spark the suicidal urge. (29)

29. Assist the client in making a list of her most prominent stressors (e.g., having no friends, experiencing constant rejection, or being emotionally and/or physically abused at home or with boyfriend) and identify emotional reactions or symptoms produced by those stressors; target those symptoms for immediate intervention and

teach coping strategies (e.g., discussing sadness in relationships with a trusted friend or therapist, contacting authorities to obtain protection from abuse, or identifying supportive relationships).

17. List solutions to these life stressors that do not require suicide. (30, 31)

30. Teach the client about her maladaptive externalizing coping patterns (e.g., running away, alcohol abuse, or self-mutilation) and internalizing coping patterns (e.g., depression, anxiety, or posttraumatic stress disorder) and replace these maladaptive coping strategies with a problem-solving focus.

31. Assign the client a treatment journal to track daily stressors, the resulting symptoms, maladaptive coping patterns, and experiences with newly acquired coping strategies; assign homework targeting symptom management. Stress to the client that the goal of therapy is healthy symptom management and *not* symptom elimination.

18. Verbalize statements of hope that stressors and symptoms can be managed in ways other than suicide. (32, 33)

32. Formulate an appropriate view of the function of suicide with the client: It stems from a need to solve a seemingly unsolvable problem; it is fueled by a sense of hopelessness and helplessness; the antidote is to develop, with the therapist's help, coping strategies for these seemingly unsolvable issues.

33. Use role-play, modeling, and behavior rehearsal to teach the client problem-solving skills (e.g., define the problem, brainstorm alternative solutions,

list the positives and negatives of each solution, select and implement a plan of action, evaluate the outcome and adjust the solution as necessary in the treatment journal).

19. Identify own biological, social, and emotional vulnerabilities that contribute to the current crisis. (34)

34. Explore the client's personal vulnerabilities contributing to her suicidal crisis (e.g., tendency for feelings of extreme self-blame, need to be perfect, feelings of isolation, or sexualized identity). Assist the client in acknowledging the existence of these traits and their influence in maladaptive coping (e.g., dissociation experiences, using sex to gain affection, self-mutilation to manage raging emotions, or eating disorders).

20. Increase the frequency of statements that communicate pride in accomplishments and improved self-confidence. (35, 36)

35. Assist the client in enhancing her self-image by encouraging her to provide reports from her treatment journal on recent incidents of improved coping and problem solving.

36. Enhance the client's self-esteem by validating examples of her growth, accomplishments, improved coping, and appropriate independent behaviors (e.g., going to school or job regularly, deciding against a dangerous behavior, or feeling self-pride in a job well done).

21. List the benefits of sharing thoughts, feelings, and activities with friends and family. (37)

37. Teach the client the value of verbalizing her emotions in the context of personal relationships (e.g., sharing feelings promotes empathy from others, sharing of burdens reduces their intensity, and sharing allows others to give their perspective and offer

solutions). Encourage the client to see herself in a social context by emphasizing the benefits of her participation in friendships and group activities.

22. List healthy ways to manage and express anger and frustration. (38, 39)

38. Stress how the maladaptive anger coping patterns of self-mutilation and eating disorders can lead to the suicidal urge; focus on constructive methods of managing anger (e.g., acknowledging that anger is healthy, engaging in physical exercise, or talking it out with a safe third party).

39. Assist the client in identifying her dissociative patterns and their triggering stressors; educate her in healthy ways to cope with these triggering stressors (e.g., self-calming techniques, verbalizing emotions, or journaling).

23. Develop a suicide prevention plan that incorporates the treatment journal and all completed homework assignments. (40, 41)

40. Educate the client about preventing relapse into suicidal behavior (e.g., be aware of strategies for positive coping with stressors and symptoms, be aware of vulnerable parts, avoid isolation and maintain social network, and allow permission to fail and restart).

41. Assist the client in writing a personal suicide prevention plan that lists actions she will take in the future to manage suicidal urges (including contacting supportive others); refer to lessons learned in the treatment journal and the homework assignments to enhance confidence.

___. _____   ___. _____
    _____   _____
___. _____   ___. _____
    _____   _____
___. _____   ___. _____
    _____   _____

DIAGNOSTIC SUGGESTIONS:

Axis I:

296.3x	Major Depressive Disorder, Recurrent
300.4	Dysthymic Disorder
304.80	Polysubstance Dependence
307.51	Bulimia Nervosa
309.21	Separation Anxiety Disorder
305.00	Alcohol Abuse
300.15	Dissociative Disorder NOS
307.1	Anorexia Nervosa
298.9	Psychotic Disorder NOS
300.21	Panic Disorder with Agoraphobia
309.81	Posttraumatic Stress Disorder
312.9	Disruptive Behavior Disorder NOS

_____ _____

_____ _____

CAUCASIAN FEMALE—ADULT

BEHAVIORAL DEFINITIONS

1. Verbalizes unbearable psychological pain caused by frustrated environmental, social, and psychological needs.
2. Verbalizes a devalued self-image.
3. Demonstrates significant cognitive rigidity that significantly limits effective problem solving.
4. Verbalizes feelings of desertion, isolation, aloneness, and a loss of support from significant others.
5. Displays symptoms of a major depressive disorder (e.g., anhedonia, dysphoria, fatalistic despair, lack of energy, and social withdrawal).
6. Verbalizes that the suicide intent is the *only* method available of escaping or solving the problem of unbearable psychological pain.
7. Demonstrates a life-long pattern of perfectionism and a dysfunctional need to please others.
8. Gives clear verbal and/or behavioral indications of the impending suicide event.
9. Has a history of engaging in suicide activity (e.g., chronic ideation, nonfatal gesturing, or attempts).
10. Verbalizes feelings of being "bored with life" and feels no stability in current life situation.
11. Demonstrates behaviors commonly associated with personality disorders (e.g., borderline, histrionic, or narcissistic).
12. Uses alcohol to cope with feelings of depression.

—. _____

_____

—. _____

_____

—. _____

_____

LONG-TERM GOALS

1. Embrace life with an expression of hope for the future.
2. Resolve feelings of worthlessness, self-devaluation, or isolation, which contribute to depressive reactions and suicide impulses.
3. Enhance the development of coping strategies and problem-solving skills.
4. Increase a sense of self-acceptance and an enhanced ability to cope with failures and periodic aloneness.
5. Develop a supportive social network that enhances affirmation of self.
6. Develop the capacity to accept pain as a part of the life experience.

—. _____
   _____
   _____
—. _____
   _____
   _____
—. _____
   _____

SHORT-TERM OBJECTIVES

1. Describe the specifics of the current suicide plan and/or intent. (1, 2, 3, 4)

THERAPEUTIC INTERVENTIONS

1. Explore the client's goal for the intended suicide act (e.g., cessation of intolerable psychological pain, elimination of self because of extreme self-devaluation, or a solution to a seemingly unsolvable problem).

2. Explore the amount of time and energy the client spent in planning the suicide event (e.g., has a lethal means been decided on, especially note whether firearms have been chosen for the lethal means; have a date and a place been assigned; has the suicide intent been communicated to anyone and, if so, what was the reaction).

2. Identify specifics of any historic pattern of suicide ideation, gestures, or attempts. (5)

3. Provide information on personal experiences with high-risk *behavioral* markers in adult Caucasian females. (6, 7, 8)

3. Explore whether any sense of calm, peace, tranquility, or a renewed energy level has been experienced by the client since the planning for the suicide has started or has been completed.

4. Explore the client's barriers to the plan to die (e.g., religious beliefs, fear of emotional impact on survivors, or accidentally being discovered, saved, and then surviving; responsibility for dependent children; or a wish to attend some future event); note whether there is any ambivalence displayed about her completed suicide attempt.

5. Examine the client's previous suicide activity and explore her motivation and the outcome; pay close attention to those activities that were self-interrupted or calculated for rescue (suicide gestures) versus those activities that were accidentally interrupted against the client's wishes (suicide attempts).

6. Assess the client for the high-risk adult Caucasian female suicide marker of substance abuse (e.g., age of onset, use designed to cope with stress and/or depression, use in previous suicide activity, perceived benefits gained, and readiness to change).

7. Assess the client for the high-risk adult Caucasian female suicide marker of faulty problem-solving skills (e.g., behaviors of escape, denial,

social withdrawal used as coping strategies during times of stress).

8. Assess the client for the high-risk adult Caucasian female suicide marker of lifetime patterns of runaway behaviors, eating disorder behaviors, self-mutilation, sexualized self-image, and anger management problems.

4. Provide information on personal experiences with high-risk *emotional* markers in adult Caucasian females. (9, 10, 11, 12)

9. Assess the client for the high-risk adult Caucasian female suicide marker of depression (e.g., depth of sadness, melancholic despair, global fatalism, hopelessness, low energy, anhedonia, social withdrawal, low self-esteem, or sleep disturbance).

10. Assess the client for the high-risk adult Caucasian female suicide marker of perfectionism (e.g., dysfunctional need to please others, confused sense of self-identity, significant issues of self-criticism, cognitive rigidity, or inability to tolerate mistakes or failures).

11. Assess the client for the high-risk adult Caucasian female suicide marker of anxiety (e.g., level and pervasiveness of worry, restlessness and agitation, sleep problems, concentration difficulties, irritability, or panic attacks).

12. Assess the client for the high-risk adult Caucasian female suicide marker of posttraumatic stress symptoms (e.g., history of childhood sexual and/or physical

5. Provide information on personal experiences with high-risk *social* markers in adult Caucasian females. (13, 14, 15)

6. Cooperate with psychological testing designed to evaluate suicide ideation or intent levels in adult Caucasian females. (16)

7. Provide complete information on current mood, affect, and thought process in a psychiatric evaluation and take

abuse or distinct dissociative experiences).

13. Assess the client for the high-risk adult Caucasian female suicide marker of relationship turmoil (e.g., romantic relationship termination, abuse patterns in romantic relationships, amount of time spent alone, experiences with grieving, death of significant others, or sexual orientation conflicts).

14. Assess the client for the high-risk adult Caucasian female suicide marker of employment issues (e.g., if employed, issues of self-esteem, feelings of autonomy, or sense of coping with stress; if unemployed, feelings of adequacy, self-determination, or future hopes and ambitions).

15. Assess the client for the high-risk adult Caucasian female suicide marker of loss (e.g., loss of health, self-esteem, financial security, or autonomy).

16. Administer an objective assessment inventory to reveal and evaluate suicide ideation and intent levels in the client (e.g., Suicide Probability Scale, Reasons for Living Inventory, or Beck Depression Inventory); provide feedback to the client on test results and treatment implications.

17. Refer the client for a psychiatric evaluation to determine her need for psychotropic medication and to validate any at-risk

psychotropic medication as prescribed. (17, 18)

8. Medical personnel provide relevant, current information on general health issues. (19)

9. Accept feedback gathered from all sources and the treatment plan developed from the evaluation process. (20)

10. Comply with placement in a more protective and, possibly, restrictive environment. (21)

11. Affirm a plan that allows for a safe return to the community. (22)

diagnoses (e.g., major depressive disorders; borderline, histrionic, or narcissistic personality traits; generalized anxiety disorder).

18. Monitor the client's compliance with the psychotropic medication prescription, chart her subjective and objective behavioral changes, and monitor side effects.

19. After obtaining appropriate confidentiality and privacy releases, contact the client's medical providers for a report on her health history (e.g., psychosomatic complaint pattern, signs of physical abuse, or mental health concerns).

20. Summarize and give feedback to the client on high-risk markers found in her presentation; outline the treatment plan and, if possible, engage caregivers in the client's treatment.

21. If at any time in the treatment process the client displays the presence of behaviors correlated to completed suicide (e.g., dramatic increase in depressive or anxiety symptoms), place her in a structured, therapeutic setting that will protect her from suicide impulse and decrease her perturbation and monitor treatment effectiveness.

22. Develop a discharge plan with the client and her inpatient treatment team that includes consideration of medication program, activities of daily living, support systems, and psychotherapy.

12. Agree to a crisis response plan for dealing with situations when suicide risk is strong. (23)

23. Develop a written crisis intervention plan to be implemented during trigger events and emotions (e.g., failures that lead to intolerable feelings of self-devaluation or rejections that lead to intolerable feelings of aloneness) that includes contacting the therapist, trusted friend, or local help line to process and calm the emotions; ask the client to agree, as a verbal contract of therapy, to call someone on an emergency phone list to process these emotions.

13. Identify the locus of the intolerable psychological pain that challenges problem-solving capacity, creates feelings of hopelessness, and triggers the wish to die by suicide. (24)

24. Assist the client in making a list of her most prominent stressors (e.g., loss of a loved one, rejection in a relationship, chronic conditions of depression/anxiety, or inability to meet the needs of significant others) and identify emotional reactions or symptoms produced by those stressors (e.g., intolerable grief, self-criticism, aloneness, or despair).

14. Identify specifics of faulty problem-solving strategies. (25, 26)

25. Examine the client's history of coping strategies and problem-solving techniques during times of crisis (e.g., question whether she has ever had this experience before and, if so, how did she deal with it).

26. Explore the client's impediments to problem-solving skills (e.g., chronic messages of devaluation from caregivers, chronic messages of negation in relationships, chronic anxiety preventing clear thinking, or psychological issues of posttraumatic stress disorder).

15. Identify individual personality vulnerabilities and traits that contribute to suicide ideation. (27, 28)

27. Explore the client's personal vulnerabilities and personality traits that are contributing to the current suicidal crisis (e.g., inability to access and process painful emotions, extreme need to be perfect and conform to others expectations, or extreme feelings of self-hate that stem from patterns of child abuse).

28. Assist the client in acknowledging the existence of the personality traits that make her vulnerable to a suicide crisis and their influence in maladaptive coping (e.g., self-mutilation to manage raging emotions, eating disorders, social withdrawal to manage feelings of failure, or using sex to gain affection).

16. Identify specific strategies that will diminish the influence of the personality vulnerabilities on coping capacity and the intent to die by suicide. (29, 30)

29. Assist the client in understanding the source of her personality vulnerabilities (e.g., psychological imprint from child abuse, lived in an emotionally constrictive home environment, or raised in an atmosphere where love and affirmation were tied to performance).

30. Teach the client (a) that she must respect her core self-image of intrinsic worth, (b) that she doesn't have to please the therapist, (c) that expressions of emotions are honored and accepted without judgment, (d) that she is safe and respected, (e) that she can make mistakes and fail in an atmosphere of understanding and respect, and (f) that to be vulnerable is to be human.

17. Identify specific problem-solving strategies that will aid

31. Encourage the client to write her autobiography and focus on

in the management of painful symptoms and increase a sense of hope that these symptoms can be continuously managed in ways other than suicide. (31, 32, 33, 34)

times when appropriate problem-solving strategies were developed to manage crisis; assist her in reframing and/or redefining incidents that she may not have seen as successful coping. Expand and apply these noted experiences to present-day crisis and coping strategies.

32. Use role-play, modeling, and behavioral rehearsal to teach the client problem-solving skills (e.g., define the problem, explore alternative solutions, list the positives and negatives of each solution, select and implement a plan of action, evaluate the outcome, and adjust the strategies as necessary); apply these skills to her daily life issues.

33. Assign the client a treatment journal to track daily stressors, the resulting symptoms, maladaptive coping patterns, and experiences with newly acquired coping strategies (e.g., verbalizing emotions to a friend or the therapist to experience normalization and catharsis); assign homework targeting symptom management.

34. Formulate an appropriate view of the function of suicide with the client: It stems from a need to solve a seemingly unsolvable problem; it is fueled by a sense of hopelessness and helpless-ness; the antidote is to develop, with the therapist's help, adaptive coping strategies for these seemingly unsolvable issues.

18. Increase the frequency of social contact in which feelings are shared with others. (35)

35. Teach the client the value of verbalizing her emotions in the context of personal relationships; stress that self-definition in a social context can greatly reduce some of the primary symptoms (e.g., isolation, abandonment, or aloneness) that incite suicide urges and that sharing feelings can lead to their normalization (e.g., an awareness that psychological pain is an expected human experience).

19. Increase the frequency of statements that communicate pride in accomplishments and improved confidence in self. (36)

36. Assist the client in enhancing her self-image by encouraging her to provide reports from her treatment journal on recent incidents of improved coping and problem solving.

20. Write a suicide prevention plan that incorporates the treatment journal's homework assignments. (37)

37. Assist the client in writing a personal suicide prevention plan that lists the actions she will take in the future to manage suicidal urges (e.g., avoid isolation and maintain social network, continue to practice adaptive problem-solving strategies, and continued awareness of personal vulnerabilities); refer to lessons learned in the treatment journal and the successful homework assignments to enhance confidence.

__. _____
   _____

__. _____
   _____

__. _____
   _____

__. _____
   _____

__. _____
   _____

__. _____
   _____

DIAGNOSTIC SUGGESTIONS:

Axis I: 296.xx   Major Depressive Disorder
                 300.4   Dysthymic Disorder
                 305.00   Alcohol Abuse
                 307.51   Bulimia Nervosa
                 309.21   Separation Anxiety Disorder
                 300.15   Dissociative Disorder NOS
                 307.1   Anorexia Nervosa
                 300.21   Panic Disorder with Agoraphobia
                 309.81   Posttraumatic Stress Disorder

                 _____   _____

                 _____   _____

Axis II: 301.83   Borderline Personality Disorder

                 _____   _____

                 _____   _____

CAUCASIAN MALE—ADOLESCENT

BEHAVIORAL DEFINITIONS

1. Verbally indicates a wish to die.
2. Demonstrates dangerous at-risk behaviors (e.g., reckless driving or heavy substance abuse) that are ascribed to a wish to die.
3. Verbally indicates a wish to escape from an intolerable situation and/or a painful psychological state.
4. Verbalizes a wish to join a deceased acquaintance.
5. Verbalizes a sense of hopelessness that a currently painful life event will get better.
6. Verbalizes a sense of helplessness about management of a painful life event.
7. Demonstrates behaviors positively correlated to a diagnosis of depression (e.g., anhedonia, dysphoria, irritability, sleep problems, or social isolation).
8. Frequently verbalizes feelings of worthlessness, self-hate, intense guilt, or self-criticism.
9. Consistently verbalizes feelings of failure, rejection, and isolation.
10. Experienced a recent loss of a loved one or significant acquaintance to suicide.
11. Demonstrates a chronic pattern of substance abuse where the stated goal is to escape reality.
12. Demonstrates a history of suicide gesturing (e.g., the activity is either calculated for rescue or self-interrupted) and/or attempts (the activity is accidentally interrupted, against the person's wishes).
13. Demonstrates considerable impulsivity and resides in a home where firearms are readily available.

—. _____
_____
—. _____
_____
—. _____
_____

LONG-TERM GOALS

1. Report a wish to live.
2. Develop a sense of hope for the future and an ability to define self in a futuristic context.
3. Enhance and strengthen a sense of competence in managing daily stress.
4. Resolve feelings of worthlessness, self-hate, and isolation that contribute to the suicide impulse.
5. Eliminate at-risk, dangerous behavior patterns that increase suicidal thoughts, urges, or actions.
6. Manage the perturbation caused by thought or mood disorder.
7. Develop a view of self in a social context and enhance the capacity to formulate intimate relationships.

—. _____
_____
—. _____
_____
—. _____
_____

SHORT-TERM OBJECTIVES

1. Describe the specifics of the current suicide ideation and/or intent. (1, 2, 3, 4, 5)

THERAPEUTIC INTERVENTIONS

1. Explore the goal for the intended suicide act (e.g., cessation of emotional pain, solution to a seemingly unsolvable problem, or elimination of self because of

extreme self-hate issues) with the client.

2. Examine any previous suicide activity with the client and classify as either lethal attempt (accidentally interrupted against the individual's wishes) or gesture (self-interrupted or calculated for rescue).

3. Explore the amount of time and energy spent in planning the suicide event (e.g., has a lethal means or a weapon been chosen and/or obtained; has a date or place been assigned; have prize possessions been distributed to others; have symbolic good-byes been said; has anyone been told of the suicide intent and, if so, what was the perceived reaction) with the client.

4. Explore whether the client's feelings of anxiety or depression have eased or calmed since the planning or decision to die has been made.

5. Explore any barriers to the plan to die (e.g., fear of emotional impact on survivors, religious beliefs, or fear of pain) with the client.

2. Identify current stressors and resultant symptoms that trigger the wish to die by suicide. (6, 7, 8)

6. Assist the client in making a list of his most prominent stressors (e.g., living in an alcoholic home, dealing with a physically abusive caregiver, or dealing with repeated failure in school); explore his emotional reactions or symptoms (e.g., depression, anxiety, or self-hate) produced by those stressors.

7. Assist the client in developing a complete symptom inventory that includes identifying the most disruptive symptoms (symptoms that seriously affect functioning), current management of symptoms (e.g., substance abuse, missing school, or dangerous at-risk behaviors), and whether these symptoms create other reactions (e.g., self-devaluation) that eventually overwhelm him.

8. Establish a therapeutic alliance with the client that ensures the therapist's help in targeting the most serious symptoms for immediate attention (e.g., medication, solution-oriented therapy, or hospitalization).

3. The client and caregivers provide information on facts and feelings surrounding family history and family relationships. (9, 10)

9. Explore the client's family dynamics (e.g., perceived quality of the support system; nature of sibling relationships; consistency of caregivers; stability of home environment; firearm availability in the current home; early childhood abandonment issues; family member substance abuse and history of mental illness; and issues of emotional, sexual, physical abuse patterns); explore his emotional reaction to the stressors within the home environment.

10. If possible, meet with the caregivers to explore the client's history and current functioning from their perspective; focus on issues such as prenatal care, school performance, social network, substance abuse, signs

of depression, recent rejections, and self-esteem.

4. The client and caregivers provide information on the client's personal experience with high-risk *behavioral* markers for adolescent male suicide. (11, 12)

11. Assess the client for the high-risk adolescent Caucasian male suicide marker of substance abuse by administering a thorough evaluation (e.g., mood-altering drug use history and frequency, age of onset, variety of drugs used, peer use patterns, physiological dependency signs, family member use, legal involvement, parental reaction, or history of drug use in a suicide activity).

12. Assess the client for the high-risk adolescent Caucasian male suicide marker of legal conflicts (e.g., arrest record convictions, juvenile detentions, peer arrests, gang involvement, probation/ parole compliance, family legal involvement, or parental reaction); determine whether a diagnosis of antisocial personality/conduct disorder is appropriate.

5. The client and caregivers provide information on the client's personal experience with high-risk *emotional* markers for adolescent male suicide. (13, 14)

13. Assess the client for the high-risk adolescent Caucasian male suicide marker of depression (e.g., depth of sadness, expressed hopelessness, low energy, lack of interest or pleasure in activities, social withdrawal, low self-esteem, reduced appetite, sleep disturbance, or irritability).

14. Assess the client for the high-risk adolescent Caucasian male suicide marker of panic and anxiety (e.g., level and pervasiveness of worry, motor tension and restlessness, rapid

heartbeat, shortness of breath, dry mouth, concentration difficulty, sleep disturbance, or irritability).

6. The client and caregivers provide information on the client's personal experience with high-risk *social* markers for adolescent male suicide. (15, 16)

15. Assess the client for the high-risk adolescent Caucasian male suicide marker of perceived rejection (e.g., romantic relationship termination, peer group rejection, depth of social network, amount of time spent alone, family support network, and sexual orientation issues that conflict with family).

16. Assess the client for the high-risk adolescent Caucasian male suicide marker of separation issues (e.g., pending military service; college-bound status; parent's divorce; death of close friend, acquaintance, loved one, or pet).

7. Medical personnel provide relevant, current information on the client's general health issues. (17)

17. After obtaining the appropriate confidentiality releases, contact the client's medical providers for a report on his childhood health (e.g., perinatal distress, attention deficit/hyperactivity disorder, diseases, bodily injuries, or medications); continue consultation with the primary care provider during the therapy process.

8. School personnel provide information on behavior and academic issues. (18)

18. After obtaining the appropriate confidentiality releases, contact school officials for a report on the client's attendance, behavioral, and academic patterns; continue consultation with school personnel throughout the therapy process.

9. Provide complete information on current mood, affect, and thought process in a psychiatric evaluation and take psychotropic medications as prescribed. (19, 20)

19. Refer the client for a psychiatric evaluation to determine his need for psychotropic medication and to validate any at-risk diagnoses (e.g., major depression).

20. Monitor the client's compliance with the psychotropic medication prescription; chart his subjective and objective behavioral changes and monitor side effects.

10. Cooperate with psychological testing designed to validate suicide intent/ideation. (21)

21. Administer testing most commonly used to reveal and evaluate suicide ideation and intent levels (e.g., Hopelessness Scale, Suicide Probability Scale, Reasons for Living Inventory, or Suicide Risk Measure).

11. The client and, if available, the caregivers accept feedback gathered from all sources and the treatment plan developed from the evaluation process. (22)

22. Summarize and give feedback to the client and his caregivers on high-risk markers found in the evaluation process; outline the treatment plan for all parties and integrate supportive members into the strategy (e.g., providing safety during high-risk times, encouraging effort on homework assignments, or remaining alert to an increase in risk factors).

12. Comply with placement in a more protective and, possibly, restrictive environment. (23)

23. Place the client in a supervised, structured therapeutic setting that will protect him from suicidal impulse, decrease perturbation, remove him from environmental stress, decrease his isolation, and monitor treatment effectiveness if assessments reveal high-risk suicide markers that significantly challenge his coping capacity (e.g., increase in isolative behavior, increase in substance abuse, increase in symptoms of

13. Affirm the safety of the discharge plan that allows for a return to a home and family environment. (24, 25)

14. Agree to a crisis response plan for dealing with situations when suicidal risk is strong. (26, 27)

15. Identify coping and management skills for stressors and symptoms that do not include suicide and increase verbalized statements of hope. (28, 29, 30, 31)

depression, or increase in comments of self-hate).

24. Note changes in the client's family equilibrium and hold family sessions to focus on effecting system change to accommodate his return to a home environment (e.g., improving communication patterns, resolving issues of autonomy, or setting reasonable behavioral expectations).

25. Review the inpatient treatment team's discharge plan that includes placement, school responsibilities, support system, individual and family psycho-therapy treatment, activities of daily living, and knowledge of helping services with the client and caregivers.

26. Develop a crisis intervention plan to be implemented during trigger events and feelings (e.g., arguments, failures, or rejections) that includes contacting therapist, trusted friend, or local help line to discuss emotional reactions to events that seem to be overwhelming.

27. Ask the client to agree, as a verbal contract of therapy, to call a trusted friend, local help line, the therapist, or hospital emergency room in case of strong suicide urges.

28. Formulate an appropriate view of the function of suicide with the client: It stems from a need to solve a seemingly unsolvable problem; it is fueled by a sense of helplessness and hopeless-

ness; the antidote to the suicide risk is to develop coping strategies for these seemingly unsolvable stressors and symptoms; this can be done with the therapist's help.

29. Assign a treatment journal to track daily stressors, the resulting symptoms, maladaptive coping patterns, and experiences with newly acquired coping strategies; assign homework targeting symptom management. Stress to the client that the goal of therapy is healthy symptom management and *not* symptom elimination.

30. Teach the client about his maladaptive externalizing coping behaviors (e.g., substance abuse) and internalizing coping behaviors (e.g., depression) and replace them with a problem-solving focus.

31. Use role-play, modeling, and behavior rehearsal to teach the client problem-solving skills (e.g., define the problem, brainstorm alternative solutions, list the positives and negatives of each solution, select and implement a plan of action, evaluate the outcome in the treatment journal and adjust the solution as necessary).

16. Identify own biological, social, and psychological vulnerabilities that contribute to the risk of suicide. (32, 33)

32. Explore the client's personal vulnerabilities that contribute to the suicidal crisis (e.g., issues of self-devaluation, need to be perfect, depressed affect, or inability to access emotions).

33. Assist the client in acknowledging the existence of these traits, their sources, how they were acquired, and their influences in maladaptive coping (e.g., self-injurious behavior, isolative behaviors, feelings of aloneness, inability to tolerate failure, missing school, or cheating on exams); ask him to track these traits and their influence in the treatment journal.

17. Increase the frequency of statements that communicate pride in accomplishments and improved confidence in self. (34, 35)

34. Monitor the client's suicide risk at appropriate intervals through interview and by administering standardized suicide risk assessment instruments (e.g., Beck Depression Inventory, Beck Scale for Suicide Ideation, or Suicide Probability Scale).

35. Assist the client in enhancing his self-image by encouraging him to provide self-reports from the treatment journal and the homework assignments on recent incidents of improved coping, symptom management, and problem-solving skills (e.g., going to school or job regularly, deciding against a dangerous activity, or talking to a friend about a difficult emotion).

18. List the benefits of sharing thoughts, feelings, and activities with friends. (36, 37)

36. Encourage the client to see himself in a social context by emphasizing the benefits of his participation in friendships and group activities (e.g., decreased sense of isolation); incorporate this into the homework assignments.

37. Teach the client the value of verbalizing his emotions in the

context of personal and caring relationships (e.g., sharing feelings promotes empathy from others, sharing of burdens reduces their intensity, and sharing breaks down the sense of isolation); use role play to teach him to share feelings.

19. Verbalize the capacity to see self in a future context with hope, confidence, and a balanced view of life. (38)

38. Review the client's growth, challenging him to trust the value of himself during times of temporary failure; provide him with examples of others who have risen from failure to enjoy success (e.g., Abraham Lincoln, Nelson Mandela, Johnny Cash, and Michael Jordan).

20. Develop a suicide prevention plan that incorporates the treatment journal's homework assignments. (39, 40)

39. Educate the client to prevent relapse into suicidal behavior (e.g., be aware of strategies for coping with trigger stressors and symptoms, rely on trusted others, validate his own successes without discounting them, avoid isolation and maintain social network, and remain on any prescribed medication).

40. Assist the client in writing a personal suicide prevention plan that lists actions he will take in the future to avoid the impulse to suicide.

—. _____   —. _____
   _____   _____
—. _____   —. _____
   _____   _____
—. _____   —. _____
   _____   _____

DIAGNOSTIC SUGGESTIONS:

Axis I:

296.3x	Major Depressive Disorder, Recurrent
300.4	Dysthymic Disorder
305.00	Alcohol Abuse
303.90	Alcohol Dependence
298.9	Psychotic Disorder NOS
300.01	Panic Disorder without Agoraphobia
309.81	Posttraumatic Stress Disorder
304.30	Cannabis Dependence
315.9	Learning Disorder NOS
312.82	Conduct Disorder/Adolescent-Onset Type
314.9	Attention-Deficit/Hyperactivity Disorder NOS
312.9	Disruptive Behavior Disorder NOS
307.23	Tourette's Syndrome

_____ _____

_____ _____

Axis II: V71.09   No Diagnosis

_____ _____

_____ _____

CAUCASIAN MALE—ADULT

BEHAVIORAL DEFINITIONS

1. Demonstrates behaviors positively correlated with major depression (e.g., sleep disturbances, anhedonia, irritability, or social withdrawal).
2. Expresses intense self-directed anger, rage, and devaluation.
3. Presents personality traits of extreme cognitive constriction, lack of resilience, inability to adapt to change, and high level of rigidity.
4. Does not demonstrate or verbalize suicide intent.
5. Expresses feelings of overwhelming guilt and shame.
6. Verbalizes a significant sense of aloneness, isolation, and lack of trust in others.
7. Preoccupied with past with no capacity for futuristic thinking.
8. Increase in chronic patterns of alcohol and/or illicit drug abuse.
9. Demonstrates behaviors positively correlated to an anxiety disorder (e.g., inability to concentrate, feelings of dread, or psychomotor agitation).
10. Lacks coping strategies for major issues of loss, failure, and rejection.
11. Reports a chronic pattern of suicide ideation.

—. _____

_____

—. _____

_____

—. _____

_____

LONG-TERM GOALS

1. Resolve feelings of depression and anxiety while developing a future time perspective with hopefulness.

2. Develop personality traits of resiliency, flexibility, and adaptability.
3. Develop a positive social support network.
4. Develop a sense of trust in self and others, which will promote a capacity for intimate relationships.
5. Accept a balanced life that can incorporate failure, loss, and unexpected change.

—. _____

_____

—. _____

_____

—. _____

_____

SHORT-TERM OBJECTIVES

1. Describe the conditions of previous suicide activity. (1, 2, 3)

THERAPEUTIC INTERVENTIONS

1. Explore the client's history and nature of previous suicide experiences and note incidents of suicidal ideation (e.g., thinking about suicide as a problem-solving strategy, ambivalence about the suicidal act, communicating with others about suicide intent; or obtaining help through medication and/or counseling).

2. Explore the client's history of previous suicide experiences and note incidents of suicide gesturing (e.g., acts of self-harm are designed to relieve anxiety or control emotions or relationships; suicidal gestures are often calculated for rescue or are self-interrupted; gestures are normally of low lethality).

3. Explore the client's history of previous suicide experiences and note incidents of suicide

attempts (e.g., acts clearly designed to terminate existence, fueled by emotions of dramatic despair and hopelessness, well planned to eliminate interruption and/or rescue potential, motivated by significant loss and issues of self-directed rage, accidentally interrupted and rescued with significant anger because he is still alive).

2. Identify the nature of the current suicidal ideation and/or intent. (4, 5, 6, 7)

4. Explore the client's goal of current suicide intention (e.g., poor problem-solving and coping skills, designed to relieve intolerable psychological pain and terminate the existence of the hated self, motivated by revenge factors, and fueled by severe levels of hopelessness and despair).

5. Explore the amount of energy the client spent in planning the suicide event (e.g., have lethal means been obtained, have a date and place been assigned, have financial concerns been resolved, is there any ambivalence about the plan, or have notes been written).

6. Explore whether any impediments to the plan exist (e.g., social stigma concerns, finding a place and time so that he will not be caught, fear of the emotional impact on survivors, or religious beliefs) with the client.

7. Explore any decrease in agitation and increase in energy and calm with the client since the plan has been considered;

3. Cooperate with psychological testing designed to evaluate conditions related to suicide risk in the adult Caucasian male. (8)

4. Provide complete information on current mood, affect, and thought processes in a psychiatric evaluation, taking psychotropic medication as prescribed. (9, 10)

5. Medical personnel provide relevant, current information on general health issues. (11)

6. Provide information on personal experiences with

explore continued ambivalence about the suicide act.

8. Administer testing used to reveal and evaluate suicidal ideation and intent levels in the adult Caucasian male (e.g., Reasons for Living Inventory, Suicide Probability Scale, or Beck Depression Scale); provide feedback to the client regarding test results and treatment implications.

9. Refer the client for a psychiatric evaluation to determine the need for psychotropic medication or a medically managed electroconvulsive therapy (ECT) series and validate any at-risk diagnoses (e.g., major depression, anxiety disorder, post-traumatic stress disorder, or antisocial personality disorder or traits).

10. Monitor the client's compliance with the prescribed medical interventions (e.g., medications and/or ECT); chart the effectiveness of the medication and monitor side effects.

11. After obtaining appropriate confidentiality and privacy protection releases, contact the client's primary care physician for a medical report and evaluation, paying specific attention to recent, multiple somatic complaints and any indicators of depression and/or anxiety that the physician may have noted.

12. Assess the client for the high-risk adult Caucasian male

high-risk *behavioral* markers for suicide in adult Caucasian males. (12, 13, 14)

suicide marker of substance abuse/dependency (e.g., alleviating depression and/or anxiety, polysubstance abuse patterns, history of suicide activity while under the influence of substances, social network disruption or legal involvement because of substance abuse, or violent behavior while under the influence of substances).

13. Assess the client for the high-risk adult Caucasian male suicide marker of history of violent behavior (e.g., legal involvement, history of spouse abuse, impulsivity, or uncaring reaction to violence toward others).

14. Assess the client for the high-risk adult Caucasian male suicide marker of history of childhood trauma and pathology (e.g., victim of verbal, emotional, physical, or sexual abuse; history of fire-setting, cruelty to animals, attention-deficit/hyperactivity disorder, conduct disorder, or oppositional-defiant disorder).

7. Provide information on personal experiences with high-risk *emotional* markers for suicide in adult Caucasian males. (15, 16, 17)

15. Assess the client for the high-risk adult Caucasian male suicide marker of depression (e.g., feelings of hopelessness, helplessness, melancholic despair; inquire about anhedonia, dysphoria, increase in irritability, sleep disturbance, sense of devaluation, and self-hate).

16. Assess the client for the high-risk adult Caucasian male

suicide marker of anxiety disorder (e.g., feelings of dread, panic attacks, inability to concentrate, or irrational fears).

17. Assess the client for the high-risk adult Caucasian male suicide marker of a personality disorder (e.g., antisocial, borderline, or narcissistic).

8. Provide information on personal experiences with high-risk *social* markers for suicide in adult Caucasian males. (18, 19)

18. Assess the client for the high-risk adult Caucasian male suicide marker of loss (e.g., financial, health, relationships, family, social network, or self-esteem); be attentive to issues of living alone, unemployment, and subjective feelings of isolation.

19. Assess the client for the high-risk adult Caucasian male suicide marker of help negation (e.g., lack of suicide communi-cation, and significant anger and denial when the question of suicide is approached).

9. Accept feedback on the assessments and treatment plan developed from the evaluation process. (20)

20. Summarize and give feedback to the client on high-risk markers found in his evaluation; develop a treatment plan including, if possible and appropriate, members of his social network.

10. Comply with placement in a more protective and, possibly, a more restrictive environment. (21)

21. If at any time during the therapy process the client displays an increase in the behavioral, emotional, or social risk factors, place him in a supervised and structured therapeutic setting that will protect him from suicide impulse, decrease perturbation, decrease social isolation, and allow monitoring of treatment effectiveness.

11. Affirm a plan that allows for a safe return to the community. (22, 23)

22. Monitor the client's suicide risk at appropriate intervals through a risk assessment interview and by administering standardized suicide risk assessment instruments (e.g., Beck Depression Inventory, Suicide Probability Scale, or Reasons for Living Inventory).

23. Explore community-based resources (e.g., employment services, support groups) with the inpatient treatment team that will enhance the client's psychosocial adjustment in combination with outpatient therapy; obtain his participation and affirmation of this plan.

12. Agree to a written plan for dealing with situations when suicidal urges become strong. (24, 25)

24. Develop a written crisis intervention plan to be implemented during times when the client experiences suicidal trigger events and feelings (e.g., isolation, shame, or loss) that includes contacting the therapist, a trusted member of the social network, or a family member and discussing emotional reactions to the concerning events.

25. Ask the client to agree, as a verbal contract in the therapeutic relationship, to call someone on the emergency contact list in case he experiences strong suicidal urges.

13. Identify current stressors and resultant symptoms that trigger the wish to die. (26, 27, 28)

26. Assist the client in making a list of his most prominent stressors (e.g., criticism about performance, disruption in relationships, failure at a task, or dealing with loss) and emotional reactions or symptoms (e.g., shame, internally directed rage,

isolation, or fear) produced by those stressors.

27. Assist the client in producing a complete symptom inventory that includes identifying the most disruptive symptoms (e.g., internally directed rage, shame, or isolation), how these symptoms are currently managed (e.g., alcohol abuse, violent acting out, or suicide gestures), and other reactions created by these symptoms (e.g., alienation of social network, loss of employment, depression, or anxiety).

28. Establish a therapeutic alliance with the client that ensures the therapist's help in targeting the most serious symptoms (e.g., despair due to depression, agitated anxiety, or shame) for immediate attention (e.g., inpatient hospitalization, ECT, medications, solution-oriented therapy, or increase in weekly treatment appointments).

14. Verbalize statements of hope that symptoms can be managed in ways other than suicide. (29, 30, 31, 32)

29. Formulate an appropriate view of suicide for the client: It stems from a desire to solve a seemingly unsolvable problem, it is fueled by elements of hopelessness and helplessness, and the antidote is to acquire safe, simple coping and problem-solving skills over identified stressors and symptoms.

30. Assign the client a treatment journal to track daily stressors, the resulting symptoms (feelings), maladaptive coping patterns, and experiences with newly acquired coping

strategies; assign homework targeting symptom management. Stress to him that the goal of therapy is symptom management and *not* symptom elimination.

31. Assist the client in noting in his treatment journal a plan with specific instructions on responding to and managing the perturbation associated with his immediate symptoms (e.g., implement self-calming strategies when confronted by internalized rage, engaging social network resources when feeling isolation, contacting Alcoholics Anonymous (AA) and/or sponsor when challenged to use alcohol to cope with anxiety/ depression).

32. Use role-play, modeling, and behavior rehearsal to teach the client to implement the symptom-management skills that are structured in a way to assist him during extreme emotional upset (e.g., safe, sound, and simple skills); have him note these coping strategies in the treatment journal.

15. Identify own biological, social, and emotional traits and vulnerabilities that contribute to suicidal thinking and intent. (33)

33. Explore the client's personal vulnerabilities and personality traits that contribute to the suicidal crisis and hinder adaptive coping (e.g., perfectionism, which contributes to an inability to cope with failure; emotional constriction, which prevents the client from healthy emotional access during severe life crisis; and self-devaluation, which leads to shame and internalized

rage during relationship disruptions and loss).

16. Identify strategies that will diminish the influence of personal vulnerabilities that reduce coping and problem solving. (34)

34. Assist the client in the acknowledgment of his personal vulnerabilities; explore sources of the personal vulnerabilities (e.g., early childhood trauma experiences) and develop strategies for their management (e.g., replace perfectionism with a sense of self-acceptance, replace emotional constriction with permission to explore and access emotions, and replace self-hate with a capacity to self-nurture).

17. Increase experiences of personal resiliency, flexibility, and adaptability to change. (35)

35. Assist the client in recognizing the negative influence of cognitive rigidity on healthy coping; teach him a menu of problem-solving skills (e.g., self-calming strategies, decrease external referencing, or decrease controlling patterns in relationships); redirect failure experiences with compassion and understanding and model resiliency in coping by exploring alternatives.

18. Increase a sense of belonging, identity in a social context, and intimacy. (36, 37)

36. Teach the client the value of verbalizing emotions in the context of personal and intimate relationships (e.g., sharing feelings promotes empathy from others and breaks down a sense of isolation and may lead to the normalization of emotions).

37. Encourage the client to see himself in a social context by emphasizing the benefits of participation in friendships and group activities, while empathizing with his reluctance; if

appropriate, assign participation in selected social activities (e.g., AA or support groups).

19. Review an insightful life history and develop a plan for the future based on past experiences and strengths. (38, 39)

38. As part of his treatment journal, ask the client to write his auto-biography; review the material together, encouraging a balanced view of his history, recognizing guilt or pride where it is appro-priate, shame where justified, and praise when due.

39. Drawing from the client's history, help him develop a positive perspective of himself; assist him in the development of a future life plan based on his revealed strengths.

20. Develop a suicide prevention plan that incorporates the treatment journal and all completed homework assignments. (40, 41)

40. Educate the client on preventing relapse into suicidal behavior (e.g., rely on the treatment journal for reminders of strategies for coping with trigger events, feelings, and symptoms; avoid isolation and maintain social network; monitor personality vulnerabilities and traits; remain on medications; and monitor relapse behavior in substance abuse).

41. Assist the client in writing a personal suicide prevention plan that lists individualized actions that will be taken in the future to manage suicidal urges.

__. _____   __. _____
    _____   _____
__. _____   __. _____
    _____   _____
__. _____   __. _____
    _____   _____

DIAGNOSTIC SUGGESTIONS:

Axis I:

296.xx	Major Depressive Disorder
300.4	Dysthymic Disorder
296.90	Mood Disorder NOS
300.02	Generalized Anxiety Disorder
303.90	Alcohol Dependence
308.3	Acute Stress Disorder
309.81	Posttraumatic Stress Disorder
————	————————————————
————	————————————————

Axis II:

301.7	Antisocial Personality Disorder
301.81	Narcissistic Personality Disorder
301.4	Obsessive-Compulsive Personality Disorder
————	————————————————
————	————————————————

CHEMICALLY DEPENDENT

BEHAVIORAL DEFINITIONS

1. Openly discusses the wish to die, including details on the method, place, and time.
2. Has a history of early onset of substance abuse, polysubstance dependence, substance abuse to self-medicate, and is in the latter stages of a substance dependence pattern.
3. Has experienced multiple losses (e.g., relationships, family, health, or employment) because of substance abuse patterns.
4. Has co-occurring mental illness (e.g., depression, anxiety disorder, schizophrenia, posttraumatic stress disorder, or bipolar disorder) that makes an impact on the wish to die.
5. Has a positive history of suicide activity of two or more episodes (e.g., either gesturing activity where the act was calculated for rescue or self interrupted and/or attempting activity where the act was accidentally interrupted against the person's wishes) while under the influence of mood-altering substances.
6. While using mood-altering substances has demonstrated increased violence and assaultive behavior (e.g., domestic violence).
7. Has experienced multiple relapses after brief periods of sobriety.
8. Displays significant narcissistic traits (e.g., self-aggrandizing, refuses ownership or responsibility for any dysfunctional behavior, controls relationships, or lacks capacity for empathy).
9. Has demonstrated, in the past two years, a very chaotic employment history with many job changes.
10. Has shown extreme difficulty in sharing emotions and accessing feelings.
11. Has a history of chaotic relationships.
12. Has a family of origin history of extreme dysfunction related to alcohol and/or drug abuse.
13. Demonstrates behaviors correlated to antisocial or borderline personalities.

—. _____
_____
—. _____
_____
—. _____
_____

LONG-TERM GOALS

1. Report a wish to live.
2. Develop a sense of hope for the future and an ability to define self in a futuristic context.
3. Establish a recovery pattern from substance dependence that includes social supports and relapse prevention guidelines.
4. Establish a recovery pattern from mental illness that includes therapy, social supports, and, if necessary, medication.
5. Establish a social network that enhances efforts to maintain a clean and sober lifestyle.
6. Engage in healthy activities of daily living that include employment and care of physical, spiritual, and emotional well-being.
7. Acknowledge him- or herself as a person suffering from the disease of chemical dependence and mental illness.

—. _____
_____
—. _____
_____
—. _____
_____

SHORT-TERM OBJECTIVES

THERAPEUTIC INTERVENTIONS

1. Cooperate with interview and testing designed to evaluate level of substance abuse, mental illness, and conditions correlated to elevated suicide risk. (1)

1. Administer testing to reveal and evaluate the client's level of substance use and readiness for change (e.g., University of Rhode Island Change Assessment Scale [URICA],

The Alcohol and Illegal Drugs Decisional Balance Scale, Michigan Alcohol Screening Test [MAST], or Alcohol Use Inventory [AUI]), nature of co-occurring disorders (e.g., MMPI or Beck Depression Inventory), and suicidal ideation and intent levels (Suicide Probability Scale or Beck Scale for Suicide Ideation); provide feedback to the client and, if available and appropriate, the caregivers on test results and treatment implications.

2. Comply with placement in a medically supervised detoxification program. (2)

2. If at any time during the therapy process the client has a relapse into substance abuse at a level of intensity that appears life threatening or destabilizing, refer him/her to a medically supervised detoxification setting for stabilization.

3. Identify specifics of previous suicide activity. (3)

3. Explore the circumstances and conditions of previous suicide activity (e.g., how much planning was used; was the activity self-interrupted, calculated for rescue, or was it accidentally interrupted against the person's wishes; was he/she intoxicated at the time of the activity; what was the goal of the activity; what identifiable stressors led to the activity) with the client.

4. Examine patterns of substance use in family of origin and childhood abuse experiences. (4, 5)

4. Explore the substance abuse history in the family of origin (e.g., identify family members who used mood-altering substances, were children exposed and/or encouraged to participate, and did substance abuse lead to

domestic violence or child abuse) with the client.

5. Explore the client's history for child abuse patterns in his/her family of origin and his/her perception of how this history affects his/her current addiction patterns and coping strategies (e.g., violence toward others and/or self, escapism through drugs and alcohol, emotional constriction, criminal behaviors, or difficulty in forming relationships).

5. Provide information on personal experiences with high-risk *behavioral* markers for suicide in the chemically dependent population. (6, 7, 8)

6. Assess the client for the high-risk chemically dependent suicide marker of legal involvement (e.g., number of driving violations, jail or prison time because of substance-use-related activities, current probation or parole status, or any other criminal behaviors fueled by substance abuse).

7. Assess the client for the high-risk chemically dependent suicide marker of financial difficulty (e.g., termination of employment, money spent on drugs, or legal fees because of drug related charges).

8. Assess the client for the high-risk chemically dependent suicide marker of anger/rage management problems (e.g., history of attention-deficit/ hyperactivity disorder, multiple fighting at a younger age, closed head injuries or traumatic brain injury or experiences when substance use muted or excited anger).

6. Provide information on personal experiences with high-risk *emotional* markers for suicide in the chemically dependent population. (9, 10, 11, 12, 13)

9. Assess the client for the high-risk chemically dependent suicide marker of depression (e.g., depth of hopelessness, internalized rage, shame, guilt, feelings of isolation, or social withdrawal patterns).

10. Assess the client for the high-risk chemically dependent suicide marker of posttraumatic stress disorder (PTSD; e.g., history of victimization by violence, nightmares, emotional constriction, flashback episodes, hypervigilance, and distressing and intrusive recollections).

11. Assess the client for the high-risk chemically dependent suicide marker of anxiety disorder (e.g., fears of imminent death, panic attacks, pervasive worry, restlessness, and inability to concentrate).

12. Assess the client for the high-risk chemically dependent suicide marker of psychosis (e.g., thought disorganization, delusions, and hallucinations).

13. Assess the client for the high-risk chemically dependent suicide marker of a personality disorder (e.g., antisocial, border-line, narcissistic, or histrionic).

7. Provide information on personal experiences with high-risk *social* markers for suicide in the chemically dependent population. (14)

14. Assess the client for the high-risk chemically dependent suicide marker of personal loss (e.g., loss of health, social network, family cohesion, self-esteem, employment, or financial security).

8. Medical personnel provide relevant, current information

15. After obtaining appropriate confidentiality releases, contact

on the client's general health issues. (15)

the client's primary care physician for a report on the client's health (e.g., somatic complaints, accidents, signs of depression or anxiety, general disease patterns, and history of medications).

9. Provide complete information on current mood, affect, and thought process in a psychiatric evaluation and take psychotropic medication as prescribed. (16, 17)

16. Refer the client for a psychiatric evaluation to determine the need for psychotropic medication and to validate any at risk diagnosis (e.g., PTSD, depression, psychosis, anxiety, and personality disorder).

17. Monitor the client's compliance with the psychotropic medication prescription; chart the subjective and objective behavioral changes and monitor the side effects.

10. The client and, if available, the caregivers accept feedback on the assessment for high-risk markers and the treatment plan developed from the evaluation. (18, 19)

18. Summarize and give feedback to the client and, if available and appropriate, the caregivers on the high-risk chemically dependent suicide markers found during the assessment and evaluation process.

19. Formulate an integrated treatment plan based on the client's co-occurring disorders; explain the details of the treatment plan to the client and attempt to engage the caregivers and other supportive people of his/her choosing in the treatment process.

11. Comply with placement in a more protective and restrictive environment. (20, 21)

20. If at any time during the therapy process the client displays an increase in the number or the intensity of the high-risk chemically dependent suicide markers, place him/her in a

therapeutic setting that will provide protection from suicide impulse, decrease perturbation, remove environmental stress, decrease isolation, and monitor treatment effectiveness.

21. Monitor the client's suicide risk at appropriate intervals through interview and by administering standardized suicide risk assessment instruments (e.g., Suicide Probability Scale, Suicide Risk Measure, or Reasons for Living Inventory); monitor his/her readiness for change stage at appropriate intervals by administering the URICA.

12. Affirm a safety plan that allows for a return to caregivers and/or the community. (22)

22. Coordinate outpatient planning that will, along with psychotherapy, aggressively and simultaneously treat substance abuse and psychiatric disorders, provide services that promote healthy psychosocial adjustment (e.g., case management, vocational training, housing, or medical treatment), including early relapse prevention planning, and assistance in efficient management of social stressors; obtain the client's input and affirmation of this plan.

13. Agree with a written plan for dealing with situations when suicidal urges become strong. (23)

23. Develop a written crisis intervention plan to be implemented when the client relapses into substance abuse or at times of psychiatric stress (e.g., coping with social stress and its resulting anxiety by abusing alcohol) that includes contacting a valued friend or AA/NA sponsor, therapist, case

manager and talking out emotional reaction to these events or placement into a detox unit or safe house facility; provide telephone numbers of all resources, asking the client to agree to call someone on the telephone list in such an emergency.

14. Identify people, places, and things that trigger cravings, use, social consequences, psychiatric symptoms, and the wish to die. (24)

24. Assist the client in identifying trigger events that led to relapse into substance abuse (e.g., family arguments, job frustrations, rejection in relationships, or failure at tasks).

15. Identify dysfunctional coping strategies related to experiencing strong emotions. (25, 26)

25. Assist the client in identifying emotional reactions that trigger events (e.g., uncontrollable rage, feelings of failure, feelings of isolation, increased intensity of depression, anxiety, or PTSD symptoms); teach him/her how he/she has used suicide and substance abuse as coping strategies.

26. Identify and challenge the client's cognitive distortion that the only coping strategies available are substance abuse or suicide.

16. Identify stress-management skills that do not include suicide or substance abuse. (27, 28, 29, 30)

27. Formulate an appropriate view of suicide for the client: It stems from a need to solve a seemingly unsolvable problem; it is fueled by elements of hopelessness and helplessness; it is compounded by addiction, and the antidote is to acquire safe and simple coping and problem-solving skills, in the context of sobriety, to manage identified triggers and emotional reactions.

28. Teach or refer the client for relapse prevention training, focusing on situations that pose a high risk for relapse (e.g., interpersonal conflict that creates anger and frustration, being offered a drink after going into a bar because of loneliness, or criticism at work creates feelings of failure) and modeling or role-playing coping skills for each high-risk situation (e.g., problem-solving skills, increased prosocial activities, or assertiveness skills).

29. Assign the client a journal to track daily triggers, the resulting symptoms, maladaptive coping patterns (relapse into substance abuse), and experiences with newly learned coping strategies; assign homework targeting symptom management (e.g., the client has a fight with his/her spouse over finances, and begins to feel extreme rage, but instead of coping with alcohol, he thinks about a positive consequence of staying sober in that situation).

30. Assist the client in noting in his/her journal a detailed plan for managing strong urges to relapse (e.g., using delay—this urge will pass—as an active cognitive coping skill; thinking about negative consequences to substance abuse in a specific situation; or using behavioral substitution techniques).

17. Challenge forms of negative thinking and increase statements of hope that

26. Identify and challenge the client's cognitive distortion that the only coping strategies

problems have solutions other than suicide. (26, 27, 31)

available are substance abuse or suicide.

27. Formulate an appropriate view of suicide for the client: It stems from a need to solve a seemingly unsolvable problem; it is fueled by elements of hopelessness and helplessness; it is compounded by addiction, and the antidote is to acquire safe and simple coping and problem-solving skills, in the context of sobriety, to manage identified triggers and emotional reactions.

31. Encourage the client to see the benefits of newly acquired coping skills and to recognize the decrease in the urge to abuse substances when these skills are applied at high-risk times; reinforce his/her confidence that the future will bring decreased urges if these skills are applied consistently.

18. Identify personality traits that increase vulnerability to suicide intent. (32, 33)

32. Explore the client's personality traits that increase vulnerability to suicide because of weakened coping capacity (e.g., rigid performance anxiety tied to a need to be in control and to achieve perfection, emotional constriction tied to a fear of intimacy and extreme anxiety when emoting is expected, self-loathing because of internalization of childhood messages of devaluation or negation).

33. Assist the client in understanding that his/her personality traits have been learned through social and environmental messages from childhood and have a role in the suicide

process (e.g., weakened coping ability because of emotional constriction can produce a situation where death by suicide is preferable to continued living with painful emotions).

19. Implement behaviors that reflect a positive change in personality traits and a decreased vulnerability to suicide. (34, 35, 36, 37)

34. Assist the client in effecting change in any existing suicide vulnerability traits by challenging his/her cognitive distortions and teaching new coping strategies; use homework assignments in the treatment journal for exercises directly related to effecting change in the coping patterns of the suicide vulnerable personality traits (e.g., diminish feelings of self-hate by writing a positive journal entry each day, diminish feelings of perfectionism and performance anxiety by practicing acceptance of limitations and failures, or diminish emotional constriction by sharing difficult emotions in a trusting social environment).

35. Assist the client in overcoming his/her performance anxiety (e.g., explore areas where he/she can surrender control in relationships, admit mistakes, or feel vulnerable).

36. Assist the client in overcoming his/her emotional constriction (e.g., explore areas where he/she purposely distances himself/herself from emotions; promote sharing in relationships, and feeling emotionally vulnerable).

37. Assist the client in overcoming his/her self-hate (e.g., explore areas where anger/rage creates

self-harm conditions, encourage reliance on the therapy relationship for building feelings of self-worth, and promote integration of positive feelings into the client's self-image).

20. Discuss ways to improve relationships and develop a social network. (38, 39, 40)

38. Explore with the client methods to make amends to those who have been hurt and damaged by the client's substance abuse patterns; assist in using his/her feelings of guilt and shame as motivators for reintegration into damaged social networks (e.g., displaying ownership of addiction to spouse and children).

39. Educate the client on appropriate communication skills that can be used to reintegrate into social networks or manage risky social situations (e.g., assertively refusing an offer of drugs or a drink, developing listening skills, giving positive feedback, learning effective approaches to conflict resolution, or accepting criticism for substance abuse).

40. Encourage the client to participate in friendships and groups of sober people; refer him/her to AA/NA and sponsors.

21. Develop a personal suicide prevention plan that incorporates the treatment journal, supportive social network, and all homework assignments. (41, 42)

41. Educate the client about how to prevent relapse into suicidal behavior (e.g., rely on the treatment journal for reminders of strategies for coping with trigger events, feelings, and symptoms; avoid isolation and maintain a sober supportive social network; accept help from others; remain on medications;

use trigger coping skills; and maintain futuristic thinking).

42. Assist the client in writing a personal suicide prevention plan that lists individualized actions that will be taken in the future to manage suicidal urges.

__. _____   __. _____
    _____   _____
__. _____   __. _____
    _____   _____
__. _____   __. _____
    _____   _____

DIAGNOSTIC SUGGESTIONS:

Axis I:	296.2x	Major Depressive Disorder, Single Episode
	296.3x	Major Depressive Disorder, Recurrent
	300.4	Dysthymic Disorder
	296.xx	Bipolar I Disorder
	296.89	Bipolar II Disorder
	300.02	Generalized Anxiety Disorder
	304.80	Polysubstance Dependence
	303.90	Alcohol Dependence
	305.00	Alcohol Abuse
	304.40	Amphetamine Dependence
	305.70	Amphetamine Abuse
	304.30	Cannabis Dependence
	305.20	Cannabis Abuse
	304.20	Cocaine Dependence
	305.60	Cocaine Abuse
	304.0	Opioid Dependence
	305.50	Opioid Abuse
	304.10	Sedative, Hypnotic, or Anxiolytic Dependence
	305.40	Sedative, Hypnotic, or Anxiolytic Abuse
	309.81	Posttraumatic Stress Disorder

_____ _____
_____ _____

Axis II: 301.7   Antisocial Personality Disorder
                   301.83   Borderline Personality Disorder
                   301.50   Histrionic Personality Disorder
                   301.81   Narcissistic Personality Disorder

_____   _____

_____   _____

CHILD

BEHAVIORAL DEFINITIONS

1. Expressing the wish to die under the age of 12.
2. Demonstrates the stage of development in which the finality of death is not understood.
3. Yearns for death as a way to be reunited with a deceased loved one.
4. Demonstrates developmental disabilities that create humiliation experiences and impaired self-esteem.
5. Lives within a chaotic, dysfunctional family environment.
6. Demonstrates behaviors positively correlated to significant childhood psychopathology (e.g., depression or conduct disorder).
7. Has been victimized by significant sexual and/or physical abuse.
8. Verbalizes significant despair and hopelessness that a current condition of turmoil can ever be resolved.
9. Demonstrates extreme impulse control problems and has easy access to firearms.
10. Experiences feelings of being unwanted by the family because of chronic patterns of emotional abuse.

—. _____

_____

—. _____

_____

—. _____

_____

LONG-TERM GOALS

1. Express the wish to live and sees a future with hope and promise.
2. Resolve the bereavement process of a deceased loved one with hope based on an age-appropriate spiritual foundation.
3. View him- or herself as a victim of family turmoil and pathology and not the cause.
4. Develop an appropriate sense of personal responsibility based on integrated self-worth and self-acceptance.
5. Live in a safe environment where protection, respect, and acceptance are promoted by the caregivers.

—. _____

_____

—. _____

_____

—. _____

_____

SHORT-TERM OBJECTIVES

THERAPEUTIC INTERVENTIONS

1. Identify the goal of the current suicidal ideation. (1)

1. Explore the client's goal of the intended suicidal act (e.g., a desire to be reunited with a deceased loved one, escape the humiliation experiences by peer group because of developmental disabilities, escape from a punishing or terrorizing home environment, or response to a chronic message from caregivers of being expendable).

2. Identify any planning activities connected to the suicidal ideation. (2)

2. Explore the amount of energy and planning devoted to thinking about how they would die (e.g., has a place and time been chosen, has a lethal means been discovered and do they have access to it, are the plans realistic and is the client convinced

3. Cooperate with psychological testing designed to evaluate conditions related to suicide risk in the child. (3)

4. Provide information on personal experiences with high-risk *behavioral* markers for suicide in children. (4, 5, 6)

that the plan will accomplish its goal, have good-bye notes been written) with the client.

3. Administer testing used to reveal and evaluate suicidal ideation and intent in the child (e.g., Corder-Haizlip Child Suicide Checklist, Kiddie-Schedule of Affective Disorders and Schizophrenia, or Spectrum of Suicidal Behavior Scale).

4. Assess the client for the high-risk child suicide marker of the inability to comprehend or explain the finality of death (e.g., ideas of being present and aware at their own funeral, ideas of dying for only a brief period to visit a deceased loved one, or display of high-risk and dangerous play patterns with no fear of dangerous consequences).

5. Assess the client for the high-risk child suicide marker of significant displays of general psychopathology usually associated with conduct disorder (e.g., violence toward others, preoccupation with death, poor impulse control, projection of blame onto others, inability to assume ownership of behaviors, self-mutilation, fire-setting, acts of cruelty to animals, or bedwetting).

6. Assess the client for the high-risk child suicide marker of experiences of humiliation and poor self-esteem because of the conditions of a developmental disability (e.g., a learning

5. Provide information on personal experiences with high-risk *emotional* markers for suicide in children. (7, 8)

6. Provide information on personal experiences with high-risk *social* markers for suicide in children. (9, 10, 11, 12, 13)

disorder that causes chronic teasing from peers).

7. Assess the client for the high-risk child suicide marker of depression and mood disorders (e.g., social withdrawal, tearfulness, low energy, low self-esteem, or irritability).

8. Assess the client for the high-risk child suicide marker of hopelessness (e.g., depth of despair in the context of a mood disorder, cruelty of the child's environment from which he/she sees no escape).

9. Assess the client for the high-risk child suicide marker of loss of special role within the family system (e.g., caused by divorce, death of a parent, birth or sibling moving out of the house, or illness of a parent).

10. Assess the client for the high-risk child suicide marker of family chaos (e.g., many moves, people move in and out of the home, no cohesion, episodes of spousal abuse, or episodes of substance abuse).

11. Assess the client for the high-risk child suicide marker of emotional abuse from family members (e.g., messages given to the child that they are unimportant, parents wish that the child was never born or would leave, parents claim the child interferes with their happiness, and other messages to the child of "go away").

12. Assess the client for the high-risk child suicide marker of

physical and/or sexual abuse from family members (e.g., pattern of the abuse, potential harm to the client, emotional impact of the abuse pattern on him/her); report all findings to local Social Service authorities or law enforcement agencies.

13. Assess the client for the high-risk child suicide marker of loss by death of a loved one (e.g., parent, grandparent, friend, sibling, pet, or child hero); attend to his/her concept of the finality of death.

7. Medical personnel provide relevant, current information on general health issues. (14)

14. After obtaining appropriate confidentiality releases, contact the client's primary care physician and/or pediatrician for a medical report, paying particular attention to any issues of suspected abuse and/or demonstrations of childhood psychopathology that came to the physician's attention.

8. School personnel provide relevant, current information on overall school adjustment and performance. (15)

15. After obtaining appropriate confidentiality releases, contact the client's school for a current report on academic and social adjustment, paying particular attention to reported acts of aggression, special education needs, parental involvement, or signs of abuse or neglect.

9. Provide complete information on current mood, affect, and thought process in a psychiatric evaluation. (16)

16. Refer the client for a psychiatric evaluation for any at-risk diagnoses (e.g., depression or conduct disorder) to provide consultation on the course of treatment.

10. The client and family accept feedback on the assessments

17. Summarize and give feedback to the client and family or

and the treatment plan developed from the evaluation process. (17, 18, 19)

caregivers on the high-risk child suicide markers found in the evaluation process; formulate his/her treatment program to include family engagement and schedule the number of weekly sessions based on an evaluation of risk and family support (e.g., children at high risk could be seen three times a week with a gradual decrease as the risk factors diminish and family support increases).

18. Engage community resources (e.g., school) and refer the client to other group resources to address his/her specific needs (e.g., groups for child grieving, child victims of abuse, or children of divorce).

19. Explain in understandable detail the treatment plan, putting emphasis on the relationship between the child and the therapist; stress to the parents or the caregivers that their participation, understanding, and support are essential and arrange appropriate scheduling for them.

11. Comply with placement in a more protective environment. (20, 21)

20. Monitor the client's suicide risk at appropriate intervals during the therapy process by interviewing for high-risk markers and by administering standardized suicide risk assessment measures.

21. If at any time during the therapy process the assessments reveal the presence of high-risk childhood suicide markers that significantly challenge the client's coping capacity (e.g., increased verbalizing of the

wish to die, increase in aggressive behavior toward himself/herself and others, or increase in abuse experiences), place him/her in a therapeutic setting that will protect him/her from suicidal impulse, decrease perturbation, remove environmental stress, and decrease isolation.

12. Affirm a plan that allows for a safe return to the family or designated caregivers, school, and community. (22)

22. In combination with psychotherapy, coordinate referrals to adjunct agencies (e.g., a group to assist in the grieving process, working through issues of abuse, or helping mainstream the developmentally disabled) that will assist in the client's psychosocial adjustment and make his/her safety the priority issue.

13. Agree to a written plan for dealing with situations when suicidal urges become strong. (23, 24)

23. Develop a written crisis intervention plan to be implemented by the client and parents/caregivers during times when the client experiences trigger events and feelings (e.g., terror, shame, self-directed anger, sorrow, or grieving) that includes contacting the therapist, trusted family member, or school counselor and discussing emotional reaction to events.

24. Explain, in an easily understandable fashion, the crisis intervention plan steps to the client and family and ask them to agree, as a verbal contract in the therapeutic relationship, to call someone on the emergency phone list in case the child experiences strong suicidal urges; develop as many resources as possible (five to

seven involved persons) for the resource list.

14. Identify current stressors and resultant symptoms that trigger the wish to die. (25, 26, 27)

25. Assist the client in making a list of his/her most prominent stressors (e.g., exposed to parent's physical fights; being teased by peers because of learning disabilities; grieving the death of a loved one; being demeaned by parents; or being physically and/or sexually abused by a trusted adult) and the symptoms (e.g., fear, humiliation, self-hate, unbearable sorrow, or feeling unloved) produced by the stressors.

26. Assist the client in producing a complete symptom inventory that includes identifying the most disruptive symptoms (e.g., terror in the home or shame caused by parental abuse), how these symptoms are currently dysfunctionally managed (e.g., running away, contemplating suicide, sexual acting out, or social withdrawal), and other results of these maladaptive behaviors (e.g., involvement with the juvenile justice system or missing school).

27. Establish a therapeutic alliance with the child by showing that treatment can help him/her (e.g., giving examples of how other children have gained benefit from therapy), ensuring that the therapist and child will work together to help manage these problems, that the therapist's goal is to keep the child safe, and that encourages the child to inform the therapist

15. Verbalize statements of hope that problems can be managed in ways other than suicide. (28, 29, 30, 31, 32)

when suicidal urges become overwhelming.

28. Formulate an appropriate view of suicide for the client and gently instruct him/her, with the parent's involvement and a respect for the family's spiritual base, about an appropriate view of the finality of death; teach that suicidal urges stem from a desire to solve a temporarily unsolvable problem (e.g., escaping from an intolerable situation at school or reuniting with a deceased loved one) with a permanent, unnecessary solution.

29. Emphasize to the child that feeling suicidal is under-standable (e.g., it gives the hopeless a sense of power over problems), but it can never be seen as a good way to solve problems (e.g., stress the age-appropriate view of the finality of death and that hope for the future goes away or discuss the hurt it would bring to certain special people), and safe and simple problem-solving alternatives will be acquired with the therapist's help.

30. Assign the child an age-appropriate treatment journal to track daily stressors, the result-ing symptoms or harmful emo-tions, their currently dangerous coping patterns, and any experi-ences he/she has with newly acquired coping strategies; assign homework (e.g., reading children's self-help books, viewing age-appropriate movies

with hopeful messages) that targets symptom management.

31. Assist the client in noting in his/her treatment journal a detailed plan with specific instructions on responding to and managing the perturbation associated with his/her immediate, priority symptoms (e.g., writing a note to a deceased loved one when feeling extreme sorrow); these responses should be detailed in a safe and simple fashion and structured to assist him/her during extreme emotional upset.

32. Use play therapy (with special attention paid to those children who destroy toys or act out self-directed rage), role-play, modeling, and behavior rehearsal to teach the client to implement the symptom management skills noted in his/her treatment journal.

16. Verbalize increased feelings of self-esteem. (33, 34)

33. Review daily accomplishments, newly acquired coping skills, and appropriate independent behaviors; assist him/her in recording these positive events in his/her treatment journal and compliment his/her progress and efforts to behave independently and successfully.

34. Accept with respect the client's shortcomings, frustrations, and failures, while continuing to support his/her efforts at problem solving.

17. Modify and/or decrease the frequency of aggressive behavior. (35, 36, 37)

35. Teach the client to identify the emotions (e.g., anger, rage, sadness, or loneliness) that

frustrating events (e.g., being teased at school or being demeaned at home) produce and normalize these emotions, using empathic reflecting, stress to him/her that the issue is *not* the emotions but the manner in which they are expressed and record suggestions for healthy expression in his/her journal.

36. Use role-play and modeling to teach the client to implement alternative ways of responding to normal emotions (e.g., talking to an accepting, empathic adult about the way he/she feels after a frustrating event); help him/her feel a sense of satisfaction and pride in the way he/she expresses emotions.

37. Stress to the child that it is never acceptable for anyone (including him/her) to be hurt, emotionally or physically by another person's anger or frustration; therefore, he/she must learn and implement healthy ways to express feelings.

18. Demonstrate increased trust of others by sharing feelings in a social context. (38, 39)

38. Support the client's attempt to form relationships; encourage him/her to see himself/herself in a social context by emphasizing the benefits of participation in friendships and group activities.

39. Teach the client the value of verbalizing emotions in the context of personal and loving relationships (e.g., sharing feelings reduces the burden of his/her intensity and lessens the feelings of isolation; sharing feelings allows another person to give his/her perspective and

helps normalize feelings); assist him/her in identifying those trustworthy adults with whom he/she can share frightening feelings and thoughts.

19. Develop a suicide prevention plan that incorporates the treatment journal and all completed homework assignments. (40, 41, 42)

40. Educate the client and the family about how to prevent relapse into suicidal behavior (e.g., rely on the treatment journal for reminders of strategies for coping with trigger events, feelings, and symptoms; avoid isolation; feel trust in and confide in safe adults; be a child, have fun, and look hopefully to the future).

41. Assist the client in writing a personal suicide prevention plan that lists individualized actions that will be taken in the future to manage suicidal urges; make an agreement with the client and the family that he/she will return to treatment if the suicidal urges become overwhelming.

42. Discuss and process feelings of sadness, anger, isolation, or grieving with the client about ending the therapy relationship.

__. _____   __. _____
   _____   _____
__. _____   __. _____
   _____   _____
__. _____   __. _____
   _____   _____

DIAGNOSTIC SUGGESTIONS:

Axis I:

296.xx	Major Depression
300.4	Dysthymic Disorder
296.xx	Bipolar Disorder
995.54	Physical Abuse of Child (Victim)
995.53	Sexual Abuse of Child (Victim)
309.0	Adjustment Disorder with Depressed Mood
312.81	Conduct Disorder/Childhood-Onset Type
313.81	Oppositional Defiant Disorder
314.9	Attention-Deficit/Hyperactivity Disorder
V71.02	Child Antisocial Behavior
V61.20	Parent-Child Relational Problem
V62.82	Bereavement
309.81	Posttraumatic Stress Disorder
308.3	Acute Stress Disorder
307.47	Nightmare Disorder
309.21	Separation Anxiety Disorder
300.23	Social Phobia

_____   _____

_____   _____

CHRONIC MEDICAL ILLNESS

BEHAVIORAL DEFINITIONS

1. Verbalizes a wish to die.
2. Expresses a wish to die during the early phases of a diagnosed chronic illness or a period of intractable pain.
3. Diagnosed with a chronic medical condition (especially high risk are HIV/AIDS, brain cancer, multiple sclerosis, renal failure, Parkinson's, or Huntington's disease) with comorbid conditions of depression, alcoholism, advanced age, and/or psychosis.
4. Diagnosed with a chronic medical condition related to an unsuccessful suicide activity (e.g., spinal injuries, amputations, or traumatic brain injury) with comorbid conditions of major depression, anxiety disorder, antisocial personality disorder, or substance abuse.
5. Displays personality characteristics (e.g., need to be in control, inability to accept failure, emotional constriction, or internalized rage) that render psychological coping with chronic illness a significant challenge.
6. Has required numerous inpatient hospital episodes and has experienced an increase in depressive symptoms (e.g., increased irritability, significant decrease in social functioning, isolation, or anhedonia) before and after each inpatient episode.
7. Has a positive history of suicidal ideation where the expressed goal of suicide is problem solving.
8. Displays consistent noncompliance with medical advice and engages in indirect self-destructive behaviors (e.g., refusing medications, refusing physical therapy, failure to eat and drink appropriately, smoking, or drinking alcohol).
9. Has experienced numerous losses (e.g., financial security, cognitive capacity, independence, family supports, or disruptions in relationships) because of a chronic medical condition.
10. Has a history of extremely impulsive behavior and has just received traumatic information about a chronic, debilitating medical condition.

11. Verbalizes the perception of having a serious disability or medical condition that is believed to be life threatening even though not diagnosed with a serious medical condition.
12. Expresses feelings of being useless or being a burden to others because of a chronic illness or disability.

—. _____

_____

—. _____

_____

—. _____

_____

LONG-TERM GOALS

1. Report a wish to live.
2. Engage in futuristic thinking with respect to the chronic medical condition.
3. Actively participate in and cooperate with rehabilitation efforts designed to manage the effects of the chronic medical condition.
4. Engage with caring, knowledgeable professionals for continued monitoring of the chronic medical condition.
5. Engage in healthy activities of daily living in spite of the chronic medical condition.
6. Grieve the losses experienced because of the chronic medical condition.

—. _____

_____

—. _____

_____

—. _____

_____

SHORT-TERM OBJECTIVES

1. Identify specifics of the goals and degree of planning and impediments to current suicide ideation. (1, 2, 3, 4)

THERAPEUTIC INTERVENTIONS

1. Explore the client's intended goal of the suicide act (e.g., cessation of physical pain, alleviate feelings of helplessness

in coping with the effects of chronic illness, elimination of self for the benefit of others or society, or solution to seemingly unsolvable conditions of depression and anxiety).

2. Explore the amount of energy the client has spent in planning his/her suicide event (e.g., has a weapon been obtained or a lethal method chosen; has a routine been established to stop medications, physical interventions, nourishment, or hydration; has a date or a place been assigned).

3. Probe the client for decreased feelings of anxiety and/or depression and a sense of calm and increased energy since planning started.

4. Explore whether any impediments to the implementation of his/her suicide plan exist (e.g., fear of the emotional impact on survivors, religious beliefs, or social stigma concerns) with the client.

2. Cooperate with psychological testing designed to evaluate conditions correlated to elevated suicide risk in the chronic medically ill population. (5)

5. Administer testing to reveal and evaluate the client's suicidal ideation and intent levels (e.g., MMPI-2, MCMI-III, Beck Scale for Suicide Ideation, Reasons for Living Inventory, or Suicidal Behavior Questionnaire) and provide feedback to him/her and, if available and appropriate, caregivers on test results and treatment implications.

3. Provide information on personal experiences with high-risk *behavioral* markers for suicide in the chronic

6. Assess the client for the high-risk chronic medically ill suicide marker of alcohol abuse and/or dependence (e.g., since the

medically ill population. (6, 7, 8, 9)

diagnosis of HIV/AIDS, cancer of the brain, or multiple sclerosis, has the client been abusing alcohol at an elevated rate; is his/her condition of spinal injury, amputation, or traumatic brain injury due to an accident that occurred under the influence of alcohol; inquire about current and prior poly-substance abuse patterns relative to the medical condition; is the renal failure and peptic ulcer client continuing to abuse alcohol).

7. Assess the client for the high-risk chronic medically ill suicide marker of previous suicide activity (e.g., a history of suicide ideation and the intended goal, suicide gesturing where the activity was self-interrupted or calculated for rescue, suicide attempts where the activity was accidentally interrupted and the client survived a lethal event; assess the client with spinal injuries, amputation, traumatic brain injury to determine whether these conditions were the result of an unsuccessful suicide activity).

8. Assess the client for the high-risk chronic medically ill suicide marker of noncompliance with treatment (e.g., prescribed medications, rehabilitation regimens, or medical appoint-ments) that comes from a sense of helplessness and hopelessness about his/her condition.

9. Assess the client for the high-risk chronic medically ill suicide

marker of impulsive behavior (e.g., anger management issues, risk-taking behaviors, or ADHD); assess the client for his/her reaction on initial revelation of the diagnosis of the serious medical condition.

4. Provide information on personal experiences with high-risk *emotional* markers for suicide in the chronic medically ill population. (10, 11, 12, 13)

10. Assess the client for the high-risk chronic medically ill suicide marker of depression (e.g., depth of sadness, isolation, helplessness, self-directed anger, attacks to self-esteem, or anhedonia).

11. Assess the client for the high-risk chronic medically ill suicide marker of anxiety (e.g., pervasive worry, restlessness, or fears of imminent death).

12. Assess the Parkinson's disease client for the high-risk suicide marker of adverse reactions to antiparkinsonian medication (e.g., paranoid hallucinations, assaultive behaviors to self and others, and intense feelings of depression).

13. Assess the Huntington's disease client for the high-risk suicide marker of progressive dementia, neurologic deterioration, and personality changes (e.g., impulsivity, emotional instability, and irritability).

5. Provide information on personal experiences with high-risk *social* markers for suicide in the chronic medically ill population. (14, 15, 16)

14. Assess the client for the high-risk chronic medically ill suicide marker of personal loss (e.g., financial security, self-esteem, independence, or family/social cohesion); probe the AIDS/HIV client for feelings of abandonment and stigmatization.

15. Assess the client for the high-risk chronic medically ill suicide marker of age (e.g., in the multiple sclerosis, spinal cord injury, amputation, and traumatic brain injury client, assign high-risk to clients under 40; in the cancer client, assign high-risk to clients over 70).

16. Assess the client for the high-risk chronic medically ill suicide marker of death in his/her social network (e.g., history of suicide in the immediate family or history of death in the immediate family or social network from the same illness as the client).

6. Medical personnel provide relevant, current information on the client's general health issues. (17)

17. After obtaining appropriate confidentiality releases, contact the client's primary care physician, specialty physician, or treatment team for a report on the client's health issues (e.g., general health issues, pattern of disease, prognosis, prescriptions, rehabilitation plan, and concerns about mental health issues); continue close consultation with the physician or treatment team on the client's progress in therapy and educate him/her, if needed, on signs indicating elevated suicide risk for the client.

7. Provide complete information on current mood, affect, and thought process in a psychiatric evaluation and take psychotropic medication as prescribed. (18, 19)

18. Refer the client for a psychiatric evaluation and, if needed, a neurologic evaluation to determine the need for psychotropic medication and to validate any at-risk diagnoses (e.g., major depression, borderline and antisocial personality disorders, dementia, delirium, or psychosis).

19. Monitor the client's compliance with the psychotropic medication prescription, charting subjective and objective behavioral changes and monitoring the side effects; share this information with the physician or treatment team. Remain alert to medication use by this population for suicide activity; engage caregivers, if possible, to monitor medication use.

8. The client and, if available and appropriate, caregivers accept feedback on the assessment for high-risk markers for suicide in the client's presentation. (20)

20. Summarize and give feedback to the client and, if available and appropriate, the caregivers about high-risk markers found during the assessment and evaluation process; explain details of the treatment plan and attempt to engage the caregivers. Share this information with the physician or treatment team.

9. Comply with placement in a more protective and restrictive environment if the assessment reveals high-risk markers for completed suicide. (21, 22)

21. If at any time during the therapy process the client displays an increase in the number or intensity of the examined high-risk markers, place him/her in a therapeutic setting that will protect him/her from suicide impulse, attend to the needs of his/her chronic illness or disability, decrease perturbation, remove environmental stress, decrease isolation, and monitor treatment effectiveness; remain alert to elevated suicide risk for clients with chronic medical conditions during and immediately following inpatient stays.

22. Monitor the client's suicide risk at appropriate intervals through interview and by administration of standardized suicide risk

assessment instruments (e.g., Beck Hopelessness Scale, Suicide Risk Measure, or Suicide Probability Scale); share this information with the client's physician and the treatment team.

10. Affirm a safety plan that allows for a return to the caregivers or the community. (23)

23. Coordinate planning that will, along with psychotherapy, aggressively treat the client's psychiatric problems (including any substance abuse disorders), establish a continuum of care for the chronic illness or disability, promote healthy psychosocial adjustment, and efficiently decrease social stressors; obtain the client's affirmation of this plan.

11. Agree to a written plan for dealing with situations when suicidal urges become strong. (24)

24. Develop a written crisis intervention plan to implement during trigger events or feelings (e.g., excessive physical pain, hopelessness, self-hate, fear, or isolation) that includes him/her calling a member of the treatment team, a trusted friend, a caregiver, or the therapist and processing his/her emotional reactions; encourage the client to agree to call someone on the telephone list as needed and in a responsible fashion.

12. Identify the stressors and symptoms that trigger the wish to die by suicide. (25, 26)

25. Assist the client listing of his/her most prominent stressors (e.g., chronic pain, loss of ambulation, uncomfortable dependence on others, intrusive medical procedures to maintain health, or financial burden placed on the family because of chronic illness); assess his/her emotional reactions (e.g., feelings of being

a burden, useless, isolated, self-hate, or hopelessness and help-lessness) and current coping skills (e.g., thoughts of suicide as an escape, problem-solver, or taking the burden away from the family).

26. Assist the client in developing a complete symptom inventory that includes what stressors stimulate the symptoms, how these stimulating stressors can be avoided, how he/she currently manages these stressors and symptoms, and whether these stressors cause other painful reactions and symptoms that eventually overwhelm the client.

13. Identify solutions or stress management skills that do not include suicide or the wish to die. (27)

27. Assist the client in identifying the *most* disruptive stressors and resulting symptoms (e.g., the symptoms that cause the highest level of impairment in his/her activities of daily living and psychosocial adjustment); target those symptoms for immediate intervention techniques and teach coping strategies (e.g., managing the feelings of being a burden by giving self permission to be cared for and managing feelings of hopelessness and helplessness by engaging in rehabilitation efforts and medical regimens in cooperation with treatment teams and physicians).

14. Increase verbalized statements of hope that symptoms can be managed in ways other than suicide. (28, 29, 30, 31)

28. Formulate an appropriate view of the function of suicide with the client: It stems from a need to solve a seemingly unsolvable problem, it is fueled by a sense of hopelessness and

helplessness, and the antidote is to develop coping strategies and management techniques for these seemingly unsolvable issues. Avoid leading the client to believe that the therapy process will eliminate stress symptoms, emphasizing the treatment goal of stress management.

29. Assign the client a treatment journal to track daily stressors, the resulting symptoms, maladaptive coping patterns, and experiences with newly acquired coping strategies; assign homework targeting symptom management.

30. Assist the client in identifying his/her maladaptive externalizing coping behaviors (e.g., alcohol abuse, refusing medical prescriptions, or rejecting help from others) and internalizing coping behaviors (e.g., denial, anger/rage, or suicidal thoughts of escape) and help him/her replace these maladaptive coping responses with a problem-solving focus.

31. Use role-play, modeling, and behavior rehearsal to teach the client symptom-management skills (e.g., identifying with the client a basis for self-worth by reviewing his/her talents and importance to others, identify and implement enjoyable activities that can be accomplished alone or in a group considering the medical condition, verbalizing feelings of fear and anger, provide impulse control exercises to be

15. Identify own personality traits that create vulnerabilities in coping and contribute to the risk of suicide. (32, 33)

16. Examine the function of these personality traits in the suicidal process and develop strategies for change. (34)

17. Increase the frequency of verbalizing statements that indicate improved coping with the chronic medical illness or disability. (35)

implemented during times of high stress).

32. Assess the client for personal vulnerabilities that contribute to the suicidal crisis (e.g., inability to access emotions, need to be in control or perfect or issues of self-hate and devaluation).

33. Assist the client in acknowledging the existence of his/her personal vulnerability traits and their influence on his/her maladaptive coping skills (e.g., unwillingness to accept help because of a strong need to be in control, inability to grieve because of lack of access to one's emotions, or isolating self from caring about others because of rage at self); encourage him/her to track awareness of these traits and their influence in coping in his/her treatment journal.

34. Assist client in the recognition that his/her dysfunctional traits were acquired through life lessons (e.g., being told not to cry, only perfection is acceptable, and he/she is useless); and teach him/her that these traits can be replaced with adaptive traits (e.g., having access to emotions, accepting help by accepting one's disability).

35. Teach the client to use a treatment journal to note all incidents of improved symptom management of the stressor of chronic medical illness (e.g., freely expressing grief and sadness about the medical condition, engaging in physical

and mental exercises appropriate for the chronic medical condition, accepting the treatment team's regimen for rehabilitation); encourage him/her to use positive, affirming comments toward himself/herself as he/she develops better symptom-management skills.

18. Increase social contact with a positive social support network. (36, 37)

36. Refer the client to a support group of others living with the same, or similar, chronic medical conditions.

37. Encourage the client's engagement in group social, educational, and recreational activities that are possible with his/her chronic medical condition.

19. Increase the frequency of verbalizing statements that indicate improved self-acceptance as a person with a chronic medical condition or disability. (38, 39)

38. Review the client's treatment journal and note significant patterns of decrease in the presence of high-risk symptoms in response to variety of stressors (e.g., decrease in alcohol or drug abuse patterns to cope with anxiety, increased investment in rehabilitation efforts to cope with feelings of hopelessness and helplessness, improved engagement with helping caregivers, or enhanced expressions of sorrow and sadness to cope with grieving) and any increase in comments of acceptance of the chronic medical condition and confidence in coping strategies; reinforce such positive gains.

39. Elicit feelings of confidence in the future and a sense of confidence in self (e.g., recognizing that positive coping encourages a sense of management over

20. Develop a written suicide prevention plan. (40, 41)

one's life) from the client and the caregivers.

40. Educate the client about preventing relapse into suicidal behavior (e.g., relying on the treatment journal for reminders of strategies for coping with stress-induced symptoms, remaining alert to the personality traits that make him/her vulnerable to suicidal thoughts, maintaining involvement with the medical treatment regimen, maintaining healthy activities of daily living appropriate for the chronic medical condition, continuing grief work, remaining on psychotropic medications, and maintaining futuristic thinking).

41. Assist the client in writing a personal suicide prevention plan that incorporates and respects the individual aspects of the client's life; include actions needed to continue symptom management, manage suicidal urges, and maintain confidence in himself/herself.

__. _____   __. _____
    _____   _____

__. _____   __. _____
    _____   _____

__. _____   __. _____
    _____   _____

DIAGNOSTIC SUGGESTIONS:

Axis I:

309.0	Adjustment Disorder with Depressed Mood
309.28	Adjustment Disorder with Mixed Anxiety and Depressed Mood
309.3	Adjustment Disorder with Disturbance of Conduct
309.4	Adjustment Disorder with Mixed Disturbance of Emotions and Conduct
309.24	Adjustment Disorder with Anxiety
296.xx	Major Depressive Disorder
300.4	Dysthymic Disorder
311	Depressive Disorder NOS
316	Psychological Symptoms Affecting Axis III Disorder
305.00	Alcohol Abuse
300.02	Generalized Anxiety Disorder
300.00	Anxiety Disorder NOS
312.34	Intermittent Explosive Disorder
293.xx	Psychotic Disorder Due to General Medical Conditions

—————— ————————————————————

—————— ————————————————————

Axis II:

301.7	Antisocial Personality Disorder

—————— ————————————————————

—————— ————————————————————

COLLEGE STUDENT

BEHAVIORAL DEFINITIONS

1. Communicates to someone (e.g., friend, counselor, resident assistant, help line, or teacher) a wish to die (e.g., "Life just isn't worth living," "I feel like giving up," "I wish my life would end," or "There is no solution to my problems other than taking my own life").
2. Demonstrates symptoms of major depression (e.g., social withdrawal, lack of interest in college activities, sleep disturbance, or feelings of despair and hopelessness).
3. Demonstrates behaviors correlated to the emergence of schizophrenia (e.g., social withdrawal, feelings of persecution, hyperalert, intrusive thoughts, inability to concentrate, thought disorganization, delusional thoughts, or bizarre behaviors).
4. Has extended the educational process longer than the traditional four years because of disruptions caused by major psychiatric illnesses (e.g., schizophrenia, depression, anxiety disorders, or suicidal episodes).
5. Expresses feelings of social isolation because of geographic distance from home (e.g., foreign or out of state students).
6. Demonstrates personality traits of being quiet and socially isolated, drawing very little attention to self.
7. Expresses feelings of being under severe pressure to perform academically or athletically to gain a measure of acceptance and self-worth.
8. Refrains from alcohol use because it would detract from the intense efforts to perform academically and would require social interaction.
9. Verbalizes feelings of self-hate and worthlessness connected to feelings of rejection from family.
10. Expresses need to win parental love and/or approval through academic and/or athletic excellence.
11. Displays an intolerance of academic or social failure experiences with maladaptive coping (e.g., projection of blame onto others, denial, withdrawal, or depressive episodes).

12. Does not normally talk about suicide since it would draw unwelcome attention to self.
13. Uses campus medical facility excessively because of feelings of fatigue, tiredness, or lack of energy.

—. _____
   _____
   _____
—. _____
   _____
   _____
—. _____
   _____

LONG-TERM GOALS

1. Report a wish to live.
2. Develop a sense of hope for the future and an ability to define self in a futuristic context.
3. Develop an integrated self-concept, rejecting the belief that love, affirmation, and value are gained only through performance.
4. Develop a social support network.
5. Develop a balanced self-concept that can accept temporary failures and integrate them into the growth experience.
6. Develop strategies that enable a smooth transition to the autonomy of adulthood.
7. Develop an excitement toward academic pursuits replacing the sense of anxiety centered on performance.

—. _____
   _____
—. _____
   _____
—. _____
   _____

SHORT-TERM OBJECTIVES

1. Describe general feelings about the college experience. (1, 2)

2. Provide information on personal experiences with high-risk *behavioral* markers for suicide in college students. (3, 4, 5)

THERAPEUTIC INTERVENTIONS

1. Explore the motivations for choosing the current college (e.g., proximity to home, distance from home, academic standards, athletic opportunities, elitist reputation, parental pressure, or desire to be with close friend) with the client and note any motivations that could be considered problematic for a healthy adjustment.

2. Explore, in general terms, the client's current feelings toward the college experience (e.g., very satisfied, a balanced view, dissatisfied, or very unhappy) and isolate current emotional reactions that could be problematic for a healthy adjustment (e.g., homesickness, absence from a significant relationship, feeling lost, or missing high school identity).

3. Assess the client for the high-risk college student suicide marker of escape and/or avoidance behaviors (e.g., missing classes, isolative substance abuse patterns, attitudes of passivity, or social isolation by choice where he/she makes a conscious effort to avoid drawing attention to himself/herself).

4. Assess the client for the high-risk college student suicide marker of fascination with issues of death and suicide demonstrated in a subtle fashion in study groups, dormitory

discussions, or class assigned writing projects.

5. Assess the client for the high-risk college student suicide marker of excessive medical consultations (e.g., complaints of fatigue, tiredness, lack of energy but denying or not discussing issues of depression or suicide ideation and/or intent).

3. Provide information on personal experiences with high-risk *emotional* markers for suicide in college students. (6, 7, 8, 9)

6. Assess the client for the high-risk college student suicide marker of hopelessness and helplessness (e.g., significant despair that renders current coping strategies inadequate).

7. Assess the client for the high-risk college student suicide marker of depression (e.g., sadness, self-directed anger, reduced appetite, sleep disturbances, low self-esteem, or family history of depression and psychiatric illnesses).

8. Assess the client for the high-risk college student suicide marker of emerging schizo-phrenia (e.g., social withdrawal, feelings of persecution, intrusive thoughts, inability to concentrate, or thought disorganization).

9. Assess the client for the high-risk college student suicide marker of socially prescribed perfectionism (e.g., examine closely the linkage of perfec-tionism to depression, hopeless-ness and the suicide intent, inquire about the object of the need to please, and examine the

4. Provide information on personal experiences with high-risk *social* markers for suicide in college students. (10, 11)

history of the socially prescribed perfectionism).

10. Assess the client for the high-risk college student suicide marker of termination of a romantic relationship or social network disruption because of college bound status.

11. Assess the client for the high-risk college student suicide marker of rigid family expectations (e.g., school and course of study were chosen by parents because of family tradition or prestige and parental expectations are seen as exceedingly high and beyond the student's capacity).

5. Identify the nature of current suicidal ideation, planning, and/or intent. (12, 13, 14, 15)

12. Explore the client's intended goal for the suicidal act (e.g., cessation of psychological pain or provides a sense of control by solving a seemingly unsolvable problem when other coping strategies are failing).

13. Explore the amount of energy the client spent in planning his/her suicide event (e.g., has a date and place been assigned, have notes been written, or have prize possessions been distributed).

14. Probe the client for decreased feelings of anxiety and/or depression and a sense of calm since planning either started or concluded.

15. Explore the client's impediments to implementing his/her suicide plan (e.g., fear of the emotional impact on survivors, religious

6. Cooperate with psychological testing designed to evaluate conditions related to suicide risk in the college student. (16)

7. Medical personnel, especially the college clinic and primary care physician, provide relevant, current information on the client's general health issues. (17)

8. Provide complete information on current mood, affect, and thought process in a psychiatric evaluation, taking psychotropic medication as prescribed. (18, 19)

9. The client and, if available and appropriate, caregivers accept feedback on the assessments

beliefs, or social stigma concerns).

16. Administer testing to reveal and evaluate suicidal ideation and intent levels (e.g., MMPI-2, Suicide Probability Scale, Suicide Ideation Scale, or College Student Reason for Living Inventory) and provide feedback to the client and, if available and appropriate, the caregivers on test results and treatment implications.

17. After obtaining the appropriate confidentiality releases, contact the client's primary care physician and/or the college medical clinic for a report on the client's overall general health (e.g., general disease patterns, excessive somatic complaints history, medication history, or concerns about mental health issues); continue consultation with the clinic or physician especially on mental health issues.

18. Refer the client for a psychiatric evaluation to determine the need for psychotropic medication and to validate any at-risk diagnoses (e.g., issues of emerging schizophrenia, depressive disorder, or anxiety disorder).

19. Monitor the client's compliance with the psychotropic medication prescription; chart the subjective and objective behavioral changes and monitor side effects.

20. Summarize and give feedback to the client and, if available and appropriate, the caregivers on

and the treatment plan developed from the evaluation process. (20)

10. Comply with placement in a more protective and, possibly, a more restrictive environment. (21)

11. Affirm a safety plan that allows for a return to the college community. (22)

12. Agree to a written plan for dealing with situations when suicidal urges become strong. (23, 24)

high-risk markers found during the assessment and evaluation process; explain details of the treatment plan and, if appropriate, attempt to engage the caregivers.

21. If at any time during the treatment process the client displays an increase in the number or intensity of the examined high-risk markers, place him/her in a therapeutic setting that will protect him/her from suicide impulse, decrease perturbation, remove environmental stress, decrease isolation, and monitor treatment effectiveness.

22. Coordinate planning that will, along with psychotherapy, aggressively treat psychiatric problems, promote services that foster healthy psychosocial adjustment on return to the college campus/community and efficiently decrease social stressors from the college experience; obtain the client's input and affirmation in this plan; only under extreme circumstances (e.g., significant medical condition) or his/her wishes should the student be dismissed from the college program.

23. Develop a written crisis intervention plan to be implemented during trigger events and feelings (e.g., test failure and resultant feelings of self-hate) that includes contacting a trusted friend, a resident assistant or, if available,

the therapist and talking about emotional reactions to events; provide telephone numbers to the client and, as a part of the therapy alliance, verbally contract with the client to use these resources.

24. Monitor the client's suicide risk at appropriate intervals during the therapy process through interview and by administering standardized suicide risk assessment instruments (e.g., Beck Hopelessness Scale, Suicide Ideation Scale, or College Student Reasons for Living Inventory).

13. Acknowledge the nature and source of perfectionism. (25, 26, 27)

25. Explore the client's current academic and/or athletic performance and examine any issues of perfectionism; examine the perfectionism for linkage with feelings of failure, guilt, and low self-esteem.

26. Explore the source and nature of perfectionistic feelings (e.g., self-oriented perfectionism: the person sets unrealistically high self-expectations and is unusually harsh in judging self-behavior; other-oriented perfectionism: the person establishes his/her standards of performance based on comparison with the performance of others; socially prescribed perfectionism: the standards of performance are placed on the student by significant others often with punitive consequences if the standards are not achieved).

27. Explore the client's current coping strategies developed for feelings of perfectionism and isolate those that could be problematic and foster suicide intent and/or ideation (e.g., lying about performance, cheating on tests, unrealistic criticism of professors, depression, or feelings of self-hate).

14. Identify actions to be taken that will decrease the influence of the socially prescribed perfectionism personality trait. (28, 29)

28. Assist the client in acknowledging the existence of socially prescribed perfectionism and its influence on maladaptive coping (e.g., cheating on tests, social withdrawal, depression, anxiety, isolative substance abuse to escape pressure, suicidal ideation, or inability to cope with failure); have him/her note the influence of perfectionism on his/her self-image during times of crisis (e.g., fear of loss of love because of failure to achieve socially prescribed expectations).

29. Assist the client in separating himself/herself from the socially prescribed perfectionism initiated by the significant other; engage in family therapy if the client and family show a willingness to engage in this process.

15. Identify the stressors and symptoms that trigger the wish to die by suicide. (30, 31, 32)

30. Assist the client in making a list of his/her most prominent stressors (e.g., absence from social support network, excessive performance demands, experiencing failure) and emotional reactions or symptoms (e.g., feelings of isolation and abandonment,

anxiety over being perfect, or issues of self-hate) produced by those stressors.

31. Assist the client in producing a complete symptom inventory that includes identifying the most disruptive symptoms (e.g., fear of failure, self-hate, or performance anxiety), how these symptoms are currently managed (e.g., isolative substance abuse, eating disorders, cheating on exams, or suicidal ideation), and other reactions created by these symptoms (e.g., distancing from social network, sleep disturbances, or self-mutilation).

32. Establish a therapeutic alliance with the client that ensures the therapist's help in targeting the most serious symptoms for immediate attention (e.g., hospitalization, medication, or solution-oriented therapy).

16. Identify solutions and coping strategies that do not include suicide or the wish to die. (33, 34, 35, 36)

33. Formulate an appropriate view of suicide for the client: It stems from a desire to solve a seemingly unsolvable problem; it is fueled by elements of hopelessness and helplessness; and the antidote is to acquire, with the therapist's help, safe, simple coping and problem-solving skills for identified stressors and symptoms.

34. Assign a treatment journal to track daily stressors, the resulting symptoms, maladaptive coping patterns, and experiences with newly acquired coping strategies; assign homework targeting

symptom management. Stress to the client that the goal of therapy is healthy symptom management *not* symptom elimination.

35. Assist the client in noting in his/her treatment journal a detailed plan (e.g., self-calming techniques, focus on the positive aspects of efforts to accomplish tasks, cognitive restructuring leading the client to replace his/her focus on failure to a sense of "I did good enough" or "I did the best I could") with specific instructions responding to and managing the perturbation associated with his/her immediate, priority symptoms; these responses should be detailed and structured to assist the client during extreme emotional upset (e.g., safe and simple skills).

36. Use role-play, modeling, and behavior rehearsal to teach the client to implement the symptom-management skills noted in his/her treatment journal.

17. Increase verbalized statements of hope that symptoms can be managed in ways other than suicide. (37)

37. Assist the client in reviewing the treatment journal during each session; identify and reinforce strengths and an improved sense of self-image because of enhanced problem and symptom management.

18. Increase the frequency of verbalizing statements indicating improved comfort with the college experience, appropriate anxiety with academic

38. Assist the client in finding and utilizing enjoyable aspects of campus life (e.g., creating a life balance between fun and work); encourage a sense of

demands, and smoother transition to autonomy. (38, 39)

autonomy by emphasizing decisions made that reflect self-determination.

39. Encourage the client to see himself/herself in a social context by emphasizing the benefits of participation in friendships and group activities; assign participation in selected campus activities or community volunteer activities. Reinforce success and redirect experiences of failure.

19. Verbalize increased acceptance of self as a vulnerable person, capable of mistakes and failures, while keeping intact a core image of self-regard. (40)

40. Teach the client (1) to respect his/her core self-image of intrinsic worth (e.g., always welcoming the client with a genuine caring attitude), (2) that he/she doesn't have to be perfect in the therapy relationship, (3) that expressions of vulnerability are honored and accepted without judgment, (4) that he/she doesn't have to please the therapist, (5) that he/she can experience failures safely (e.g., missed homework assignments in the treatment journal) in a relationship of understanding and respect, and (6) that to be vulnerable is to be human (e.g., use well guided and appropriate self disclosure vignettes of failure from the therapist's life experience).

20. Develop a suicide prevention plan that incorporates the treatment journal and all completed homework assignments. (41)

41. Assist the client in writing a personal suicide prevention plan that lists individualized actions that will be taken in the future to manage suicidal urges (e.g., rely on the treatment journal for reminders of strategies for coping with trigger events,

feelings, and symptoms; avoid isolation and maintain social network; respect autonomy and core self-image of intrinsic worth; remain safely respectful of failure experiences; remain on physician prescribed medication; maintain futuristic thinking; and trust the value of self).

—. _____   —. _____
    _____   _____
—. _____   —. _____
    _____   _____
—. _____   —. _____
    _____   _____

DIAGNOSTIC SUGGESTIONS:

Axis I: 296.xx   Major Depressive Disorder
                300.4   Dysthymic Disorder
                296.90   Mood Disorder NOS
                305.00   Alcohol Abuse
                305.20   Cannabis Abuse
                295.xx   Schizophrenia
                298.9   Psychotic Disorder NOS
                308.3   Acute Stress Disorder
                300.02   Generalized Anxiety Disorder
                300.81   Somatization Disorder

                _____   _____
                _____   _____

Axis II: 301.4   Obsessive-Compulsive Personality Disorder

                _____   _____
                _____   _____

ELDERLY

BEHAVIORAL DEFINITIONS

1. Expresses an intense, unequivocal, unambiguous desire to die.
2. Expresses the belief that he or she is in the way, a burden, or harmful to others.
3. Expresses the belief that he or she is in a hopeless condition or state.
4. Expresses a belief in ageism, especially that the aged should be allowed to accept suicide as a solution to their problems.
5. Demonstrates a life-long pattern of depression that is now transformed into extreme suspiciousness and hostility toward family and society.
6. Demonstrates an intense, angry rejection of help from caregivers especially when a loss of independence is perceived.
7. Expresses feelings of uselessness, devaluation, or being unnecessary.
8. Demonstrates a life-long pattern of self-centered, controlling, narcissistic behavior that makes the current conditions of dependency unbearable.
9. Demonstrates a recent pattern of social isolation and a tendency toward hypochondriasis, hostility, and rigidity.
10. Demonstrates a lack of resiliency to cope with typical age-related issues (e.g., retirement, decrease in income, loss of meaningful activities, or health problems).

—. _____
_____
—. _____
_____
—. _____
_____

LONG-TERM GOALS

1. View self in a futuristic context.
2. Develop a social support network.
3. Accept age-related changes in lifestyle.
4. Accept help from a variety of sources while integrating this into an emerging self-image.
5. Resolve dysfunctional thinking that creates psychological conflict with the aging process and its associated dependency issues.

—. _____
   _____
   _____
—. _____
   _____
   _____
—. _____
   _____

SHORT-TERM OBJECTIVES

1. Identify maladaptive responses to age-related changes. (1, 2)

2. Identify the nature of current suicidal ideation, planning, and/or intent. (3, 4, 5)

THERAPEUTIC INTERVENTIONS

1. Explore the client's negative responses to the aging process (e.g., a fierce level of pride and independence that motivates an angry refusal of assistance from others; sense of self is damaged because of being too closely tied to productivity as a worker; lack of tolerance for change and limitations; or increasing despair about the future).

2. Explore the client's history of inpatient psychiatric episodes (e.g., age of first episode, cause of episode, or outcome of episode) as evidence of previous maladaptive coping skills or depressive disorder.

3. Explore the client's goal of the intended suicide act (e.g., cessation of physical or

emotional pain; solution to social, economic, or physical problems; or reaction to increasing level of disgust and anger at his/her current mental or physical state).

4. Explore the amount of energy the client spent in planning the suicide event (e.g., has a weapon been purchased; has a date and place been assigned; have notes been written; or have financial concerns been resolved).

5. Explore whether any impediments to the plan exist (e.g., fear of the emotional impact on survivors; finding a time and place so he/she will not be caught; religious beliefs; or social stigma concerns) with the client.

3. Cooperate with psychological testing designed to evaluate conditions related to suicide risk in the elderly. (6)

6. Administer testing used to reveal and evaluate suicidal ideation and intent levels in the elderly (e.g., Geriatric Depression Scale, or Center for Epidemiological Studies Depression Scale) and provide feedback to the client and, if possible, caregivers on test results and treatment implications.

4. Provide information on personal experiences with high-risk *behavioral* markers for suicide in the elderly. (7, 8, 9)

7. Assess the client for the high-risk elderly suicide marker of a major loss (e.g., death of a spouse or major lifestyle change, such as retirement or moving to assisted living; loss of income; or loss of independence, when dependency is unacceptable).

8. Assess the client for the high-risk elderly suicide marker of communication of intent

(e.g., writing suicide notes that are dominated by hopelessness; direct expression of the wish to die; giving away prized possessions; strangely calm, peaceful attitude when talking of death; a history of previous suicide attempts; or a family history of suicide completions and/or attempts).

9. Assess the client for the high-risk elderly suicide marker of somatic complaints (e.g., numerous visits to the physician with complaints of unrelenting, unremitting physical pain; using alcohol; logical, clear argument on the "right to die" and the use of suicide as a solution to pain).

5. Provide information on personal experiences with high-risk *emotional* markers for suicide in the elderly. (10, 11, 12)

10. Assess the client for the high-risk elderly suicide marker of depression (e.g., deep despair, hopelessness, incapable of futuristic thinking, morbid, guilt-ridden preoccupation with the past, social withdrawal, low energy, devalued self-image, feelings of being a burden, increase in rage outbursts, or rejection of help).

11. Assess the client for the high-risk elderly suicide marker of narcissistic trauma (e.g., uncharacteristically expressing feelings of inferiority; lack of trust in others; inability to cope with physical decline, accept help from others in activities of daily living, cope with the natural aging process, or historical base of self-image focused on work and productivity).

12. Assess the client for the high-risk elderly suicide marker of rigidity in thought and inflexibility in attitude (e.g., uses denial as a primary coping mechanism; experiences overwhelming states of pain and anxiety; or views suicide as a control and mastery device over physical and mental decline).

6. Provide information on personal experiences with high-risk *social* markers for suicide in the elderly. (13)

13. Assess the client for the high-risk elderly suicide marker of social disruption (e.g., engages in behaviors designed to alienate family, social network, and/or caregivers; death of close friends; loss of autonomy, or loss of work-related relationships).

7. Medical personnel, especially the physician, provide relevant, current information on general health issues. (14, 15)

14. After obtaining appropriate confidentiality releases, contact the client's primary care physician for a medical report and evaluation, paying particular attention to recent, multiple somatic complaints and any indicators of depression that the physician noted.

15. Maintain communication with the client's primary care physician to facilitate the sharing of information on the client, enhance the physician's knowledge base about symptoms of depression in the elderly and their management, and respect that the elderly seek assistance from their physician before they confide in mental health professionals.

8. Provide complete information on current mood, affect, and thought process in a

16. Refer the client for a psychiatric evaluation to determine the need for psychotropic medication or a

psychiatric evaluation, taking psychotropic medication as prescribed. (16, 17)

medically managed electro-convulsive therapy series (ECT) and validate any at-risk diag-noses (e.g., single episode of nonpsychotic major depression or narcissistic personality).

17. Monitor the client's compliance with the prescribed medical interventions (e.g., medication and/or ECT); chart the subjec-tive and objective behavioral changes and monitor side effects, sharing observations with the primary care physician.

9. The client and, if available, caregivers accept feedback on the assessments and the treatment plan developed from the evaluation process. (18)

18. Summarize and give feedback to the client and, if available, caregivers on high-risk elderly suicide markers found in the evaluation process; formulate his/her treatment plan and engage the caregivers (e.g., monitor medications, mood, or activities).

10. Comply with placement in a more protective and, possibly, a more restrictive environment. (19)

19. If assessments reveal the presence of high-risk elderly suicide markers that signifi-cantly challenge coping capacity (e.g., increase in verbalized wishes to die, unwillingness to care for self, physical combat-iveness, or increase in comments of self-hate), place the client in a therapeutic setting that will protect him/her from suicidal impulse, decrease perturbation, remove environmental stress, decrease isolation, and monitor treatment effectiveness.

11. Affirm a safety plan that allows a return to the caregivers and the community. (20, 21)

20. Refer the client to a community-based clinical case management program that has the capacity to monitor and coordinate medical management, respite services,

crisis intervention, home medical and nutritional services, and family support as the client returns to home and the community from an inpatient stay; obtain the client's affirmation of this plan.

21. Monitor the client's suicide risk at appropriate intervals through high-risk elderly suicide markers interview and by administering standardized suicide risk assessment (e.g., Suicide Probability Scale).

12. Agree to a written plan for dealing with situations when suicidal urges become strong. (22, 23)

22. Develop a written crisis intervention plan to be implemented during times when the client experiences trigger events and feelings (e.g., isolation, fears, or loss) that includes contacting the case manager, therapist, trusted friend or family member and discussing emotional reactions to events.

23. Ask the client to agree, as a verbal contract in the therapeutic relationship, to call someone on the emergency phone list in case he/she experiences strong suicidal urges.

13. Identify current stressors and resultant symptoms that trigger the wish to die. (24, 25, 26)

24. Assist the client in making a list of his/her most prominent stressors (e.g., residing in an assisted living facility, retiring from a job that made him/her feel good about himself/herself, or physical maladies that hinder autonomy) and emotional reactions or symptoms (e.g., depression, anxiety, anger, or self-hate) produced by those stressors.

25. Assist the client in producing a complete symptom inventory that includes identifying the most disruptive symptoms (e.g., depression, anxiety, anger, or self-hate), how these symptoms are managed (e.g., physical outbursts, refusing help, or denial), and other reactions created by these symptoms (e.g., alienated of family and friends, loneliness, or boredom).

26. Establish a therapeutic alliance with the client that ensures the therapist's help in targeting the most serious symptoms for immediate attention (e.g., hospitalization, ECT, medication, or solution-oriented therapy).

14. Verbalize statements of hope that symptoms can be managed in ways other than suicide. (27, 28, 29, 30)

27. Formulate an appropriate view of suicide for the client: It stems from a desire to solve a seemingly unsolvable problem, it is fueled by elements of hopelessness and helplessness; and the antidote is to acquire safe, simple coping and problem-solving skills over identified stressors and symptoms with the therapist's help.

28. Assign the client a treatment journal to track daily stressors, the resulting symptoms, maladaptive coping patterns, and experiences with newly acquired coping strategies; assign homework targeting symptom management; stress to the client that the goal of therapy is healthy symptom management and *not* symptom elimination.

29. Assist the client in developing in his/her treatment journal a

detailed plan with specific instructions on responding to and managing the perturbation associated with his/her immediate, priority symptoms; these responses should be detailed and structured to assist the client during extreme emotional upset.

30. Use role-play, modeling, and behavior rehearsal to teach the client to implement the symptom-management skills noted in his/her treatment journal.

15. Identify own biological, social, and emotional vulnerabilities that contribute to suicidal thinking. (31, 32)

31. Explore the client's personal vulnerabilities that contribute to the suicidal crisis (e.g., narcissistic personality traits, need to be in control, or performance anxiety).

32. Assist the client in acknowledging the existence of his/her personal vulnerabilities and their influence on maladaptive coping (e.g., inability to accept help, inappropriately high level of rigid independence, inability to accept the aging process gracefully, or judging value based solely on work performance).

16. Review the life history and develop a plan for the future based on past experiences and strengths. (33, 34)

33. As part of his/her treatment journal, ask the client to write his/her autobiography; review the material together, encouraging a balanced view of his/her history, recognizing guilt or pride where it is appropriate, shame where justified, and praise when due.

34. Drawing from the client's history, help him/her develop a

17. Increase the frequency of sharing life experiences with others. (35, 36)

18. Verbalize a sense of confidence that physical impairments and changes in functioning can be managed with assistance. (37, 38)

positive perspective of himself/herself; assist him/her in the development of a future life plan based on his/her revealed strengths.

35. Teach the client the value of verbalizing emotions in the context of personal and intimate relationships (e.g., sharing feelings promotes empathy from others, sharing burdens reduces their intensity, sharing allows others to give their perspective on problems and offer solutions, and sharing breaks down a sense of isolation and helps normalize the issues of aging); assist the client in identifying those trusted individuals with whom he/she could share thoughts and feelings.

36. Encourage the client to see himself/herself in a social context by emphasizing the benefits of participation in friendships and group activities; assign participation in selected social activities or community volunteer, reinforcing success and redirecting for failure.

37. Assist the client in listing ways that the tendency toward help negation, expressing hostility to helping others, holding on to an unrealistic desire for independence can be replaced with alternate, constructive methods of accepting help and being comfortable with a degree of dependence; ask the client to accept help (e.g., write a thank you note to someone who has

offered assistance) from someone in the coming week.

38. Review the client's growth, challenging him/her to trust the value of himself/herself and his/her wisdom gained from life experience.

19. Develop a suicide prevention plan that incorporates the treatment journal and all completed homework assignments. (39, 40)

39. Educate the client about preventing relapse into suicidal behavior (e.g., rely on the treatment journal for reminders of strategies for coping with trigger events, feelings, and symptoms; avoid isolation and maintain social network; accept help from others; remain on medications; or maintain futuristic thinking).

40. Assist the client in writing a personal suicide prevention plan that lists individualized actions that will be taken in the future to manage suicidal urges.

__. _____   __. _____
    _____   _____

__. _____   __. _____
    _____   _____

__. _____   __. _____
    _____   _____

DIAGNOSTIC SUGGESTIONS:

Axis I:	296.23	Major Depressive Disorder, Single Episode, Severe
	296.xx	Major Depressive Disorder
	300.4	Dysthymic Disorder
	300.3	Obsessive-Compulsive Disorder
	300.21	Panic Disorder with Agoraphobia

	303.90	Alcohol Dependence
	305.00	Alcohol Abuse
	296.90	Mood Disorder NOS
	308.3	Acute Stress Disorder
	300.02	Generalized Anxiety Disorder
	300.81	Somatization Disorder
	307.80	Pain Disorder Associated with Psychological Factors
	300.7	Hypochondriasis with Poor Insight

————— ————————————————————————

————— ————————————————————————

Axis II:

	301.7	Antisocial Personality Disorder
	301.83	Borderline Personality Disorder
	301.81	Narcissistic Personality Disorder
	301.4	Obsessive-Compulsive Personality Disorder

————— ————————————————————————

————— ————————————————————————

GAY/LESBIAN/BISEXUAL

BEHAVIORAL DEFINITIONS

1. Verbalizes a wish to die.
2. Engages in dangerous at-risk behaviors (e.g., reckless, unsafe sexual activity, or polysubstance abuse) that are ascribed to a wish to die.
3. Demonstrates an internalizing of societal homophobia and negative attitudes in ways that manifest as shame, hostility, and self-hatred.
4. Indicates that the process of self-identification and disclosure of homosexual orientation to family and friends causes fear and anxiety.
5. Demonstrates a significant pattern of suicide attempt activity that is both calculated for rescue and/or self-interrupted and is accidentally interrupted against the victim's wishes.
6. Demonstrates signs and symptoms of depression (e.g., sad affect, irritability, lack of energy, social withdrawal, sleep disturbance, or a sense of hopelessness).
7. Verbally indicates a sense of isolation and being different.
8. Lacks a positive social support system that is accepting and affirming.
9. Demonstrates anxiety, stress, and inadequate coping ability when discussing sexual orientation issues.
10. Indicates being victimized by criminally violent behavior because of sexual orientation with resulting posttraumatic stress.
11. Is HIV positive with resulting loss of employment, loss of insurance coverage, repeated infections, painful or disfiguring physical deterioration, treatment failures, and lack of social support.

—. _____
   _____
—. _____
   _____
—. _____
   _____

LONG-TERM GOALS

1. Report a wish to live.
2. Develop a sense of hope for the future and an ability to define self in a futuristic context.
3. Enhance the skill to cope with societal homophobic attitudes.
4. Develop internalized pride and ownership in sexual orientation.
5. View self in a social context that is global and not isolated by sexual orientation criteria.
6. Enhance the capacity to grieve the loss of loved ones to disease, discrimination, or pathological behavior such as substance abuse.

—. _____

_____

—. _____

_____

—. _____

_____

SHORT-TERM OBJECTIVES

1. Identify specifics of the development and identity formation of homosexual orientation. (1, 2, 3, 4)

THERAPEUTIC INTERVENTIONS

1. Explore the process of the client's recognition of himself/ herself as lesbian or gay; examine whether this process entailed any difficulties (e.g., conflicting feelings associated with the homosexual orientation, feelings of low self-esteem, or experiences of peer or family rejection) and determine the age range of the experience, expecting that more conflicts will be experienced at a younger age.

2. Explore how the client gained information about homosexuality and the gay and lesbian community; examine whether this process was accomplished in a positive, healthy way or

whether the experience was in a high-risk setting (e.g., drug use, prostitution, or sexual abuse).

3. Explore the client's experience with disclosing his/her sexual orientation to others and whether it was affirming or traumatic (e.g., resulted in abandonment by family and/or peers, harassment at school or workplace, or physical assault).

4. Explore whether the client is comfortable with and accepting of his/her sexual orientation or whether conflict yet prevails; examine the depth of conflict or existing denial (e.g., holds negative attitudes toward homosexuality or engages in reckless heterosexual activity).

2. Identify the nature of current suicidal ideation, planning, and/or intent. (5, 6, 7)

5. Explore the client's intended goal of the suicidal act (e.g., cessation of psychological pain, revenge against perpetrators, need to eliminate himself/herself for the benefit of others or society, or the solution to a seemingly unsolvable problem).

6. Explore the amount of energy the client spent in planning his/her suicide event (e.g., has a weapon been obtained or a lethal method chosen, has a date or a place been assigned, have notes been written, have prized possessions been distributed, has a sense of calm replaced turmoil since the planning began or was completed).

7. Explore whether any impediments to the implementation of his/her suicide plan exist

(e.g., fear of the emotional impact on survivors, religious beliefs, or social stigma concerns) with the client.

3. Cooperate with psychological testing designed to evaluate conditions correlated to elevated suicide risk in the gay/lesbian/bisexual (GLB) population. (8)

8. Administer testing to reveal and evaluate suicidal ideation and intent levels (e.g., Suicide Ideation Questionnaire, Beck Depression Inventory, Beck Scale for Suicide Ideation, Suicide Probability Scale, or Reasons for Living Inventory) and provide feedback to client and, if available, caregivers on test results and treatment implications.

4. Provide information on personal experiences with high-risk *behavioral* markers for suicide in the GLB population. (9, 10, 11)

9. Assess the client for the high-risk GLB suicide marker of substance abuse by administering a thorough evaluation (e.g., in lesbians, inquire about an increase in alcohol abuse; in gays and bisexuals, inquire about polysubstance abuse patterns, age of onset, family member use, physiologic dependency signs, and types of drugs used and frequency).

10. Assess the client for the high-risk GLB suicide marker of maladaptive coping patterns associated with early attraction to same-gender individuals (e.g., denial, avoidance, suppression, or escape) and examine with him/her the behaviors associated with these maladaptive coping patterns (e.g., reckless engagement in heterosexual sex, voicing extremely negative attitudes about homosexuals, excessive

use of alcohol or a variety of drugs, attempting to get pregnant or father a child to validate heterosexuality, or affiliation with a highly rigid social or religious environment).

11. Assess the client for the high-risk GLB suicide marker of gender nonconforming behavior (e.g., disclosing sexual orientation in a social setting that is unsafe and nonaccepting; engaging in same-sex behavior in a setting that is unsafe and predatory) which may lead to harassment, victimization by violence, prostitution, or STD exposure.

5. Provide information on personal experiences with high-risk *emotional* markers for suicide in the GLB population. (12, 13, 14)

12. Assess the client for the high-risk GLB suicide marker of depression (e.g., depth of sadness, isolation, hopelessness, self-directed anger, low energy, social withdrawal, low self-esteem, lack of interest or pleasure in activities, reduced appetite, or sleep disruptions).

13. Assess the client for the high-risk GLB suicide marker of posttraumatic stress (e.g., dissociative flashback episodes, nightmares, distressing, intrusive recollections, emotional constriction, sleep disorders, hypervigilance, or increase irritability).

14. Assess the client for the high-risk GLB suicide marker of panic anxiety (e.g., pervasive worry, motor tension and restlessness, rapid heartbeat, fears of imminent death, sleep

6. Provide information on personal experiences with high-risk *social* markers for suicide in the GLB population. (15, 16)

7. School personnel provide information on the client's behavior and academic issues. (17)

8. Medical personnel provide relevant, current information on the client's general health issues. (18)

9. Provide complete information on current mood, affect, and thought process in a psychiatric evaluation and take psychotropic medication as prescribed. (19, 20)

disturbance, irritability, or difficulty in concentration).

15. Assess the client for the high-risk GLB suicide marker of social rejection (e.g., romantic relationship termination, peer-group rejection, college bound status and fears, nature of social support network, or military experiences of rejection).

16. Assess the client for the high-risk GLB suicide marker of family rejection (e.g., physically abused by a family member, disowned by family, or thrown out of the home).

17. After obtaining appropriate confidentiality releases, contact school officials for a report on the client's social network, absence record, academic pattern, and victimization episodes because of gender-nonconformity behavior.

18. After obtaining the appropriate confidentiality releases, contact the client's primary care physician for a report on the client's health (e.g., STD history, bodily injuries, evidence of sexual abuse, general disease patterns, medications, or concerns about mental health issues); continue periodic consultation with the physician.

19. Refer the client for a psychiatric evaluation to determine the need for psychotropic medication and to validate any at-risk diagnoses (e.g., major depression, anxiety disorder, PTSD issues).

20. Monitor the client's compliance with the psychotropic medication prescription; chart subjective and objective behavioral changes, and monitor the side effects.

10. The client and, if available, caregivers accept feedback on the assessment for high-risk markers for suicide in the client's presentation. (21)

21. Summarize and give feedback to the client and, if available and appropriate, the caregivers, on high-risk markers found during the assessment and evaluation process; explain details of the treatment plan and attempt to engage the caregivers.

11. Comply with placement in a more protective and restrictive environment if the assessments reveal high-risk markers for completed suicide. (22, 23)

22. If at any time during the therapy process the client displays an increase in the number or intensity of the examined high-risk markers, place him/her in a therapeutic setting that will protect him/her from suicide impulse, decrease perturbation, remove environmental stress, decrease isolation, and monitor treatment effectiveness.

23. Monitor the client's suicide risk at appropriate intervals through interview and by administering standardized suicide risk assessment instruments (e.g., Beck Hopelessness Scale, Suicide Probability Scale, Suicide Risk Measure, or Reasons for Living Inventory).

12. Affirm a safety plan that allows for the return to caregivers or the community. (24)

24. Coordinate planning that will, along with psychotherapy, aggressively treat psychiatric problems and substance abuse disorders, provide services that promote healthy psychosocial adjustment, diminish the effects

of discrimination, and efficiently decrease social stressors; obtain the client's affirmation of this plan.

13. Agree to a written plan for dealing with situations when suicidal urges become strong. (25)

25. Develop a written crisis intervention plan to be implemented during trigger events and feelings (e.g., isolation, self-hate, or fear) that includes contacting a trusted friend or, if available, a family member or therapist and talking out emotional reactions to events; provide telephone numbers in writing to the client, and as part of the therapeutic relationship, have the client enter into a verbal agreement to call the resources on an as-needed basis.

14. Identify the stressors and symptoms that trigger the wish to die by suicide. (26, 27)

26. Assist the client in making a list of his/her most prominent stressors (e.g., facing rejecting friends or family members, visiting a substance-dependent friend, seeing close friend die of AIDS, or being harassed at school); assess his/her emotional reactions or symptoms (e.g., fear, self-hate, or sorrow) produced by those stressors.

27. Assist the client in developing a complete symptom inventory that includes stressors-symptoms stimulation and current dysfunctional management of symptoms (e.g., self-mutilation, substance abuse, reckless heterosexual activity, or emotional constriction); do these stressors cause other painful reactions that eventually overwhelm him/her (e.g., loss of self-respect, depression, or suicidal thoughts).

15. Identify solutions or stress-management skills that do not include suicide or the wish to die. (28)

28. Assist the client in identifying the *most* disruptive stressors and resulting symptoms (i.e., the symptoms that cause the highest level of impairment in their activities of daily living); target those symptoms for immediate intervention techniques and teach coping strategies (e.g., managing the sadness and anger generated by rejection of family or former friends through the development of a supportive social network, learning the value of verbal expression of those harmful emotions from the therapist).

16. Increase verbalized statements of hope that symptoms can be managed in ways other than suicide. (29, 30, 31, 32)

29. Formulate an appropriate view of the function of suicide with the client: It stems from a need to solve a seemingly unsolvable problem, it is fueled by a sense of hopelessness and helpless-ness, and the antidote is to develop coping strategies and management techniques for these seemingly unsolvable issues; avoid leading the client to believe that the therapy process will eliminate stress symptoms, emphasizing the treatment goal of symptom management.

30. Assign the client a treatment journal to track daily stressors, the resulting symptoms, maladaptive coping patterns, and experiences with newly acquired coping strategies; assign homework targeting symptom management; stress to the client that the goal of therapy is healthy symptom

management and *not* symptom elimination.

31. Assist the client in identifying his/her maladaptive externalizing coping behaviors (e.g., drug abuse, sexual acting out, or fighting) and internalizing coping behaviors (e.g., eating disorders, anxiety reactions, or depression) and help him/her replace these maladaptive coping responses with a problem-solving focus. Use homework assignments in the treatment journal for exercises.

32. Use role-play, modeling, and behavior rehearsal to teach the client symptom management skills (e.g., verbalizing feelings of anxiety or confusion with a trusted friend, engaging in a prescribed physical exercise program when feelings of anxiety are heightened, focusing on self-integrity when anxiety over sexual orientation is heightened).

17. Identify own personality traits and vulnerabilities that contribute to the risk for suicide. (33, 34)

33. Assess the client for personal vulnerabilities that contribute to the suicidal crisis (e.g., emotional constriction, issues of self-hate, the need to be perfect, feelings of isolation, or a pathological disruption in the developmental process of acquiring sexual orientation).

34. Assist the client in acknowledging the existence of his/her personal vulnerability traits and their influence on his/her maladaptive coping skills (e.g., inability to express powerful

emotions, need to conform to others' expectations, or impulse toward self-injurious or high-risk behaviors); teach him/her how to diminish influence on coping strategies (e.g., enabling the client to become less dependent on the approval of others or teaching the client the benefits of free expression of emotions).

18. Increase the frequency of verbalizing statements indicating improved comfort with sexual orientation and coping with homophobic attitudes. (35)

35. Teach the client to use a treatment journal to note all incidents of improved symptom management of the stressor of homophobic attitudes and attacks (e.g., walking away or using calming techniques in the face of verbal harassment); encourage him/her to use positive, affirming comments toward himself/herself as he/she develops better symptom-management skills.

19. Reach out to build a positive, accepting social support network. (36)

36. Encourage the client to seek out social settings with mature, sensitive, respectful, gay, lesbian, and heterosexual friends; review these attempts to reach out, reinforcing success and redirecting for failures.

20. Verbalize increased self-acceptance and the related ability to self-disclose to others. (37, 38)

37. Review the client's treatment journal to note significant patterns of decrease in the presence of high-risk symptoms in response to a variety of stressors (e.g., decrease in sexual acting out to cope with isolation, substance abuse patterns to cope with anxiety, self-mutilation to cope with self-hate) and any increase in comments of pride in sexual

orientation, confidence in self-disclosing, or feelings of life management; stress to the client that as self-acceptance increases, so does the capacity to disclose to others.

38. Elicit from the client his/her feelings of confidence in the future and sense of confidence in self (e.g., recognizing that positive coping encourages a sense of management over one's life); stress to the client that self-acceptance is the capacity to embrace the good, bad, positive, and negative into an integrated self-concept.

21. Develop a suicide prevention plan that incorporates the treatment journal and all completed homework assignments. (39, 40)

39. Educate the client about how to prevent relapse into suicidal behavior (e.g., rely on the treatment journal for reminders of strategies for coping with stress-induced symptoms, share feelings with trusted others, avoid isolation, maintain a healthy and global social network, remain on medications, and maintain futuristic thinking).

40. Assist the client in writing a personal suicide prevention plan that incorporates and respects the individual aspects of the client's life; include all of the actions needed to continue symptom management, manage suicidal urges, and maintain confidence in himself/herself.

___. _____   ___. _____
      _____   _____
___. _____   ___. _____
      _____   _____
___. _____   ___. _____
      _____   _____

DIAGNOSTIC SUGGESTIONS:

Axis I: 296.23   Major Depressive Disorder, Single Episode,
                        Severe
              296.xx   Major Depressive Disorder
              300.4   Dysthymic Disorder
              303.9   Alcohol Dependence
              296.90   Mood Disorder NOS
              300.02   Generalized Anxiety Disorder
              302.85   Gender Identity Disorder
              300.21   Panic Disorder with Agoraphobia
              305.00   Alcohol Abuse
              304.20   Cocaine Dependence
              304.80   Polysubstance Dependence
              309.81   Posttraumatic Stress Disorder

              _____   _____
              _____   _____

HISPANIC MALE

BEHAVIORAL DEFINITIONS

1. Expresses a generalized fatalism about life and an absence of hope for the future.
2. Demonstrates behaviors positively associated with the diagnosis of depressive disorder (e.g., lack of energy, anhedonia, dysphoria, or social withdrawal).
3. Family of origin is characterized by extreme turmoil and dysfunction (e.g., parental substance abuse or child emotional and physical abuse).
4. Experiences considerable acculturation stress (e.g., language barriers; employment; education; or lack of contact with cultural, ethnic, and traditional activities).
5. Demonstrates poorly defined coping and problem-solving skills and will often use escape and denial to deal with stress.
6. Engages in psychoactive substance abuse (e.g., crack, alcohol, opiates, or cocaine) to cope with acculturation stress.
7. Demonstrates ethnic and cultural identity confusion, which may lead to a sense of social isolation for the Hispanic/Anglo (e.g., mixed race) population.
8. Lacks involvement or is passively involved in traditional Hispanic support systems or religious organizations (e.g., Catholic Church).

—. _____
   _____
—. _____
   _____
—. _____
   _____

LONG-TERM GOALS

1. Resolve feelings of worthlessness, self-hate, and isolation that contribute to depressive reactions and the impulse to suicide.
2. Enhance the development of coping strategies and problem-solving skills.
3. Enhance self-identity based on cultural and ethnic traditions.
4. Engage in the acculturation process while maintaining a linkage to cultural, spiritual, and religious supports.

__. _____
_____
_____

__. _____
_____
_____

__. _____
_____

SHORT-TERM OBJECTIVES

1. Describe the specifics of acculturation stress. (1, 2)

2. Identify specifics of family turmoil and/or dysfunctional patterns. (3, 4)

THERAPEUTIC INTERVENTIONS

1. Assess whether the client's efforts to adjust to American culture have had positive outcomes (e.g., employment was obtained, social life was enhanced, and educational opportunities were available) or negative outcomes (e.g., feelings of isolation were predominant, discrimination was experienced, and traditional Hispanic values were abandoned).

2. Explore any sense of social isolation, low self-esteem, poor futuristic outlook, and ambivalence with the client about ethnic identification because of mixed race (Hispanic/Anglo) ancestry.

3. Explore the client's family of origin and nuclear family for turmoil and/or dysfunction

(e.g., parental abandonment; issues of emotional, physical, or sexual abuse; parental or spousal substance abuse patterns; or incidents of spousal physical abuse).

4. Assist the client in identifying and clarifying the emotional impact of his family turmoil (e.g., fear, isolation, rage, or depression with helplessness).

3. Cooperate with psychological testing designed to evaluate suicide ideation or intent levels. (5)

5. Administer testing most commonly used to reveal and evaluate suicide ideation and/ or intent levels (e.g., Beck Hopelessness Scale, Reasons for Living Inventory, or Suicide Risk Measure).

4. Provide complete information on current mood, affect, and thought process in a psychiatric evaluation and take psychotropic medication as prescribed. (6, 7)

6. Refer the client for a psychiatric evaluation to determine his need for psychotropic medication and to validate any at-risk diagnoses (e.g., major depressive disorder).

7. Monitor the client's compliance with the psychotropic medication prescription; chart the effectiveness of the medication and monitor the side effects.

5. Medical personnel provide relevant current information pertaining to general health issues. (8)

8. After obtaining appropriate confidentiality releases and privacy documentation, contact the client's medical care providers for a report on general health issues.

6. The client and, if possible and appropriate, caregivers provide personal information on high-risk *behavioral* markers for the Hispanic male suicide population. (9, 10)

9. Assess the client for the high-risk Hispanic male suicide marker of substance abuse (e.g., age at onset of personal and family use, use to cope with acculturation stress during previous suicide activity, and/or during acculturation efforts).

10. Assess the client for the high-risk Hispanic male suicide marker of using coping strategies of denial, social withdrawal, and behavioral disengagement (e.g., giving up, inactivity, or fatalism).

7. The client and, if possible and appropriate, caregivers provide personal information on high-risk *emotional* markers for the Hispanic male suicide population. (11)

11. Assess the client for the high-risk Hispanic male suicide marker of depression (e.g., hopelessness, self-devaluation, anhedonia, dysphoria, or social withdrawal).

8. The client and, if possible and appropriate, caregivers provide personal information on high-risk *social* markers for the Hispanic male suicide population. (12)

12. Assess the client for the high-risk Hispanic male suicide marker of affiliation with a violence-prone peer group (e.g., degree of fulfillment of social, environmental, and psycho-logical needs through this affiliation).

9. Identify specifics of the current suicide ideation and/or intent. (13, 14, 15, 16)

13. Explore the client's goal for his intended suicide act (e.g., cessation of severe emotional pain, antidote for feelings of hopelessness, escape from extreme family turmoil, or a solution to a seemingly unsolv-able problem).

14. Explore the amount of time and energy the client has spent in planning his suicide event (e.g., has a lethal means been chosen and/or obtained, has a date or place been assigned, has the suicide intent been communi-cated to anyone and, if so, what was the reaction).

15. Explore whether the client has experienced any sense of calm, peace, tranquility, or renewed energy level since planning for

his suicide started or was completed.

16. Explore whether the client identifies any barriers to his plan to die (e.g., personal religious beliefs, fear of emotional impact on survivors, or fear of accidentally surviving); note any ambivalence he displays about completed suicide.

10. Identify specifics of any historic pattern of suicide ideation, gestures, or attempts. (17)

17. Explore the client's previous experiences with suicide activity (e.g., chronic experiences of thinking about suicide as a way to solve a problem; deliberate nonfatal, self-harm activities designed to fulfill needs other than death; or acts of self-harm where the intent was to die but the act was accidentally interrupted).

11. Identify specifics of faulty problem-solving strategies. (18, 19)

18. Explore the client's psychiatric factors that hinder his effective problem solving (e.g., depressive disorders, anxiety disorders, or obsessive-compulsive personality disorder).

19. Explore emotional and psychological factors that hinder the client's effective problem solving (e.g., overprotective childhood, delayed autonomy of adolescence, or verbal abuse as a child with a scripting message of being "stupid").

12. The client and, if possible and appropriate, the caregivers accept feedback gathered from all sources and the treatment plan developed from the evaluation process. (20)

20. Summarize and give feedback to the client and, if available and appropriate, his caregivers on high-risk markers found in the evaluation process and outline the treatment plan; if available and appropriate, engage

supportive caregivers into the treatment strategy (e.g., providing safety during high-risk times and encouraging his efforts on homework assignments).

13. Comply with placement in a more protective and, possibly, restrictive environment. (21)

21. If the assessments reveal the presence of high-risk suicide markers that significantly challenge the client's coping capacity (e.g., severe symptoms of depression or increase in statements of self-devaluation), place him in a structured, supervised therapeutic setting that will protect him from suicide impulse, decrease perturbation, remove him from environmental stress, and monitor treatment effectiveness.

14. Affirm a plan that allows for a safe return to the community. (22)

22. Review the inpatient treatment team's discharge plan with the client and the caregivers that includes placement, support systems, individual and family psychotherapy, activities of daily living, knowledge of helping services, and medication monitoring.

15. Agree to a crisis response plan for dealing with situations when the suicide risk is strong. (23)

23. Develop a crisis intervention plan to be implemented during trigger events and feelings (e.g., family violence, acculturation failures, or feelings of isolation and despair) that includes contacting the therapist, a trusted friend, or a local suicide prevention center or mental health center help line; ask the client to agree, as a verbal contract of therapy, to call someone on the phone list to

discuss emotional reactions that appear overwhelming.

16. Identify current stressors and resultant symptoms that trigger the wish to die by suicide. (24, 25, 26)

24. Assist the client in making a list of his most prominent stressors (e.g., failures in acculturation efforts, living in an abusive home, or discrimination based on mixed-race ancestry); explore his emotional reactions or symptoms (e.g., despair, hopelessness, rage, or self-devaluation) produced by those stressors.

25. Assist the client in developing a complete symptom inventory that includes identifying the most disruptive symptoms (e.g., isolation, fear, or despair), dysfunctional management of these symptoms (e.g., substance abuse, social withdrawal, hopelessness, or suicide ideation), and whether these maladaptive behaviors create other results (e.g., depression or anxiety) that eventually overwhelm him.

26. Establish a therapeutic alliance with the client that ensures the therapist's help in targeting the most serious symptoms for immediate attention (e.g., medications or solution-oriented therapy).

17. Increase verbalized statements of hope that stressors and symptoms can be managed continuously in ways other than suicide. (27, 28, 29)

27. Formulate an appropriate view of the function of suicide with the client: It stems from a need to solve a seemingly unsolvable problem (e.g., escaping abuse in the home), it is fueled by a sense of hopelessness and helplessness, and the antidote is to develop problem-solving skills,

with the therapist's help, for these seemingly unsolvable stressors and symptoms.

28. Assign the client a treatment journal to track daily stressors, the resulting symptoms, maladaptive coping behaviors, and experiences with newly acquired adaptive coping strategies (e.g., substance abuse is replaced by sharing feelings with a trusted friend); assign homework targeting symptom management.

29. Use role-play, modeling, and behavior rehearsal to teach the client to use adaptive problem-solving skills to replace maladaptive coping strategies (e.g., define the problem, seek alternative solutions, list the positives and negatives of each solution, select and implement a plan of action, evaluate the outcome, and adjust the solution as necessary).

18. Identify and diminish the influence of personality vulnerabilities and traits on problem-solving deficiencies that contribute to suicide ideation and/or intent. (30, 31, 32)

30. Explore the client's personal vulnerabilities that hinder healthy coping strategies and contribute to the suicidal crisis (e.g., perfectionism, need to please others, self-devaluation, or inability to access emotions).

31. Assist the client in acknowledging his suicide-fostering traits and vulnerabilities, their source, how they were acquired (e.g., self-devaluation from consistent parental criticism), and their influence in maladaptive coping (e.g., feelings of isolation or inability to tolerate failure); ask him to track these traits and their

influence in the treatment journal.

32. Teach the client methods and exercises that will diminish the influence of his suicide-fostering personality traits on problem-solving efforts (e.g., inability to tolerate failure replaced by a sense of self-acceptance, isolative behaviors and a sense of aloneness replaced by a capacity for intimacy and the ability to share thoughts and feelings in the therapy sessions).

19. Increase the use of personal resiliency, flexibility, and problem-solving skills during challenges from acculturation. (33, 34)

33. Encourage the client to write an autobiography focusing on times of successfully coping with stressors and symptoms created by acculturation efforts; teach him to adapt those strategies to present-day stressors and symptoms.

34. Encourage the client to retain or return to ethnic traditions and affiliations (e.g., attendance at religious ceremonies of importance or involvement in ethnic-based community support services) during efforts at acculturation.

20. Increase the frequency of statements that communicate pride in accomplishments and improved confidence in self. (35, 36)

35. Assist the client in enhancing his self-image by encouraging him to provide reports from his treatment journal and the homework assignments on recent incidents of his improved coping, symptom management, and problem-solving skills (e.g., remaining on medication for a diagnosed depressive disorder or talking to a friend about a difficult emotion).

36. Challenge the client to trust the value of himself during times of temporary failure; provide him with examples of others who rose from failure to enjoy success (e.g., *Why is Everybody Always Picking on Us?* by Webster-Doyle, *Who Belongs Here* by Knight, and other selected titles reflecting Hispanic culture and heritage).

21. Develop a suicide prevention plan that incorporates the treatment journal's homework assignments. (37)

37. Assist the client in writing a personal suicide prevention plan that lists actions he will take in the future to manage the impulse to suicide (e.g., remain aware of strategies for coping with trigger stressors and symptoms, avoid isolation, maintain culturally relevant social network, and remain on medications, if prescribed).

__. _____   __. _____

_____   _____

__. _____   __. _____

_____   _____

__. _____   __. _____

_____   _____

DIAGNOSTIC SUGGESTIONS:

Axis I:	296.xx	Major Depressive Disorder
	300.4	Dysthymic Disorder
	309.0	Adjustment Disorder with Depressed Mood
	300.02	Generalized Anxiety Disorder
	303.90	Alcohol Dependence
	305.60	Cocaine Abuse
	305.00	Alcohol Abuse
	V62.4	Acculturation Problem

V62.89   Religious or Spiritual Problem
V61.20   Parent-Child Relational Problem
V62.2   Occupational Problem
309.81   Posttraumatic Stress Disorder

_____   _____

_____   _____

HOMELESS MALE

BEHAVIORAL DEFINITIONS

1. Demonstrates behaviors correlated to the mental illness of schizophrenia (e.g., delusions, hallucinations, thought disorganization, or depersonalization) with co-occurring disorders of major depression and substance abuse/dependence.
2. Demonstrates behaviors correlated to the antisocial personality disorder (e.g., lack of empathy for the rights and feelings of others, remarkable disdain for society's regulations, inability to regulate emotions of rage, or inability to delay gratification) with co-occurring disorders of major depression and substance abuse/dependency.
3. Demonstrates behaviors correlated to posttraumatic stress disorder (e.g., impulsive behaviors, out-of-control addiction to risk-taking behaviors, inability to regulate strong emotions, or high level of distrust and guardedness toward society) with co-occurring disorders of major depression and substance abuse/dependency.
4. Rejects help from social-service agencies, religious organizations, mental health, and substance abuse programs.
5. Isolates self because of fears, rage, oppositional and defiant traits, suspiciousness, and assaultive behaviors.
6. Unable to meet necessities of daily living (e.g., food, shelter, clothing, nutrition, general health concerns, or chronic unemployment).
7. Experiences numerous, pronounced rejections from essential support networks (e.g., immediate family, children, spouse, or partner) because of an unwillingness to seek help for psychiatric impairment.
8. Demonstrates apathy about a desire to live and is unconcerned about life-threatening situations (e.g., disregard for dangerous weather conditions or dangerous levels of polysubstance abuse/dependence or disregard for general health and nutrition needs).
9. Presents an extreme challenge to health care providers because of chronic noncompliance with treatment plans and recommendations.

10. Lacks futuristic thinking, but, instead, engages in a guilt-producing obsession with the past.

—. _____

_____

—. _____

_____

—. _____

_____

LONG-TERM GOALS

1. Consistently engage in behaviors that provide for the basic needs of life (e.g., food, shelter, and clothing).
2. Obtain psychiatric care and stabilize mental and emotional condition.
3. Participate in a program of recovery from addiction.
4. Learn problem-solving and adaptive coping skills for daily life stress.
5. Engage in productive and healthy activities of daily living.

—. _____

_____

—. _____

_____

—. _____

_____

SHORT-TERM OBJECTIVES

THERAPEUTIC INTERVENTIONS

1. Identify factors contributing to current homeless condition. (1, 2, 3)

1. Examine precipitating factors in the client's social, familial, and occupational experience that instigated the homeless condition (e.g., chronic, untreated substance dependence; undiagnosed and/or untreated mental disorders; or chronic demonstration of dysfunctional behaviors in social and/or intimate relationships).

2. Identify life hopes and expectations prior to the onset of the homeless condition. (4)

3. Cooperate with psychological testing designed to evaluate conditions correlated to completed suicide. (5)

4. Provide complete information on current mood, affect, and thought process in a psychiatric evaluation and take psychotropic medication as prescribed. (6, 7)

2. Ask the client to characterize his current homelessness as satisfying, acceptable, or disappointing.

3. Assist the client in identifying what contributes to his home-lessness being a satisfying or acceptable condition (e.g., friendships, freedom, no social obligations, or psychological comfort); ask him to identify what makes homelessness a disappointing condition (e.g., psychiatric turmoil, fear of physical violence, weather conditions, lack of food, exposure to drugs, or missing old relationships).

4. Explore the client's vocational, occupational, personal, and social hopes and aspirations prior to the onset of the home-less condition; assess how his homelessness affects his hopes and aspirations; note any level of hopelessness and/or despair as a result of his homeless condition.

5. Arrange for psychological testing to evaluate the client's level and nature of current suicide ideation/intent (e.g., Suicide Probability Scale, Beck Hopelessness Scale, or Reasons for Living Inventory); share test results with the client.

6. Refer the client for a psychiatric evaluation to determine the need for psychotropic medi-cation and to verify any at-risk diagnoses (e.g., schizophrenia, polysubstance dependence, major depression, posttraumatic

stress, or antisocial personality traits).

7. Arrange a community-based action plan (e.g., utilize homeless shelter staff) to monitor the client's compliance with the psychotropic medication prescription; remain alert to his subjective and objective behavioral changes and side effects as well as co-occurring substance abuse.

5. Provide information on personal experiences with high-risk *behavioral* markers for suicide in homeless males. (8, 9, 10, 11)

8. Assess the client for the high-risk homeless male suicide marker of substance abuse/dependency by administering a thorough evaluation (e.g., age of onset, choice of substances, readiness to change issues, or use as a coping strategy for environmental/social conditions or to calm psychiatric turmoil).

9. Assess the client for the high-risk homeless male suicide marker of a history of assaultive behaviors (e.g., aggressive acting out as a response to paranoid fears; periods of incarceration because of assault; long-term history of violence to property and people; or incidents of violence linked to posttraumatic stress).

10. Assess the client for the high-risk homeless male suicide marker of previous suicide activity (e.g., age of activity, motivation for suicide, whether suicide was calculated for rescue or if it was accidentally interrupted and he is angry that he failed, risk factors present at the time of the activity and whether

those same risk factors are currently present, and family history of suicide).

11. Assess the client for the high-risk homeless male suicide marker of a history of rejecting offered mental health services and/or general assistance (e.g., medications, shelter, food, clothing, or medical assistance); examine paranoid and/or anti-social features contributing to his history of refusal of services.

6. Provide information on personal experiences with high-risk *emotional* markers for suicide in homeless males. (12, 13, 14, 15)

12. Assess the client for the high-risk homeless male suicide marker of the presence of a thought disorder (e.g., schizophrenia paranoid type, depression with psychosis, bipolar illness, drug-induced psychotic conditions); evaluate the chronicity of the condition, history of treatment, family history of mental illness, and presence of persecutory delusions or hallucinations).

13. Assess the client for the high-risk homeless male suicide marker of major depressive disorder (e.g., hopelessness and despair; anhedonia; low self-esteem; self-hate; or psychosis linked to the depressive disorder).

14. Assess the client for the high-risk homeless male suicide marker of a posttraumatic stress disorder (e.g., need to escape expectations of society; inability to respond to social norms; or fears of excessive environmental/social stimulation).

15. Assess the client for the high-risk homeless male suicide marker of antisocial personality traits or disorder (e.g., unregulated rage against society; lack of empathy for the needs of others and social expectations; need to withdraw from an intrusive society; or history of assaultive behavior).

7. Provide information on personal experiences with high-risk *social* markers for suicide in homeless males. (16, 17)

16. Assess the client for the high-risk homeless male suicide marker of chronic occupational impairment (e.g., history of employment and number of jobs held; reasons for termination of employment; ability to adapt to regulations of the workplace; history of relationships with fellow workers and supervisors; and current job status and his reaction to unemployment).

17. Assess the client for the high-risk homeless male suicide marker of social isolation (e.g., history of family rejection, current social network, feelings of isolation that are linked to the suicide intent, and feelings of being rejected by society); inquire whether the client has a social place where he is comfortable.

8. Provide specific information on the nature of the current suicide ideation/intent. (18, 19, 20, 21)

18. Assess whether the client can state a goal for his intended suicide act (e.g., to escape the hopelessness and despair of homelessness, acting on the emotion of self-directed rage and self-devaluation, revenge toward a rejecting society or specific social group, or to escape psychiatric turmoil).

19. Assess the level of planning the client is devoting to his intended suicide (e.g., time and place has been chosen, lethal means obtained, suicide pact with others has been concluded, or passively accepting and refusing to modify his serious health endangering behaviors).

20. Examine any decrease in agitation and hopelessness with the client and/or an experience of calm since the planning for suicide started (e.g., a sense of peace after a period of turmoil could be a warning sign for a pending suicide event).

21. Explore any doubts or ambivalence about the intended suicide (e.g., impact on others or religious beliefs) with the client; such doubts may diminish the urge for suicide.

9. Accept feedback gathered from all sources and the resulting treatment plan. (22)

22. Summarize and give feedback to the client on high-risk markers found in the evaluation process and outline the treatment plan; engage the client and any existing, appropriate social network in the treatment plan.

10. Comply with a placement in a more protective and restrictive therapeutic setting when risk for suicide is high. (23, 24)

23. Monitor the client's suicide risk at appropriate intervals in the treatment process through a risk assessment interview and by administering, if possible, standardized suicide risk assessment instruments (e.g., Beck Scale for Suicide Ideation, Beck Depression Inventory, or Suicide Probability Scale).

24. If at any time in the therapy process the client demonstrates

an increase in the number or intensity of noted risk factors for suicide, arrange for an immediate placement in a therapeutic setting that will protect him from suicide impulse, decrease perturbation, remove him from environmental stress, decrease his isolation, and provide close monitoring of medical and psychological treatment effectiveness.

11. Affirm a plan that allows for a safe return to the community. (25)

25. In consultation with the inpatient treatment team, discharge planning for the client should include a structured sheltering program, social support network, treatment and rehabilitation case management services, monitoring of medication, and occupational mainstreaming; obtain the client's affirmation of this plan.

12. Agree to a crisis response plan for dealing with situations when suicidal urges become strong. (26)

26. Develop a crisis intervention plan to be implemented during high suicide risk periods that includes the following: accessing shelter staff, using a local mental health help line, accessing hospital emergency services, contacting the therapist; provide all telephone numbers in writing to the client and guide him on appropriately accessing these services.

13. Comply with placement in a community-based treatment and rehabilitation program. (27)

27. Encourage and monitor the client's involvement in a community mental health treatment and rehabilitation plan that will address the following components: teach the client how to meet basic needs of food, safety,

and shelter; teach him about the psychiatric issues contributing to his current condition; teach him to monitor his medications; and teach problem-solving and coping skills.

14. Implement problem-solving skills to discover solutions to personal problems or life stresses. (28, 29)

28. Assist the client in identifying alternate solutions to his problems, challenging his perspective that suicide may be the only solution.

29. Teach the client problem-solving skills (e.g., define the problem, identify alternative solutions, list the pros and cons of each solution, select and implement a plan of action, and evaluate the outcome and adjust as necessary).

15. Verbalize statements of hope that problems can be managed continuously in ways other than suicide. (30, 31, 32)

30. Formulate an appropriate view of suicide with the client: It stems from a desire to solve a seemingly unsolvable problem, it is fueled by elements of hopelessness and helplessness, and the antidote is to acquire safe and simple coping and problem-solving skills for identified stresses.

31. Assign the client a treatment journal to track daily stresses (e.g., hunger or the threat of physical violence), the resulting emotional reactions or symptoms (e.g., fear), maladaptive coping patterns (e.g., substance abuse, need to isolate, or stealing), and experiences with newly acquired coping strategies (e.g., referring to shelter staff or case manager on issues of safety); assign

homework targeting symptom management.

32. Stress to the client that the goal of therapy is healthy symptom management and *not* symptom elimination.

16. Identify own biological, social, and emotional vulnerabilities that contribute to the suicidal condition and impair adaptive problem solving. (33)

33. Explore the client's personal vulnerabilities that contribute to the suicidal crisis and hinder effective problem solving (e.g., difficulty in regulating emotions, self-devaluation, distrust of society, or a need for isolation); encourage him to acknowledge the existence and influence of these vulnerabilities (e.g., need to isolate prevents him from seeking help) and to track these factors in the treatment journal.

17. Identify strategies that will enhance self-management of mental health and addiction issues, shelter needs, health concerns, and social deficits. (34, 35)

34. Teach the client to manage his own mental illness and addiction issues (e.g., recognize the symptoms of his psychiatric illness, understand the effects and side effects of his medication, recognize psychosocial stresses effecting symptoms, recognize the consequence of his substance abuse patterns, and continue to engage in treatment and support systems); monitor his implementation of these management processes.

35. Teach the client to manage his own shelter needs, health concerns, and social cohesion (e.g., remain in safe shelter/housing, manage hygiene to minimize health risks, maintain adequate nutrition, engage in appropriate medical and dental care, budget for basic needs within his

income, utilize free time in ways that contribute to good physical and mental health, and engage in safe and healthy relationships); monitor his implementation of these activities.

18. Increase the frequency of statements that communicate pride in accomplishments and improved self-confidence. (36, 37)

36. Assist the client in enhancing his self-image by encouraging self-reports on recent incidents on improved coping and problem solving (e.g., spending funds previously used for alcohol on a deposit for a safe, independent apartment); encourage him to record these efforts in the treatment journal for future reference.

37. Enhance the client's self-esteem by validating examples of growth, accomplishments, improved coping, and appropriate independent behaviors (e.g., going to a job regularly, medication compliance, or remaining in a social context).

19. Verbalize agreement with a written suicide prevention plan. (38, 39)

38. Educate the client on preventing relapse into suicidal behavior (e.g., remain aware of newly acquired coping strategies, avoid isolation, maintain a social network, remain on medication program, avoid substance abuse, or remain engaged in occupational endeavors).

39. Assist the client in writing a personal suicide prevention plan that lists actions that will be taken in the future to avoid suicide; list specific strategies for coping with stresses, what social activities will be engaged in and with whom, when and what medications will be taken,

what substances will be avoided, what occupational activities will be maintained, and when further counseling will be held.

—. _____   —. _____
_____   _____
—. _____   —. _____
_____   _____
—. _____   —. _____
_____   _____

DIAGNOSTIC SUGGESTIONS:

Axis I: 296.3x   Major Depressive Disorder, Recurrent
296.34   Major Depressive Disorder, Recurrent, Severe, with Psychotic Features
304.80   Polysubstance Dependence
303.90   Alcohol Dependence
295.30   Schizophrenia, Paranoid Type
295.10   Schizophrenia, Disorganized Type
295.90   Schizophrenia, Undifferentiated Type
295.60   Schizophrenia, Residual Type
295.70   Schizoaffective Disorder
297.1   Delusional Disorder
300.21   Panic Disorder with Agoraphobia
309.81   Posttraumatic Stress Disorder
300.02   Generalized Anxiety Disorder
V15.81   Noncompliance with Treatment

_____   _____
_____   _____

Axis II: 301.20   Schizoid Personality Disorder
301.7   Antisocial Personality Disorder
301.83   Borderline Personality Disorder

_____   _____
_____   _____

INCARCERATED MALE

BEHAVIORAL DEFINITIONS

1. Expresses hopelessness and melancholic despair about the future.
2. Incarcerated because of a violent or sexual crime and expresses remorse and guilt over the act.
3. Has a history of inpatient hospitalization for psychiatric illness.
4. Has a history of chemical dependence.
5. Describes the incarceration as a punishment and a disgrace, a loss of control and privacy over his life, and a loss of family and friends.
6. Expresses anxiety about a transfer, appeal, or parole request.
7. Expresses fear about the violent prison atmosphere.
8. Experienced a family background of physical/emotional abuse, criminality, and violence as a mode of communication.
9. Presents symptoms of a major depressive disorder (e.g., anhedonia or dysphoria).
10. Is in the early stages of prison custody (e.g., the initial three to six months).
11. Expresses severe anxiety about family financial problems and his lack of control.

—. _____
   _____
—. _____
   _____
—. _____
   _____

LONG-TERM GOALS

1. Express acceptance of incarcerated status and a will to live.
2. Increase contact and communication with family and/or positive community supports.
3. Enhance the ability to cope with the prison environment.
4. Enhance the capacity to process threatening emotions with prison mental health staff and/or any existing inmate peer support group.
5. Increase activities of daily living and diminish isolative behaviors.
6. Nurture physical, mental, and spiritual needs.

—. _____
_____
—. _____
_____
—. _____
_____

SHORT-TERM OBJECTIVES

1. Describe the facts and feelings related to criminal history and current incarceration. (1, 2, 3)

THERAPEUTIC INTERVENTIONS

1. Explore the client's criminal history (e.g., juvenile criminal record, chronic acts of violence toward others, history of criminal sexual conduct, chronic probation/parole violations, and specific crime(s) that led to the current incarceration).

2. Examine the client's emotional reactions to criminal history and/or lifestyle and current incarceration (e.g., genuine feelings of remorse and guilt, views incarceration as a personal disgrace and deserved punishment, demonstrated projection of blame onto others, denial of charges, or general uncaring attitude). Be attentive to those reactions (e.g., feeling of guilt) linked to suicide.

3. Determine client's current prison status (e.g., length of sentence, parole eligibility, length of time in current prison with special attention paid to the client who is in his initial three to six months, currently enforced sanctions, or length of time spent in isolation).

2. Identify the nature of any existing community and/or family support. (4, 5, 6)

4. Explore the client's current family cohesion (e.g., spouse, children, parents, or siblings) and examine the nature of these relationships; identify feelings of isolation and rejection that his incarceration and criminal history caused in this family network.

5. Examine the nature of the client's current community supports (e.g., are they supportive of his current situation, rehabilitation efforts, and possible release; or are they viewed as contributors to his current criminal lifestyle and incarceration).

6. Explore the quality of the client's social support network (e.g., letters or visits) and, if his feelings are negative, explore possible venues for improvement and enhancement.

3. Identify any history of abuse or criminality background. (7)

7. Explore any history of abuse and/or criminality in the client's family (e.g., examine issues of sexual, physical, or emotional abuse experienced as a child; witness to chronic patterns of spousal and/or sibling abuse; violence used as a mode of communication; or incarceration of parent(s) or sibling(s).

4. Provide information on personal experiences with high-risk *behavioral* markers for suicide in incarcerated males. (8, 9, 10, 11)

8. Assess the client for the high-risk incarcerated male suicide marker of substance abuse/ dependence (e.g., current use within the prison subculture, age of onset, patterns of use, poly-substance dependence; use during criminal activity and other acts of violence toward self or others; or family patterns of substance dependence).

9. Assess the client for the high-risk incarcerated male suicide marker of history of violence (e.g., childhood patterns of torturing animals and/or fire-setting; spousal or child abuse patterns; violent acts toward others during criminal behavior, with special attention paid to acts of sexual violence).

10. Assess the client for the high-risk incarcerated male suicide marker of patterns of self-mutilation; explore his emotional state and emotional response during these acts.

11. Assess the client for the high-risk incarcerated male suicide marker of faulty problem-solving skills (e.g., escape, projection, denial, and violence to psychologically cope with crisis; limited knowl-edge of adaptive problem-solving techniques; discomfort with adaptive problem-solving techniques; and cognitive rigidity).

5. Provide information on personal experiences with high-risk *emotional* markers for suicide in incarcerated males. (12, 13, 14, 15)

12. Assess the client for the high-risk incarcerated male suicide marker of depression (e.g., hopelessness, helplessness, melancholic despair, reduced

appetite, sleep disturbances, and history of psychiatric treatment, either in- or outpatient).

13. Assess the client for the high-risk incarcerated male suicide marker of psychosis (e.g., bizarre behavior, hallucinations, disorganized thoughts, thought intrusion, paranoid feelings, or inability to concentrate; note history of psychiatric treatment either in- or outpatient).

14. Assess the client for the high-risk incarcerated male suicide marker of extreme feelings of guilt or remorse about criminal acts, especially acts of violence toward others.

15. Assess the client for the high-risk incarcerated male suicide marker of extreme feelings of fear because of the atmosphere of violence in the prison and/or anxiety about a pending transfer, appeal, or parole request; explore the linkage to his feelings of hopelessness and helplessness.

6. Provide information on personal experiences with high-risk *social* markers for suicide in incarcerated males. (16, 17)

16. Assess the client for the high-risk incarcerated male suicide marker of feelings of loss (e.g., loss of membership in society or loss of control over life, privacy, family and friends, and dignity).

17. Assess the client for the high-risk incarcerated male suicide marker of distress because of personal and/or family financial problems resulting from incarceration.

7. Identify the nature of current suicidal ideation, planning, and/or intent. (18, 19, 20, 21)

18. Explore the client's intended goal for the suicide act (e.g., provides a sense of control by solving a seemingly unsolvable problem when other coping strategies are failing).

19. Explore the amount of energy the client spends in planning his suicide event (e.g., examine preoccupation with suicide, has a method been creatively devised, or has a date been set).

20. Examine whether the client's feelings of anxiety and/or depression have decreased and a sense of calm has entered since his planning started or concluded.

21. Explore any impediments to the implementation of the client's plan and have ways been considered to minimize these impediments (e.g., the lack of privacy is dealt with by planning the event after dark or the lack of lethal means has been dealt with by creatively using materials on hand).

8. Cooperate with psychological testing designed to evaluate suicide risk in the incarcerated male. (22)

22. Administer testing to reveal and evaluate the client's suicidal ideation and intent levels (e.g., Beck Hopelessness Scale or Suicide Probability Scale); provide feedback on test results and treatment implications.

9. Provide complete information on current mood, affect, and thought process in a psychiatric evaluation, taking psychotropic medication as prescribed. (23, 24)

23. Refer the client for a psychiatric evaluation to determine the need for psychotropic medication and to validate any at-risk diagnoses (e.g., psychosis, depressive disorder, generalized anxiety, or antisocial personality disorder).

10. Accept feedback on the assessments and the treatment plan developed from the evaluation process. (25)

11. Comply with placement in a more protective and, possibly, a more restrictive environment. (26, 27)

12. Affirm a safety plan that allows for a return to the prison's general population. (28)

24. Monitor the client's compliance with the psychotropic medication prescription; chart subjective and objective behavioral changes and monitor side effects.

25. Summarize and give feedback to the client on high-risk markers found during the assessment and evaluation process and outline the treatment plan.

26. If at any time during the treatment process the client displays an increase in the number or intensity of the examined high-risk markers, place him on Suicide Precaution Watch, as designated by the prison's policy and procedures; this placement should be as therapeutic as possible to allow a decrease in the suicide impulse.

27. Ensure that the prison policy and procedure does not allow the Suicide Precaution Watch implementation by placing the client in isolation, which increases his risk for suicide; access to meaningful support networks is essential at this time.

28. Coordinate planning with psychotherapy that will aggressively treat psychiatric problems and promote adaptive adjustment to the realities of the prison environment (e.g., within the context of the client's level of confinement, allow for an activities of daily living plan that permits effective time utilization).

13. Agree to a written plan for dealing with situations when suicidal urges become strong. (29, 30)

29. Develop a detailed, structured, written crisis intervention plan to be implemented during trigger events and feelings (e.g., an attacking letter from family that results in feelings of self-hate or a denial of an appeal that produces melancholic despair) that includes contacting the therapist or the prison health-care staff.

30. Monitor the client's suicide risk at appropriate intervals during the therapy process through interview and by administering standardized suicide risk assessment instruments (e.g., Beck Hopelessness Scale or Suicide Ideation Scale).

14. Identify the stressors and symptoms that trigger the wish to die by suicide. (31, 32, 33)

31. Assist the client in making a list of his most prominent stressors (e.g., violent prison atmosphere, loss of family cohesion, or loss of control over life) and emotional reactions or symptoms (e.g., unmanageable fear, shame, isolation, rejection, or despair) produced by those stressors.

32. Assist the client in producing a complete symptom inventory that includes identifying the most disruptive symptoms (e.g., those symptoms that appear to have no solution and create the most intense need to die by suicide) and how these symptoms are currently managed (e.g., isolation from the general population or substance abuse).

33. Establish a therapeutic alliance with the client that ensures the therapist's help in targeting the most serious symptoms for

immediate attention (e.g., solution-oriented therapy to enhance problem-solving skills and, if needed, medications).

15. Identify solutions and coping strategies that do not include suicide or the wish to die. (34, 35, 36)

34. Formulate an appropriate view of suicide for the client: It stems from a desire to solve and/or escape a seemingly unsolvable problem and/or painful psychological state that is temporary; it is fueled by elements of hopelessness and helplessness; and the antidote is to acquire, with the therapist's help, safe and simple problem-solving skills for identified stressors and symptoms.

35. Assign the client a treatment journal to track daily stressors, the resulting symptoms, maladaptive coping patterns, and experiences with newly acquired coping strategies; assign homework targeting symptom management.

36. Teach the client various forms of problem-solving strategies (e.g., direct action strategies aimed at modifying the stressful situation; situation redefinition and distraction strategies; catharsis skills; relaxation skills; and seeking social support) and examine with him the particular strategy that fits his personal strengths, reduces the strength of the current stressor, and are most likely to be successful.

16. Increase the frequency of verbalizing statements indicating improved coping with the realities of the prison

37. Assist the client in reviewing the treatment journal during each session; identify and reinforce strengths and an improved sense

experience that are specifically challenging to the client. (37, 38)

of self-image because of enhanced problem-solving strategies and symptom management.

38. Assist the client in his efforts to manage the prison routine and reinforce constructive means for using his time; formulate daily schedules that will identify activities that will meet his emotional, intellectual, physical, and spiritual needs.

17. Verbalize increased acceptance of self as a vulnerable person, capable of mistakes and failures, while keeping intact a core image of self-regard. (39)

39. Teach the client that he must respect his core self-image of intrinsic worth (e.g., always welcome him with a genuine caring attitude), that the catharsis of emotions are honored and accepted without judgment, that to be vulnerable is to be human, and that the value of a life is not determined by where we are but who we are.

18. Develop a suicide prevention plan that incorporates the treatment journal and all completed homework assignments. (40)

40. Assist the client in writing a personal suicide prevention plan that lists actions that will be taken in the future to manage suicidal urges (e.g., rely on the treatment journal for reminders of strategies for coping with trigger events, feelings, and symptoms; maintain a productive activities of daily living routine; trust the value of self; and continue to respond to emotional, intellectual, physical, and spiritual needs).

—. _____   —. _____
   _____   _____
—. _____   —. _____
   _____   _____
—. _____   —. _____
   _____   _____

DIAGNOSTIC SUGGESTIONS:

Axis I:

296.xx	Major Depressive Disorder
296.90	Mood Disorder NOS
308.3	Acute Stress Disorder
300.02	Generalized Anxiety Disorder
305.00	Alcohol Abuse
303.90	Alcohol Dependence
305.20	Cannabis Abuse
295.xx	Schizophrenia
298.9	Psychotic Disorder NOS
312.30	Impulse Control Disorder NOS
312.34	Intermittent Explosive Disorder
309.81	Posttraumatic Stress Disorder

_____   _____
_____   _____

Axis II:

301.7	Antisocial Personality Disorder
301.83	Borderline Personality Disorder

_____   _____
_____   _____

LAW ENFORCEMENT OFFICER

BEHAVIORAL DEFINITIONS

1. Demonstrates behaviors positively correlated to extreme psychological distress (e.g., depressive disorders, anxiety disorders, obsessive-compulsive disorder, or posttraumatic stress disorder).
2. Expresses a need to escape from an intolerable life situation and will suggest to others that suicide is a method under consideration.
3. Displays distress about job-related conflicts (e.g., no job promotion, assignment conflicts, diminished respect from the public, life-threatening elements of the job, constant exposure to conflict, or conflict with superiors).
4. Uses alcohol or other mood-altering drugs until high, intoxicated, or passed out.
5. Experiences current relationship problems because of long, irregular working hours, ignores family needs and activities, and experiences sexual dysfunction that possibly is due to depression.
6. Demonstrates a life-long problem with effective communication of emotions, resulting from a family pattern of dysfunctional communication.
7. Has recently experienced a significant psychological trauma (e.g., loss of a relationship, loss of a friend or loved one to death, loss of health, or loss of financial security).
8. Demonstrates a significant increase in social isolation and withdrawal.
9. Has a history of psychiatric treatment, or it has been recommended by superiors.
10. Has been caught in an illegal activity and is at risk of going to prison.
11. Talks about suicide as a method of gaining revenge against an insensitive police bureaucracy.
12. Demonstrates a life-long pattern of impulsive, high-risk behaviors.

—. _____
_____
—. _____
_____
—. _____
_____

LONG-TERM GOALS

1. Develop adaptive coping skills for effective management of work-related stresses.
2. Experience a positive engagement with life and hope for the future.
3. Develop a balanced lifestyle that includes meeting professional, personal, relational, and social needs.
4. Enhance the capacity for emotional expression in the context of intimate relationships.
5. Enhance and use supportive social networks.

—. _____
_____
—. _____
_____
—. _____
_____

SHORT-TERM OBJECTIVES

THERAPEUTIC INTERVENTIONS

1. Identify specifics on the choice of a law enforcement career. (1, 2)

1. Explore the client's motivations for choosing the law enforcement profession (e.g., family tradition, need for social approval, altruism, need for an action-oriented profession, or attracted to the authority aspects of the profession) and note any motivations that could be problematic for a healthy adjustment.

2. Provide information on personal experiences with high-risk *behavioral* markers for suicide in law enforcement officers. (3, 4, 5, 6)

2. Explore the client's current feelings toward his/her professional experience (e.g., very satisfied, a balanced view, dissatisfied, or very unhappy) and isolate current emotional reactions that could be problematic for a healthy adjustment (e.g., stress because of continuous exposure to violence and trauma, frustrations because of an uncaring bureaucracy).

3. Assess the client for the high-risk law enforcement officer suicide marker of alcohol abuse/dependency (e.g., use of alcohol to cope with job-related stress, use of alcohol in job-related socializing, family patterns of use/abuse, use to cope with psychological distress).

4. Assess the client for the high-risk law enforcement officer suicide marker of illegal activity with the resulting risk of going to prison (e.g., the type of activity and the motivation for this activity).

5. Assess the client for the high-risk law enforcement officer suicide marker of verbalizing masked, subtle suicide intent (e.g., "Sometimes I wish I would wake up dead," "Maybe today I'll get lucky and get shot," "Nobody around here would miss me if I died," or "Sometimes I'd like to make a permanent exit from this place").

6. Assess the client for the high-risk law enforcement officer

suicide marker of verbalizing extreme job-related stress (e.g., lack of job promotion, conflicts with superiors, assignment conflicts, or ridicule by peers).

3. Provide information on personal experiences with high-risk *emotional* markers for suicide in law-enforcement officers. (7, 8, 9, 10)

7. Assess the client for the high-risk law enforcement officer suicide marker of extreme patterns of psychiatric/psychological distress (e.g., behaviors correlated to depressive disorders, anxiety/mood disorders, obsessive-compulsive personality disorder, posttraumatic stress disorder, or issues of hopelessness and despair for the future).

8. Assess the client for the high-risk law enforcement officer suicide marker of history of, or current involvement with, psychiatric treatment (e.g., if there is current treatment, releases should be obtained; if there is past involvement, a detailed history should be obtained).

9. Assess the client for the high-risk law enforcement officer suicide marker of emotional constriction (e.g., inability to access emotions, reduced capacity for empathy, and diversion behaviors used to avoid emotional expression).

10. Assess the client for the high-risk law enforcement officer suicide marker of life-long patterns of risk-taking behaviors (e.g., correlation to issues of posttraumatic stress disorder, patterns of extreme and unnecessary risk-taking while on

4. Provide information on personal experiences with high-risk *social* markers for suicide in law enforcement officers. (11, 12, 13)

duty, history of spousal abuse, functioning as a motivator for the profession of law enforcement officer).

11. Assess the client for the high-risk law enforcement officer suicide marker of relationship turmoil (e.g., alienation from wife and/or children, history of disrupted relationship patterns, attending to the needs of his/her profession over the needs of family and/or relationships, issues of sexual dysfunction as a factor in relationship turmoil).

12. Assess the client for the high-risk law enforcement officer suicide marker of loss (e.g., relationships, partners, self-esteem, health, financial security, or job enthusiasm).

13. Assess the client for the high-risk law enforcement officer suicide marker of a pattern of social isolation (e.g., avoiding activities that had previously given social identification, isolative patterns of substance abuse, or isolative behaviors motivated by paranoia and/or generalized anger).

5. Identify the nature of current suicidal ideation, planning, and/or intent. (14, 15, 16, 17)

14. Explore the client's intended goal for the suicide act (e.g., revenge against uncaring bureaucracy, cessation of intolerable psychological pain, or motivated by self-hate or self-devaluation).

15. Explore the amount of energy the client has spent in planning his/her suicide event (e.g., has a date and/or a place been

assigned, paying special attention to allusions to using his/her police revolver in the act).

16. Examine whether the client's feelings of anxiety and/or depression have decreased and a sense of calm has entered since the planning started or concluded.

17. Explore whether the client experiences any ambivalence to the implementation of his/her suicide plan (e.g., fear of emotional impact on survivors, hope that problems may possibly have other solutions, or social stigma concerns).

6. Cooperate with psychological testing designed to evaluate conditions related to suicide risk in law enforcement officers. (18)

18. Administer testing that will reveal and evaluate the client's suicidal ideation and intent levels (e.g., MMPI-2, Suicide Probability Scale, Suicide Ideation Scale, or Reasons for Living Inventory); provide feedback to him/her on the results and treatment implications.

7. Medical personnel provide relevant current information on the client's general health issues. (19)

19. After obtaining appropriate confidentiality and privacy releases, contact the client's primary care physician for a report on his/her general health issues (e.g., health concerns that may prevent the continuation of his/her law enforcement career, health-related sexual functioning problems, patterns of accidental injuries, or mental health concerns).

8. Provide complete information on current mood, affect, and

20. Refer the client for a psychiatric evaluation to determine the need

thought process in a psychiatric evaluation, taking
psychotropic medication as
prescribed. (20, 21)

for psychotropic medication
and to validate any at-risk
diagnoses (e.g., depressive
disorders or posttraumatic stress
disorder).

21. After affirming for the client
that the prescribed medication
will not hinder, in any way,
his/her job performance,
monitor his/her compliance with
the psychotropic medication;
chart the subjective and
objective behavioral changes
and monitor side effects paying
special attention to any effects
that limit his/her job performance and, possibly, compromise
safety.

9. Accept feedback on the assessments and the treatment plan
developed from the evaluation
process. (22)

22. Summarize and give feedback to
the client and, if available and
appropriate, significant others,
on high-risk markers found
during the assessment and
evaluation process; explain
details of the treatment plan and,
if appropriate, attempt to engage
significant others.

10. Comply with placement in a
more protective and, possibly,
a more restrictive environment.
(23)

23. If at any time during the
treatment process the client
displays an increase in the
number or intensity of the
examined high-risk factors
(e.g., an exacerbation of the
depressive disorder symptoms)
and explicit warning signs
correlated to completed suicide
(e.g., increased verbalization
of the intent to die), place
him/her in a therapeutic setting
that will protect from suicide
impulse, decrease perturbation,
and remove him/her from
environmental stress.

11. Affirm a safety plan that allows for a return to the community and engagement in his/her professional duties. (24, 25)

12. Identify the stresses and symptoms that trigger the wish to die by suicide. (26, 27, 28)

24. Coordinate planning with psychotherapy that will aggressively treat psychiatric problems, provide services that promote healthy psychosocial adjustment on return to duty, and efficiently decrease social stressors of the law enforcement officer experience; obtain the client's input and affirmation of this plan for discharge from inpatient care.

25. Develop a written crisis intervention plan to be implemented during trigger events and feelings (e.g., job-related concerns that cause feelings of self-devaluation and helplessness) that includes talking to the therapist and about emotional reactions to these events; stress the adaptive coping strategy that the crisis intervention plan includes versus maladaptive coping strategies (e.g., alcohol abuse).

26. Assist the client in making a list of his/her most prominent stressors (e.g., job-related stress or peer conflicts, constant exposure to trauma) and emotional reactions or symptoms (e.g., rage, grieving, self-devaluation, humiliation, or helplessness) produced by those stressors; remain alert to his/her ability or inability to access emotional reactions to the identified stressors.

27. Assist the client in producing a complete symptom inventory that includes identifying the most disruptive symptoms (e.g.,

rage, helplessness, guilt, or grieving), how these symptoms are currently dysfunctionally managed (e.g., isolative substance abuse, unnecessary violent acts while on duty, or socially isolating behaviors), and other reactions created by these symptoms (e.g., relationship turmoil, job jeopardy, or loss of social support).

28. Establish a therapeutic alliance with the client that ensures the therapist's help and provides a sense of hope for the future by targeting the most serious symptoms for immediate attention (e.g., medication prescription or solution-oriented therapy).

13. Identify coping strategies to those stresses and symptoms that do not include suicide or the wish to die.
(29, 30, 31, 32, 33)

29. Formulate an appropriate view of suicide for the client: It stems from a desire to solve a seemingly unsolvable problem; it is fueled by elements of hopelessness and helplessness; and the antidote is to acquire, with the therapist's help, adaptive problem-solving skills for the identified stressors and symptoms.

30. Assign the client a treatment journal to track daily stressors, the resulting symptoms, maladaptive coping patterns, and experiences with newly acquired coping strategies; assign homework targeting symptom management.

31. Teach the client about his/her maladaptive, externalizing coping behaviors (e.g., alcohol abuse) and internalizing coping

behaviors (e.g., denial, avoidance, or self-devaluation) and replace these maladaptive coping strategies with a problem-solving focus.

32. Teach the client problem-solving skills (e.g., accurately define the problem by distinguishing stressors and symptoms, explore alternative solutions, identify the positives and negatives of each solution, select and implement a plan of action, evaluate in the treatment journal the outcome, and adjust the solution as necessary).

33. Detail and structure the proposed solutions to assist the client during extreme emotional perturbation (e.g., safe, sound, and simple problem-solving skills); provide him/her with a detailed plan (e.g., diversion coping strategies, action oriented strategies, or catharsis strategies) with specific instructions on responding to and managing the perturbation associated with his/her most painful symptoms.

14. Increase verbalized statements of hope that symptoms can be managed continuously in ways other than suicide. (34)

34. Assist the client in enhancing his/her self-image by encouraging him/her to provide self-reports from the treatment journal and homework assignments on recent incidents of his/her improved coping, symptom management, and problem-solving skills (e.g., talking to spouse or trusted friend about a difficult emotion versus coping with alcohol abuse).

15. Identify own personality traits and vulnerabilities that hinder adaptive coping strategies and contribute to the suicide intent. (35, 36)

35. Explore the client's personal vulnerabilities that hinder adaptive problem-solving and contribute to the suicidal crisis (e.g., inability to access emotions, need to be in control causing an inability to accept failure, need for excitement and risk-taking behavior).

36. Assist the client in acknowledging the existence of his/her suicide vulnerability traits, their source (e.g., coming from an emotionally constricted family system or a performance-oriented family or symptoms of posttraumatic stress disorder), and their influence on maladaptive coping (e.g., isolating during times of stress, inability to tolerate failures, or impulsive acting out); have him/her track these traits and their influence in the treatment journal.

16. Develop management strategies to diminish the influence of these identified personality traits on adaptive coping skills. (37)

37. Teach the client that there is value in verbalizing emotions (e.g., sharing of feelings reduces their intensity or breaks down the sense of isolation), that there are safe ways to meet excitement needs (e.g., socially acceptable, action oriented activities), and that it is safe to be vulnerable (e.g., failure is accepted in the therapy relationship).

17. Develop a supportive social network. (38)

38. Encourage the client to see himself/herself in a social context by emphasizing the benefits of his/her participation in friendships and group activities (e.g., decreased sense of isolation); incorporate this

task into the homework assignments and have him/her track these efforts in the treatment journal.

18. Develop a suicide prevention plan that incorporates the treatment journal and all completed homework assignments. (39)

39. Assist the client in writing a personal suicide prevention plan that lists actions he/she will take in the future to avoid the impulse to suicide (e.g., rely on the treatment journal for reminders of adaptive coping skills, avoid isolation, maintain social network, and remain on any prescribed medications).

_\. _____   _\. _____
_____   _____
_\. _____   _\. _____
_____   _____
_\. _____   _\. _____
_____   _____

DIAGNOSTIC SUGGESTIONS:

Axis I:

296.xx	Major Depressive Disorder
300.4	Dysthymic Disorder
311	Depressive Disorder NOS
308.3	Acute Stress Disorder
300.02	Generalized Anxiety Disorder
300.00	Anxiety Disorder NOS
305.00	Alcohol Abuse
309.28	Adjustment Disorder with Mixed Anxiety and Depressed Mood
309.81	Posttraumatic Stress Disorder
V62.82	Bereavement
312.34	Intermittent Explosive Disorder
V62.2	Occupational Problem
_____	_____
_____	_____

NATIVE AMERICAN MALE

BEHAVIORAL DEFINITIONS

1. Expresses a wish to die.
2. Demonstrates behaviors positively associated with the diagnosis of depressive disorder (e.g., lack of energy, anhedonia, dysphoria, social withdrawal, hopelessness, helplessness, and despair about the future).
3. Demonstrates behaviors positively associated with the diagnosis of substance abuse/dependence, especially binge drinking and inhalant abuse.
4. Demonstrates behaviors positively associated with the diagnosis of conduct or antisocial disorder (e.g., especially the incidence of two or more arrests in the previous 12 months).
5. Demonstrates extreme family-of-origin turmoil and dysfunction (e.g., child abandonment, child emotional and physical abuse, divorce, imprisonment of caregivers, multiple caregivers, and alcoholism).
6. Experienced removal from home because of extreme family dysfunction or his own unruly behavior and, consequently, was placed in an Indian boarding school.
7. Experienced significant loss of cultural identity because of living off the reservation.
8. Experienced significant loss of cultural identity because of tribal instability (e.g., diminished influence of spiritual, clan, tribe, or extended family traditions or diminished socioeconomic security).
9. Was adopted by an Anglo American family and now finds discrimination in employment, education, and social life, with resultant negative effects on self-esteem.
10. Failed assimilation into larger American culture with resultant feelings of despair and hopelessness, along with feelings of isolation from tribal affiliation.
11. Moved away from the tribe and its customs because of lack of socioeconomic opportunities and persistent poverty.

12. Affiliated with a tribe where norms and traditions operate against achievement and success and assimilation into the larger American culture.

—. _____
   _____
   _____

—. _____
   _____
   _____

—. _____
   _____

LONG-TERM GOALS

1. Engage life with an expression of hope for the future.
2. Resolve feelings of worthlessness, self-hate, and isolation that contribute to depressive reactions and suicide impulses.
3. Enhance development of coping strategies, self-efficacy, and problem-solving skills.
4. Enhance development of spiritual, cultural, and moral foundations based on historic tribal traditions.
5. Enhance development of self-identity based on tribal traditions.
6. Eliminate dangerous, at-risk behavior patterns that increase suicidal thoughts, urges, or actions.

—. _____
   _____
   _____

—. _____
   _____
   _____

—. _____
   _____

SHORT-TERM OBJECTIVES	THERAPEUTIC INTERVENTIONS
1. Describe the specifics of current affiliation with tribal culture, religion, and traditions. (1, 2)	1. Examine the stability of spiritual traditions in the client's tribe (e.g., tribe retains religious rituals, healing ceremonies, puberty rites, and priesthood; if

2. Identify specifics of current and/or previous breaks from tribal or reservation culture. (3, 4)

3. Identify specifics of current stressors associated with tribal norms or traditions. (5, 6)

the client is an adolescent, does he have an elder mentor).

2. Examine the stability of cultural traditions in the client's tribe (e.g., trust and respect for the tribal council and elders; traditional ways of maintaining economic stability are intact; extended families are strong; young people have economic opportunities and are encouraged to remain on the reservation).

3. Assess whether the client's efforts to adjust to American, nontribal, off-reservation culture had positive outcomes (e.g., employment was obtained, social life was enhanced, and educational opportunities were positive) or negative outcomes (e.g., feelings of isolation were predominant, discrimination was experienced, and alcohol abuse was a preferred way to cope).

4. Explore any history of being adopted into an Anglo American family and/or placement into an Indian boarding school with the client and examine any negative psychological effects from those experiences (e.g., isolation, abandonment, shame, or devaluation).

5. Examine any tribal traditions that may be contributing to current stress (e.g., tradition that states people should not strive to be better than others; tribal pressure to adapt to Anglo American economic and social standards) with the client.

6. Examine issues of instability within the traditions of the tribal framework (e.g., tribal conflicts about governmental structure, religion, clans, extended families; high rates of divorce and/or spousal abuse; high rates of alcoholism and incidence of fetal alcohol syndrome; and deterioration of the extended family) with the client.

4. Cooperate with psychological testing designed to evaluate suicide ideation/intent in Native American males. (7)

7. Administer testing most commonly used to reveal and evaluate suicide ideation and/or intent levels (e.g., Beck Hopelessness Scale, Suicide Probability Scale, Reasons for Living Inventory, or Suicide Risk Measure).

5. Provide complete information on current mood, affect, and thought process in a psychiatric evaluation and take psychotropic medications as prescribed. (8, 9)

8. Refer the client for a psychiatric evaluation to determine his need for psychotropic medication and to validate any at-risk diagnoses (e.g., major depressive disorder, anxiety disorders, or antisocial personality disorder).

9. Monitor the client's compliance with the psychotropic medication prescription; chart the effectiveness of the medication and monitor side effects.

6. Medical personnel provide relevant current information pertaining to general health issues. (10)

10. After obtaining the appropriate confidentiality releases and privacy documentation, contact the client's medical care providers for a report on general health issues (e.g., bodily injuries, diseases, nutrition problems, developmental delays, substance abuse related health issues, or signs of mental health concerns).

7. The client and, if possible and appropriate, caregivers provide information on the client's personal experience with high-risk *behavioral* markers for Native American male suicide. (11, 12, 13)

11. Assess the client for the high-risk Native American male suicide marker of substance abuse by administering a thorough evaluation (e.g., inhalant and mood altering drug use, binge drinking patterns, age of onset, family member use, legal involvement, history of substance abuse in a suicide activity, readiness for change evaluation, or tribal restrictions on substance use).

12. Assess the client for the high-risk Native American male suicide marker of legal conflicts (e.g., arrest record and convictions, record of two or more arrests in the last 12 months, alcohol-related crimes, or family legal involvement); determine whether a diagnosis of antisocial personality/conduct disorder is appropriate.

13. Assess the client for the high-risk Native American male suicide marker of risk-taking behaviors (e.g., unprotected sex with multiple partners, reckless driving or use and possession of firearms, poor nutrition habits, or smoking) that are ascribed to a passive attitude about living (e.g., "I don't really care if I live or die").

8. The client and, if possible and appropriate, caregivers provide information on the client's personal experience with high-risk *emotional* markers for Native American male suicide. (14, 15)

14. Assess the client for the high-risk Native American male suicide marker of depression (e.g., linkage to hopelessness and despair, increased self-directed rage, increase in alcohol abuse to cope, anhedonia, or dysphoria).

15. Assess the client for the high-risk Native American male suicide marker of adolescent or young adult onset of an acute or chronic disease (e.g., diabetes, cardiac disease, or leukemia); note an expressed hopelessness about the future, a threatened sense of security in body imagery, a diminished drive for autonomy and future goals, or a fear of being dependent.

9. The client and, if possible and appropriate, caregivers provide information on the client's personal experience with high-risk *social* markers for Native American male suicide. (16, 17, 18)

16. Assess the client for the high-risk Native American male suicide marker of extreme family-of-origin turmoil and dysfunction (e.g., an arrest of the primary caregiver, a history of multiple caregivers, divorce, abandonment, child or spouse abuse, family alcohol abuse patterns or suicide, or multiple school changes because of family chaos).

17. Assess the client for the high-risk Native American male suicide marker of tribal instability or failed acculturation efforts (e.g., chronic unemployment, deterioration of the extended family, placement in an Indian boarding school as a youth, ethnic confusion, lack of role models, or social isolation).

18. Assess the client for the presence of high-risk Native American male suicide marker of adoption into an Anglo American family and culture (e.g., problems with isolation and feelings of abandonment; ethnic confusion, self-devaluation, or shame; effects of

experiences with discrimination; adoptive family encouraged or discouraged activity in Native American religion, culture, and social events).

10. Identify specifics of the current suicide plan and/or intent. (19, 20, 21, 22)

19. Explore the goal for the intended suicide act (e.g., cessation of severe emotional pain; antidote for hopelessness; or elimination of self because of extreme self-hate, an extreme form of coping, or a solution to a seemingly unsolvable problem) with the client.

20. Explore the amount of time and energy spent in planning the suicide event (e.g., has a lethal means or weapon been chosen and/or obtained, has a date or place been assigned, has the suicide intent been communicated to anyone and, if so, what was the reaction, and have symbolic good-byes been communicated) with the client.

21. Explore whether the client has experienced any sense of calm, peace, tranquility, or renewed energy level since the planning for the suicide started or was completed.

22. Explore any barriers to the plan to die (e.g., tribal traditions, tribal or personal religious beliefs, or fear of emotional impact on survivors, of being discovered, or of accidentally surviving) with the client; note any ambivalence he displays about completed suicide.

11. The client and, if available and appropriate, the caregivers

23. Summarize and give feedback to the client and, if available and

accept feedback gathered from all sources and the treatment plan developed from the evaluation process. (23)

appropriate, his caregivers on high-risk markers found in the evaluation process and outline the treatment plan; if available and appropriate, engage supportive caregivers into the treatment strategy (e.g., providing safety during high-risk times, or encouraging the client's effort on homework assignments).

12. Comply with placement in a more protective and, possibly, restrictive environment. (24)

24. If assessments reveal the presence of high-risk Native American male suicide markers that significantly challenge the client's coping capacity (e.g., increase in isolative behavior, increase in symptoms of depression), place him in a supervised, structured therapeutic setting that will protect him from suicide impulse, decrease perturbation, remove him from environmental stress, decrease his isolation, and monitor treatment effectiveness.

13. Affirm a plan that allows for the safe return to the community. (25)

25. Review the inpatient treatment team's discharge plan with the client and the caregivers including placement, support system, individual and family psychotherapy, activities of daily living, and knowledge of helping services.

14. Agree to a crisis response plan for dealing with situations when suicide risk is strong. (26)

26. Develop a crisis intervention plan to be implemented during trigger events and feelings (e.g., family violence, rejections, or failures) that includes contacting the therapist, trusted friend, tribal elder, or local suicide prevention center or mental health center help line; ask the

client to agree, as a verbal contact of therapy, to call someone on the phone list to discuss emotional reactions that appear to be overwhelming.

15. Identify current stressors and resultant symptoms that trigger the wish to die by suicide. (27, 28, 29)

27. Assist the client in making a list of his most prominent stressors (e.g., persistent poverty on the reservation; lack of educational, vocational, or employment opportunities; living in an alcoholic home; failure in acculturation efforts; or autonomy-limiting traditions of the tribe); explore his emotional reactions or symptoms (e.g., hopelessness, despair, or depression) produced by those stressors.

28. Assist the client in developing a complete symptom inventory that includes identifying the most disruptive symptoms (e.g., hopelessness, despair, or self-hate), how these symptoms are dysfunctionally managed (e.g., substance abuse, violent acting out, or suicidal ideation), and whether these symptoms create other reactions (e.g., depression, anxiety, or legal involvement) that eventually overwhelm him.

29. Establish a therapeutic alliance with the client that ensures the therapist's help in targeting the most serious symptoms for immediate attention (e.g., medications or solution-oriented therapy).

16. Increase verbalized statements of hope that managing depressive symptoms can be

30. Formulate an appropriate view of the function of suicide with the client: It stems from a need

done continuously in ways other than suicide. (30, 31, 32)

to solve a seemingly unsolvable problem (e.g., depression), it is fueled by a sense of helplessness and hopelessness, and the antidote is to develop coping strategies for these seemingly unsolvable stressors and symptoms with the therapist's help.

31. Assign the client a treatment journal to track daily stressors, the resulting symptoms, mal-adaptive coping behaviors, and experiences with newly acquired coping strategies (e.g., substance abuse is replaced by sharing feelings with a trusted friend or tribal elder); assign homework targeting symptom management.

32. Use role-play, modeling, and behavior rehearsal to teach the client to use problem-solving skills to replace maladaptive coping strategies (e.g., define the problem, seek alternative solutions, list the positives and negatives of each solution, select and implement a plan of action, evaluate the outcome, and adjust the solution as necessary).

17. Identify and diminish the influence of traits and vulnerabilities that contribute to suicide ideation. (33, 34, 35)

33. Explore the client's personal vulnerabilities that hinder healthy coping strategies and contribute to the suicidal crisis (e.g., perfectionism, need to please others, self-devaluation, or inability to access emotions).

34. Assist the client in acknowledging his suicide-fostering traits and vulnerabilities, their source, how they were acquired (e.g., self-devaluation from consistent parental criticism), and their

influence in maladaptive coping (e.g., self-injurious behavior, feelings of aloneness, or inability to tolerate failure); ask him to track these traits and their influence in the treatment journal.

35. Explore methods and exercises with the client that will diminish the influence of his suicide-fostering personality traits on coping capacity (e.g., self-injurious behaviors replaced by a sense of self-regard, inability to tolerate failure replaced by a sense of self-acceptance, and isolative behaviors and feelings of aloneness replaced by a capacity for intimacy and the ability to share thoughts and feelings in a social context).

18. Increase cultural and spiritual development and ethnic identity within existing tribal traditions. (36)

36. Encourage the client to enhance engagement in tribal functions, traditions, and religious cere-monies; encourage him to seek mental health services, alcohol/ drug treatment services, and other health promotion services that are Native American specific and show the involve-ment of the Native American community.

19. Increase personal resiliency, flexibility, and the ability to cope with change during challenges from acculturation. (37)

37. Encourage the client to retain tribal traditions and affiliations (e.g., annual attendance at religious ceremonies of importance or communication with trusted tribal elder) during attempts at acculturation.

20. Increase the frequency of statements that communicate pride in accomplishments and

38. Assist the client in enhancing his self-image by encouraging him to provide self-reports from the

improved confidence in self. (38, 39)

treatment journal and the homework assignments on recent incidents of his improved coping, symptom management, and problem-solving skills (e.g., going to school or job regularly, deciding against a dangerous activity, or talking to a friend about a difficult emotion).

39. Challenge the client to trust the value of himself during times of temporary failure; provide him with examples of others who rose from failure to enjoy success (e.g., provide titles and/or readings on examples from the Native American cultural and religious history).

21. Develop a suicide prevention plan that incorporates the treatment journal's homework assignments. (40, 41)

40. Educate the client on preventing relapse into suicidal behavior (e.g., be aware of strategies for coping with trigger stressors and symptoms, rely on trusted others, avoid isolation, and maintain culturally relevant social network).

41. Assist the client in writing a personal suicide prevention plan that lists actions he will take in the future to manage the impulse to suicide.

__. _____

_____

__. _____

_____

__. _____

_____

__. _____

_____

__. _____

_____

__. _____

_____

DIAGNOSTIC SUGGESTIONS:

Axis I:

296.xx	Major Depressive Disorder
300.4	Dysthymic Disorder
309.0	Adjustment Disorder with Depressed Mood
303.90	Alcohol Dependence
305.00	Alcohol Abuse
291.89	Alcohol-Induced Mood Disorder
304.60	Inhalant Dependence
305.90	Inhalant Abuse
300.02	Generalized Anxiety Disorder
V62.4	Acculturation Problem
312.8	Conduct Disorder
V61.20	Parent-Child Relational Problem
V62.89	Religious or Spiritual Problem
V62.2	Occupational Problem
309.81	Posttraumatic Stress Disorder

_____   _____

_____   _____

Axis II:

301.7	Antisocial Personality Disorder

_____   _____

_____   _____

PATHOLOGICAL GAMBLER

BEHAVIORAL DEFINITIONS

1. Expresses a wish to die when confronted with a gambling related crisis (e.g., loss of financial security or loss of a significant relationship).
2. Views suicide as the solution when feeling hopeless about the ability to stop gambling.
3. Uses maladaptive gambling behavior as a way of escaping problems or of relieving dysphoric mood (e.g., feelings of helplessness, guilt, anxiety, or depression).
4. Restless and/or irritable when attempting to limit or stop gambling.
5. Has lost a significant relationship, employment, educational opportunity, and/or financial security as a result of gambling.
6. Experiences significant and addictive physiologic excitement while gambling.
7. Has a history of poor impulse control, risk-taking behavior, and faulty internal regulation of emotions.
8. Is actively engaged in substance abuse to manage the emotions related to gambling (e.g., guilt, shame, anger, or fear).
9. Demonstrates behaviors positively correlated to antisocial personality disorder.
10. Has a history of theft or other illegal activity designed to support his or her gambling habit.
11. Demonstrates behaviors positively correlated with obsessive-compulsive personality disorder.

__. _____
    _____
__. _____
    _____
__. _____
    _____

LONG-TERM GOALS

1. Resolve suicidal crisis and develop hope for the future.
2. Terminate maladaptive gambling behavior.
3. Resolve issues of financial concerns and develop responsible money-management skills.
4. Alleviate depressed mood and develop positive feelings toward self and the world.
5. Develop healthy internal regulation of emotions, sound problem-solving skills, healthy stress-management skills, and impulse control.
6. Assume responsibility for disruptions in social network and, if possible, make amends for their repair.

—. _____

_____

—. _____

_____

—. _____

_____

SHORT-TERM OBJECTIVES	THERAPEUTIC INTERVENTIONS
1. Identify current and historical specifics related to the gambling addiction. (1, 2, 3)	1. Explore the client's progressive onset of gambling behavior patterns (e.g., age of onset, conditions of introduction, chronic feeling state at the time of introduction, or physiologic changes while gambling).
	2. Explore benefits that the client believes result from his/her gambling behavior (e.g., relieves boredom, relieves chronic malaise, provides physiologic energy/excitement, provides a sense of management/control, provides a sense of being alive, provides a way of getting out of gambling related debt, or is

designed to recapture the initial euphoria of winning).

3. Examine the client's experience with long-standing behaviors that could be associated with conditions of dysthymia, obsessive-compulsive personality disorder, antisocial personality traits, mania, and major depression.

2. Identify specifics of previous suicide ideation or intent. (4)

4. Explore the client's suicide activity history for high-risk markers (e.g., activities where there was a clear intent to die, but the activity resulted in a nonfatal injury because of a rescue that was accidental and against the victim's wishes; suicide activities where there was no planning and could be termed *impulsive;* or history of chronic suicide ideation).

3. Identify attempts to stop or limit the gambling behaviors. (5)

5. Explore the client's previous efforts to control or manage gambling behaviors and his/her experiences with eventual relapse (e.g., resultant experiences of depression, apathy, irritability, alcohol abuse, anxiety after quitting; the client identifies the trigger to relapse into gambling as a method "of getting out of depression").

4. Cooperate with psychological testing designed to evaluate suicide ideation/intent. (6)

6. Administer testing most commonly used to reveal and evaluate suicide ideation and intent levels (e.g., MMPI, Beck Depression Inventory, Reasons for Living Inventory, or Suicide Probability Scale).

5. Provide complete information on current mood, affect, and thought process in a psychiatric evaluation, take psychotropic medications as prescribed. (7, 8)

6. Medical personnel provide relevant, current information on the client's general health issues. (9)

7. Provide information on personal experiences with high-risk *behavioral* markers for suicide in pathological gamblers. (10, 11, 12, 13, 14)

7. Refer the client for a psychiatric evaluation to determine his/her need for psychotropic medication and to validate any at-risk diagnoses (e.g., clarifying whether the pathological gambling is associated with the manic phase of the bipolar disorder; issues of major depression, dysthymia, obsessive-compulsive personality disorder, or antisocial personality).

8. Monitor the client's compliance with the psychotropic medication prescription; chart his/her subjective and objective behavioral changes and monitor side effects.

9. After obtaining the appropriate confidentiality and privacy releases, contact the client's medical provider for a report on his/her current medical problems.

10. Assess the client for the high-risk gambler suicide marker of substance abuse by administering a thorough evaluation (e.g., age of onset, use in conjunction with gambling behavior, use to cope with chronic feelings of uselessness and apathy, history of use in suicide activity).

11. Assess the client for the high-risk gambler suicide marker of criminal behavior and legal involvement (e.g., crimes of theft, embezzlement, passing bad checks, or any illegal activity to support gambling behavior; or feelings of shame, guilt, or being out of control).

12. Assess the client for the high-risk gambler suicide marker of loss of financial stability (e.g., bankruptcy; business failure; no hope of ever repaying debt; losing money designated for college education of children, retirement for spouse, savings for home; note significant threat to current socioeconomic status).

13. Assess the client for the high-risk gambler suicide marker of job loss (e.g., the number of jobs lost since gambling is out of control; numerous moves because of job loss; feelings of shame, guilt, or worthlessness connected to job loss).

14. Assess the client for the high-risk gambler suicide marker of chronic impulse-control problems (e.g., linkage to antisocial personality traits; in regard to the addiction to physiologic excitement, any linkage to posttraumatic stress disorder; other behaviors seen as risk-taking; early childhood onset).

8. Provide information on personal experiences with high-risk *emotional* markers for suicide in pathological gamblers. (15, 16)

15. Assess the client for the high-risk gambler suicide marker of depressive disorders (e.g., anhedonia; dysphoria; linkage with elements of despair and hopelessness; lifetime prevalence; addiction to gambling as a self-identified strategy to offset feelings of depression, apathy, and dysthymia).

16. Assess the client for the high-risk gambler suicide marker of

obsessive-compulsive traits (e.g., issues of guilt, shame, or discomfort with gambling urges and issues of arousal, pleasure, gratification, excitement, and absence of guilt or shame with gambling urges).

9. Provide information on personal experiences with high-risk *social* markers for suicide in pathological gamblers. (17, 18)

17. Assess the client for the high-risk gambler suicide marker of disruption of interpersonal relationships (e.g., divorce, losing friends because of debts owed, and feelings of isolation and abandonment).

18. Assess the client for the high-risk gambler suicide marker of severe pathological gambling patterns (e.g., meets all of the diagnostic criteria found in *DSM-IV-TR* for Pathological Gambling; if the game of choice is isolative such as slot machines, note consistency of habit and money spent).

10. Identify specifics of the current suicide ideation and/or intent. (19, 20, 21, 22)

19. Explore the client's intended goal of the suicide act (e.g., method of solving the gambling addiction, eliminate feelings of guilt or shame, eliminate the severe pain of depression, eliminate himself/herself because of extreme issues of self-hate, provide a sense of control and management while in a psychological state of uncontrolled turmoil).

20. Explore the amount of time and energy the client spent in planning the suicide event (e.g., has a lethal means or weapon been chosen and/or obtained, has a date or place been assigned, has the suicide

intent been shared with anyone, and are the plans specific to avoid possible rescue and/or interruption).

21. Examine whether the client has experienced an easing or relief from intense feelings of anxiety and/or depression since the planning for suicide started or concluded.

22. Explore the client's sense of ambivalence about the suicide intent (e.g., openness to exploring other problem-solving options) and/or any barriers to the plan to die (e.g., fear of suicide's emotional impact on survivors, or religious beliefs).

11. Accepts feedback gathered from all sources and the treatment plan developed from the evaluation process. (23)

23. Summarize and give feedback to the client on high-risk markers found in the evaluation process; outline an integrated treatment plan, incorporating issues of depression, gambling behavior, and substance abuse, engaging the supportive social network and/or family members, if appropriate and available.

12. Comply with placement in a more protective and, possibly, restrictive environment. (24)

24. If at any time during the treatment process the client displays an increase in risk factors (e.g., depression, agitation, or guilt) and demonstrates specific warning signs correlated to completed suicide (e.g., obtaining a weapon), placed him/her in a structured, therapeutic setting that will protect him/her from suicide impulse, decrease perturbation, and monitor medication effectiveness.

13. Affirm a discharge plan that allows for a safe return to the community. (25)

25. Review the inpatient treatment team's discharge plan with the client that includes support systems (e.g., Gambler's Anonymous meetings), individual psychotherapy appointments, activities of daily living, knowledge of helping services, and medication regimen.

14. Agree to a crisis response plan for dealing with situations when suicidal risk is strong. (26, 27)

26. Develop a crisis intervention plan to be implemented during trigger events (e.g., relapse into gambling or high-profile sporting events) and resultant emotional reactions (e.g., shame, guilt, depression, impulse control, or despair) that includes contacting the therapist, the Gambler's Anonymous sponsor, or a trusted friend to discuss emotional reactions and alternative coping strategies.

27. Ask the client to agree, as a verbal contract of therapy, to call someone on the phone list in cases of strong suicide intent.

15. Identify current stressors, and resultant symptoms, that trigger the wish to die by suicide. (28, 29, 30)

28. Assist the client in listing his/ her most prominent stressors (e.g., attempts at quitting gambling or dealing with family discord or financial debt); explore emotional reactions or symptoms (e.g., depression, irritability, shame, guilt, or isolation), produced by those stressors.

29. Assist the client in developing a complete symptom inventory that identifies the most disruptive symptoms, how these symptoms are currently dysfunctionally managed (e.g., relapse

into gambling, substance abuse, or suicide ideation), and whether these maladaptive responses lead to consequences (e.g., family rejection, or loss of job) that eventually overwhelm him/her.

30. Establish a therapeutic alliance with the client that ensures the therapist's help in targeting the most serious symptoms for immediate attention (e.g., solution-oriented therapies, medication, or hospitalization).

16. Increase verbalized statements of hope that symptoms can be managed continuously in ways other than suicide. (31, 32, 33)

31. Formulate an appropriate view of the function of suicide for the client: It stems from a need to solve a seemingly unsolvable problem, it is fueled by a sense of hopelessness and helplessness, and the antidote is to develop healthy coping strategies for these seemingly unsolvable stressors and symptoms.

32. Assign the client a treatment journal to track daily stressors, the resultant symptoms, maladaptive coping patterns, and experiences with newly acquired coping strategies (e.g., managing the urge to gamble by avoiding the stimulating event and diverting attention to another activity); assign homework targeting symptom management.

33. Teach the client healthy problem-solving skills (e.g., define the problem, explore alternative solutions, list the positives and negatives of each solution, select and implement a

plan of action, evaluate the outcome and adjust skills as necessary in the treatment journal).

17. Identify own biological, social, and psychological vulnerabilities and traits that hinder healthy coping strategies and contribute to the risk of suicide. (34, 35)

34. Explore the client's personal vulnerabilities and traits that contribute to the suicidal crisis (e.g., need for excitement, malaise, despair, need to be in control, or emotional constriction); help him/her acknowledge the existence of these traits and track them and their influence on coping patterns in the treatment journal.

35. Assist the client in developing strategies to manage the influence of vulnerability traits on coping strategies and diminish their influence on the suicide intent (e.g., treating dysthymia with medication, experiencing the benefit of emotional expression, or meeting excitement needs in a more responsible fashion).

18. Implement strategies that will enhance a balanced life and make amends for pain caused to others. (36, 37)

36. Assist the client in developing strategic plans for financial control, activities of daily living, involvement in Gambler's Anonymous and/or AA/NA, steady employment and work habits; emphasize the benefits of a managed life (e.g., security, decrease in anxiety, or sense of management).

37. Assist the client in repairing social network disruption and family cohesion (e.g., owning responsibility for disruptive behaviors, accepting anger and resentment from family and social network, remain alert to

19. Increase self-awareness and acceptance that includes self-identification as a person who craves excitement, is prone to depression, vulnerable to impulsivity, and attracted to gambling. (38, 39)

20. Develop a suicide prevention plan that incorporates the treatment journal's homework assignments. (40)

the urge to use denial and projection of blame, or respond to the needs and directions of the family and/or social network).

38. Assist the client in gaining insight on the function of gambling in his/her life (e.g., alleviate dysthymic/depressive symptoms, escape from stress, need to be in control, alleviate malaise, or addiction to excitement); incorporate an acceptance of himself/herself as vulnerable to gambling for the rest of his/her life.

39. Assist the client in enhancing self-image by encouraging him/her to provide self-reports from the treatment journal and homework assignments on recent incidents of improved coping, symptom management, and problem-solving skills (e.g., refraining from subtle opportunities to gamble, deciding against a risk-taking activity, or remaining on medication prescription for depression).

40. Assist the client in writing a personal suicide prevention plan that lists actions he/she will take to avoid the risk of impulse to suicide (e.g., remain aware of lessons from the treatment journal for coping with trigger stressors and symptoms, rely on supportive social network, or remain on prescribed medications).

___. _____   ___. _____
      _____   _____
___. _____   ___. _____
      _____   _____
___. _____   ___. _____
      _____   _____

DIAGNOSTIC SUGGESTIONS:

Axis I:

296.xx	Major Depressive Disorder
300.4	Dysthymic Disorder
311	Depressive Disorder NOS
312.31	Pathological Gambling
312.30	Impulse-Control Disorder NOS
303.90	Alcohol Dependence
305.00	Alcohol Abuse
300.01	Panic Disorder without Agoraphobia
300.3	Obsessive-Compulsive Disorder
300.02	Generalized Anxiety Disorder
309.81	Posttraumatic Stress Disorder

_____   _____

_____   _____

Axis II:

301.83	Borderline Personality Disorder
301.7	Antisocial Personality Disorder
301.4	Obsessive-Compulsive Personality Disorder

_____   _____

_____   _____

PHYSICIAN

BEHAVIORAL DEFINITIONS

1. Demonstrates personality traits of being obsessional, perfectionistic, overly ambitious, and rigid.
2. Has difficulty with emotional expression, a low tolerance for uncertainty, and inadequate coping skills to effectively deal with stress.
3. Demonstrates symptoms of a major depressive disorder (e.g., anhedonia, dysphoria, despair, increased irritability, or sleep problems) and/ or anxiety disorder (e.g., inability to concentrate).
4. Displays a tendency to deny, minimize, and rationalize psychiatric symptoms and behaviors.
5. Engages in significant patterns of alcohol abuse and drug dependency in reaction to verbalized disappointment with career, high levels of job-related stress and burn out, and marital discord.
6. Verbalizes fatigue and stress because of continuous exposure to traumatic stimuli, feeling intense responsibility to relieve suffering, confrontation with ethical dilemmas, and meeting the competing needs of clients and his/her own family.
7. Practices in a medical environment with high stress levels (e.g., rural isolation, HIV medicine, oncology, emergency departments, intensive care units, anesthesiology, psychiatry, start-up practice).
8. Reluctance to discuss personal psychiatric and/or psychological issues with a peer physician.
9. Shuns talking about suicide intent and/or ideation because of fears of stigma or feelings of vulnerability, worthlessness, shame, or guilt.
10. Motivated to choose the medical profession by social status, a need to earn other's approval, and/or parental or family pressure.
11. Experienced significant childhood trauma (e.g., exposure to family members with serious physical and/or mental health disorders) that influenced the decision to study medicine.

—. _____
_____
—. _____
_____
—. _____
_____

LONG-TERM GOALS

1. Report a wish to live.
2. Develop a balanced self-concept that can accept temporary failures and integrate them into professional and personal growth experience.
3. Develop an enhanced capacity for emotional expression that enables adaptive coping with frustration, fear, grief, and other emotions common to the practice of medicine.
4. Develop a sense of hope for the future and an ability to define self in a futuristic context.
5. Develop a supportive social network.
6. Acknowledge personal vulnerabilities that allow empathic responses and helping gestures from significant others.
7. Develop an appropriate boundary on the practice of medicine that allows energy for meeting personal and/or family needs.

—. _____
_____
—. _____
_____
—. _____
_____

SHORT-TERM OBJECTIVES

1. Describe feelings of satisfaction and/or dissatisfaction with the medical practice. (1, 2)

THERAPEUTIC INTERVENTIONS

1. Explore the client's motivations for choosing the medical profession (e.g., intellectual challenge, altruism, job security, social status, parental pressure,

approval from others, or childhood exposure to family pathology) and note any motivations that could be problematic for a healthy adjustment.

2. Acknowledge the nature of the personality trait of perfectionism. (3, 4, 5)

2. Explore the client's current feelings toward his/her medical practice (e.g., very satisfied, a balanced view, dissatisfied, or very unhappy) and isolate current emotional reactions that could be problematic for a healthy adjustment (e.g., feeling flawed and inadequate, extreme fatigue because of long hours, stress because of continuous exposure to trauma, or frustration because of lack of private life).

3. Explore the client's current professional performance and examine any issues of perfectionism (e.g., tends to be overly ambitious, obsessional, or rigid; shows a low tolerance for uncertainty; puts client's needs ahead of his/her own, or has excessively high expectations of himself/herself); examine these issues for linkage with feelings of failure, guilt, shame, or low self-esteem.

4. Explore the source and nature of the client's perfectionistic feelings (e.g., self-oriented perfectionism where he/she sets unrealistically high self-expectations and is unusually harsh with self-criticism; other-oriented perfectionism where he/she establishes standards of performance based on comparisons with others;

socially prescribed perfectionism where the standards of performance are placed on him/her by significant others).

5. Explore the client's current dysfunctional coping strategies for feelings of perfectionism and any related feelings of failure and isolate those strategies that could be risk factors for suicide intent (e.g., alcohol abuse, drug dependency, avoiding social/familial responsibilities, or working longer hours to compensate for feelings of inadequacy).

3. Provide information on personal experiences with high-risk *behavioral* markers for suicide in physicians. (6, 7, 8, 9, 10)

6. Assess the client for the high-risk physician suicide marker of alcohol abuse and drug dependency (e.g., use in isolation and/or during on-duty hours, connected to intensity of suicidal thoughts, and contributes to marital discord or unethical and/or illegal behaviors).

7. Assess the client for the high-risk physician suicide marker of inadequate coping skills to deal effectively with stress (e.g., difficulty with emotional expression, reluctant to seek help because of fear of professional stigma, replaces his/her own needs with those of clients; tends to deny, minimize, or rationalize his/her symptoms or behaviors).

8. Assess the client for the high-risk physician suicide marker of a need to sustain a presentation of power, authority, and

control (e.g., illusions of grandiosity and indispensability, an inability to view himself/herself as flawed and inadequate, or a fear of losing the social perception that doctors are omnipotent and invulnerable).

9. Assess the client for the high-risk physician suicide marker of a high stress medical specialty (e.g., emergency departments, residency program, oncology, rural isolation, or anesthesiology); examine his/her motivations for choosing this particular specialty (e.g., family pressure and/or tradition, need for a challenge and/or excitement, financial rewards, or social status).

10. Assess the client for the high-risk physician suicide marker of job burn-out (e.g., exhaustion leading to negative self-concept and professional attitude, high work load, inadequate professional support system, dealing with death and suffering, treatment failures, or extreme financial problems).

4. Provide information on personal experiences with high-risk *emotional* markers for suicide in physicians. (11, 12)

11. Assess the client for the high-risk physician suicide marker of depression and anxiety, especially in females (e.g., social withdrawal, anhedonia, dysphoria, irritability, inability to concentrate, physical and emotional agitation, post-traumatic stress disorder, or melancholic despair).

12. Assess the client for the high-risk physician suicide marker

of a life-long pattern of socially prescribed perfectionism (e.g., its linkage to feelings of hopelessness and despair, the object of the need to please, the role of socially prescribed perfectionism in choosing the medical profession, and its linkage to suicide intent).

5. Provide information on personal experiences with high-risk *social* markers for suicide in physicians. (13, 14)

13. Assess the client for the high-risk physician suicide marker of marital discord or relationship turmoil (e.g., infidelities, lack of communication, financial problems, lack of meaningful time together, devotion to work versus relationship, and his/her refusal to engage in relationship counseling).

14. Assess the client for the high-risk physician suicide marker of social isolation (e.g., the nature of any meaningful relationships, whether the medical practice eliminates most opportunities for a meaningful relationship, and the linkage of social isolation to the suicide intent).

6. Identify the nature of current suicidal ideation and/or intent. (15, 16, 17, 18)

15. Explore the client's intended goal for the suicide act (e.g., cessation of unbearable psychological pain, motivated by intense self-hate, provides a sense of control by solving a seemingly unsolvable problem when other coping strategies have failed).

16. Explore the amount of energy the client spends in planning or physically preparing for the suicide event (e.g., financial issues are resolved, lethal means

was obtained, or a date and place was assigned).

17. Inquire whether the client's feelings of anxiety and/or depression have decreased and a sense of calm has entered since planning started or concluded.

18. Explore for any impediments to the client's implementation of the suicide plan (e.g., fear of the emotional impact on survivors, fear of social and/or professional stigma, or religious beliefs).

7. Provide complete information on current mood, affect, and thought process in a psychiatric evaluation, taking psychotropic medications as prescribed. (19, 20, 21, 22)

19. Examine the client for any feelings of shame, loss of credibility, or loss of control that are implied when the issue of a psychiatric referral is discussed; caution him/her against self-diagnosis and treatment; inform him/her that the need to self-diagnose and self-treat could be viewed as a maladaptive method of managing shame and may prevent him/her from receiving optimal care.

20. Acknowledge, respect, and process the feelings of shame that the client may experience as a result of his/her changing from the role of provider to beneficiary of medical assistance; normalize these feelings, but, at the same time, do not allow them to preclude a psychiatric consultation.

21. Choose a psychiatrist, in consultation with the client, who has a history of working with physicians, the respect of physicians in the community, the respect of the client, and a

reputation of sound ethical practice; refer him/her for a psychiatric evaluation to determine the need for psycho-tropic medication and to validate any at-risk diagnoses.

22. Monitor the client's compliance with the psychotropic medica-tion prescription in consultation with the chosen psychiatrist; chart the subjective and objective behavioral changes and monitor side effects, while continuously cautioning him/her against self-treatment, emphasizing trust in the treating physician, empathizing with his/her difficulty in being a client, and focusing on the course of treatment.

8. Accept feedback on the assessments and the treatment plan developed from the evaluation process. (23)

23. Summarize and give feedback to the client and, if available and appropriate, the caregivers on high-risk markers found during the assessment and evaluation process; explain details of the treatment plan and, if appropri-ate, attempt to engage the caregivers.

9. Comply with placement in a more protective and, possibly, more restrictive environment. (24, 25)

24. Assess the client's negative views toward the mentally ill (e.g., psychiatric clients are "hard to like" and difficult to treat) or toward psychiatric hospitalization; process these issues.

25. If the client displays risk factors (e.g., divorce or loss of hospital privileges) and warning signs (e.g., the purchase of a gun) that are positively correlated to completed suicide, a decision must be made about immediate

placement in a structured, therapeutic setting; hospitalization, if necessary, should not be delayed or avoided, but an alternative site from his/her home, hospital, or practice should be considered.

10. Agree to a plan for dealing with situations when suicidal urges become strong. (26, 27, 28)

26. Acknowledge that as the client returns to the community he/she may experience an exacerbation of feelings of worthlessness and/or shame; coordinate planning that will aggressively treat psychiatric problems and efficiently decrease the stressors of his/her medical practice.

27. Monitor the client's suicide risk at appropriate intervals during the therapy process; develop a crisis intervention plan to be implemented during trigger events and feelings (e.g., treatment failures leading to a sense of worthlessness) that encourages contacting the therapist to discuss and process these emotional reactions; construct this plan as a verbal agreement in the context of the therapy alliance.

28. Emphasize to the client that talking out these difficult emotions begins a course of adaptive coping with stressful situations and works to diminish the maladaptive coping strategies (e.g., substance abuse) that fueled eventual suicide ideation.

11. Identify the stressors and symptoms that trigger the wish to die by suicide. (29, 30, 31)

29. Assist the client in making a list of his/her most prominent stressors (e.g., marital discord, job burn out, treatment failures, or financial problems) and

emotional reactions or symptoms (e.g., despair, shame, self-devaluation, or fear) produced by those stressors.

30. Assist the client in producing a complete symptom inventory that includes identifying the most disruptive symptoms (e.g., those psychological states described as "unbearable" and appear to be the prominent motivator of suicide), how these symptoms are currently dysfunctionally managed (e.g., alcohol abuse or isolative behaviors), and other reactions created by these symptoms (e.g., loss of confidence in medical skills).

31. Establish a therapeutic alliance with the client that ensures the therapist's help in targeting the most serious symptoms for immediate attention (e.g., solution-oriented therapy); focus his/her attention in identifying the locus of the most intense psychological pain (e.g., the distress that appears to be the major contributor to the suicide intent) and how the therapy will help him/her manage that pain.

12. Identify problem-solving strategies for current stressors and symptoms that do not include suicide or the wish to die. (32, 33, 34)

32. Formulate an appropriate view of suicide for the client: It stems from a desire to solve a seemingly unsolvable problem; it is fueled by elements of hopelessness and helplessness; and the antidote is to acquire, with the therapist's help, safe and simple problem-solving skills for identified stressors and symptoms.

33. Assign the client a treatment journal to track daily stressors, the resulting symptoms, maladaptive coping patterns, and experiences with newly acquired coping strategies; assign homework targeting symptom management; stress to him/her that the goal of therapy is healthy symptom management and *not* symptom elimination.

34. Guide and teach the client to implement adaptive problem-solving strategies; assist him/her in noting in his/her treatment journal a detailed strategy (e.g., cognitive redefining strategies, catharsis strategies, or diversion strategies) with specific instructions on responding to and managing the perturbation associated with his/her priority symptoms.

13. Develop strategies for diminishing the influence of personality traits and vulnerabilities on the suicide intent. (35, 36)

35. Assist the client in acknowledging and respecting his/her personality traits and vulnerabilities (e.g., difficulty with emotional expression or perfectionism) that diminish the effectiveness of adaptive coping strategies and contribute to the suicide intent; assist him/her in examining the source of these traits (e.g., overly demanding parental expectations).

36. Assist the client in a process of redefining himself/herself; engage him/her in exercises (e.g., a calm acceptance of his/her intrinsic worth during times of treatment failure or marital discord, or safely engaging in emotional catharsis in a social context) that will be experienced in the therapy

14. Increase verbalized statements of hope that stressors and symptoms can be managed continuously in ways other than suicide. (37)

15. Verbalize an increased acceptance of self as a vulnerable person, capable of mistakes and failures, while keeping intact a core image of self-regard. (38)

16. Increase activities that show an improved sense of a balanced life style. (39)

17. Develop a suicide prevention plan that incorporates a treatment journal and all completed homework assignments. (40)

session and practiced in his/her social environment.

37. Assist the client in reviewing the treatment journal during each session; identify and reinforce strengths and an improved sense of self-image because of improved problem-solving and coping strategies.

38. Teach the client (a) that his/her core self-image of intrinsic worth must be respected; (b) that expressions of vulnerability in the therapy relationship are honored and accepted without judgment; and (c) that to be vulnerable is to be human.

39. Assist the client in formulating a balanced activities of daily living program that respects the demands of his/her medical practice, but firmly structures specified times for relationship, family, personal needs; have him/her note in the treatment journal his/her experiences in responding to this schedule.

40. Assist the client in writing a personal suicide prevention plan that lists all the individualized actions that will be taken in the future to manage suicide urges (e.g., rely on the treatment journal for reminders of strategies for coping with trigger events, feelings, and symptoms; avoid isolation and maintain social network; remain on physician prescribed medication; maintain futuristic thinking; trust the value of himself/herself).

___.   _____   ___.   _____
       _____   _____
___.   _____   ___.   _____
       _____   _____
___.   _____   ___.   _____
       _____   _____

DIAGNOSTIC SUGGESTIONS:

Axis I: 296.xx   Major Depressive Disorder
             300.4   Dysthymic Disorder
             296.90   Mood Disorder NOS
             308.3   Acute Stress Disorder
             305.00   Alcohol Abuse
             303.90   Alcohol Dependence
             304.40   Amphetamine Dependence
             304.80   Polysubstance Dependence
             300.3   Obsessive-Compulsive Disorder
             300.02   Generalized Anxiety Disorder
             309.81   Posttraumatic Stress Disorder
             V62.2   Occupational Problem

             _____   _____
             _____   _____

PSYCHIATRIC INPATIENT

BEHAVIORAL DEFINITIONS

1. Demonstrates symptoms correlated to a severe mental illness (e.g., major depression, schizophrenia, or bipolar disorder) that significantly diminish adaptive coping and cloud logical thinking.
2. Demonstrates severe symptoms of psychological turmoil (e.g., grieving, rage, confusion, or loss) that limit coping options and present the client with a melancholic despair for their resolution.
3. Presents significant risk factors (e.g., chronic conditions such as depression, alcohol abuse/dependency, schizophrenia, or posttraumatic stress) and warning signs (e.g., statements of hopelessness, melancholic despair, self-directed rage, social isolation, or suicide planning) that are positively correlated to completed suicide.
4. Engages in self-harm activity that includes suicide gestures (i.e., behaviors that are either calculated for rescue or are self-interrupted, and there is no clear intent to die) and/or suicide attempts (i.e., behaviors that are accidentally interrupted against the client's wishes, and there is a clearly established intent to die).
5. Lives within a toxic environment (e.g., physically abusive home or drug and alcohol-related environment) that clearly increases stress.
6. Lacks a supportive social network because of isolation behavior.
7. Displays a rapid reduction in anxiety and/or an elevation in depressed mood that could be reflective of an ultimate decision to suicide.

—. _____

_____

—. _____

_____

—. _____

_____

LONG-TERM GOALS

1. Obtain protection from any severe suicide impulse.
2. Diminish the psychological pain associated with the symptoms of a severe mental illness.
3. Diminish the perturbation association with symptoms of severe psychological turmoil.
4. Increase a sense of hope for further healing.
5. Participate in a therapeutic milieu that encourages future therapeutic alliances.
6. Gain relief from a toxic environment, significant social stress, and social isolation.
7. Gain insight into the causes for the suicide intent.

—. _____
   _____
—. _____
   _____
—. _____
   _____

SHORT-TERM OBJECTIVES	THERAPEUTIC INTERVENTIONS
1. Identify the causes for, planning associated with, and resistance to the current suicide intent. (1, 2, 3, 4)	1. Examine with the client the meaning of and motivation for his/her suicide intent (e.g., cessation of intolerable psychological pain, elimination of self due to severe issues of self-devaluation, a cognitive problem-solving strategy when confronted with hopelessness and despair in coping with life stress, a wish to be reunited with a loved one).
	2. Examine with the client the amount of time and energy devoted to his/her suicide intent (e.g., acquisition of a lethal means, a time and

place designation, financial affairs resolved, farewell communication to significant others, planning to eliminate rescue potential, rehearsal behaviors).

3. Assess the client for any observable calm and/or tranquility that suicide planning has provided after experiencing a prolonged episode of psychological/psychiatric turmoil (e.g., he/she will show no outward signs of inner conflicts and may socially disengage and appear emotionally distant).

4. Explore the client's impediments to or ambivalence about the suicide intent (e.g., fear of emotional impact on survivors, concern with the "stigma" of suicide, religious beliefs, a reported absence of impediments and/or ambivalence).

2. Describe the history of previous suicide ideation, gestures, and/or attempts. (5, 6, 7)

5. Explore the client's history of suicide ideation (e.g., chronic patterns of suicidal thoughts, age of onset, conditions and circumstances of thoughts, intended goals, factors that diminish suicidal ideation).

6. Examine the client's history of suicide gestures (e.g., chronic patterns of self-harm behaviors for which the intent is not to die, but to achieve other social, psychological, environmental needs; evidence that self-harm activity was calculated for rescue and/or was self-interrupted; age of onset;

conditions and circumstances of behaviors; intended goals).

7. Assess the client's history of suicide attempts (e.g., reported incidents in which the intent was death; planning was precise to avoid detection; rescue was accidental and against his/her wishes; he/she demonstrates anger at being prevented from completing suicide), remaining alert to the significantly elevated risk that correlates suicide attempts, and repeated suicide gestures, to completed suicide.

3. Provide information on personal experiences with high-risk *behavioral* factors for completed suicide in the psychiatric inpatient population. (8, 9)

8. Assess the client for the high-risk psychiatric inpatient marker of substance abuse/dependency (e.g., age of onset, report of relief from psychiatric symptoms during use, negative life consequences due to use).

9. Assess the client for the high-risk psychiatric inpatient marker of a history of suicide gestures and/or attempts (e.g., precipitating events prior to each activity, distinguish between gesture and attempt, use of substances during events, psychological state during each event).

4. Provide information on personal experiences with high-risk *emotional* factors for completed suicide in the psychiatric inpatient population. (10, 11)

10. Assess the client for the high-risk psychiatric inpatient marker of a major mood or affect disorder (e.g., elements of hopelessness and despair, lack of energy, age of onset, history of treatment, co-morbid medical illness).

11. Assess the client for the high-risk psychiatric inpatient marker

5. Provide information on personal experiences with high-risk *social* factors for completed suicide in the psychiatric inpatient population. (12, 13)

of a major thought disorder (e.g., paranoid schizophrenia with active delusions and co-morbid mood disorder, history of assaultive behaviors, pre-morbid functioning).

12. Assess the client for the high-risk psychiatric inpatient marker of isolation (e.g., lack of social support, living alone, unemploy-ment, recent relationship loss, decline in socioeconomic status).

13. Assess the client for the high-risk psychiatric inpatient marker of family history of suicide (e.g., identify person, place, time, and circumstances of the event; course of processing this event).

6. Identify high-risk acute warning signs correlated to completed suicide. (14, 15)

14. Assess the client for the acute warning signs of psychological turmoil (e.g., sleep disturbance noted by early morning rising, increase in irritability, racing thoughts, inability to concen-trate), statements of self-hate, severe despair, shame, guilt, feelings of isolation, comments that suicide is the "only" way out of pain, acts of help negation, or sudden elevation of mood.

15. Reassess the client for warning signs at appropriate intervals during inpatient stay, document-ing findings to guide the inpatient staff to implement proper protective actions and optimum patient care if the warning signs increase.

7. Cooperate with psychological testing designed to evaluate the

16. Administer tests most commonly used to reveal and

risk level of the current suicide intent. (16)

evaluate suicide intent and risk levels (e.g., Suicide Probability Scale, Beck Hopelessness Scale, Reasons for Living Inventory); process assessment results with the client.

8. Provide complete information on current mood, affect, and thought process in a psychiatric evaluation, and take psychotropic medications as prescribed. (17, 18)

17. Refer the client for a psychiatric evaluation to determine his/her need for psychotropic medication and to validate any at-risk diagnoses (e.g., major depression, recurrent, severe, with psychotic features; schizophrenia, paranoid type with co-occurring major depression; bipolar II disorder in a severe depressive phase; antisocial personality disorder with co-occurring substance abuse/dependency).

18. Monitor the client's compliance with the psychotropic medication regimen; chart his/her subjective and behavioral changes and monitor any side effects.

9. Cooperate with a trial of electroconvulsive therapy to relieve acute, severe depressive turmoil. (19)

19. Refer the client for medically supervised electroconvulsive treatment in order to achieve rapid relief from severe depressive turmoil (e.g., demonstrates delusional thought content co-occurring with a high-risk mental illness) that contributes to the highly lethal suicide risk.

10. Identify current and specific general health considerations that may contribute to the suicide intent. (20)

20. After obtaining appropriate confidentiality and privacy releases, contact the client's personal care physician for a report on current health issues that may trigger suicidal behavior (e.g., HIV/AIDS; brain

cancer; Multiple Sclerosis; renal failure; Parkinson's disease; Huntington's disease with comorbid issues of depression, psychosis, and alcohol abuse; chronic injuries resulting from previous suicide attempts).

11. Accept safety rules and supervision procedures designed to prevent successful suicide behavior.
    (21, 22, 23, 24)

21. Ensure that secure architectural and environmental safety features are maintained during the client's treatment (e.g., limit access to means of hanging, asphyxiation, cutting, poisoning, or burning).

22. Establish rigid policies on staff monitoring procedures (e.g., search the client on admission for lethal objects; remove articles of clothing that could be used for hanging, asphyxiation, cutting; train nonclinical staff in all safety procedures; secure all doors; monitor police weapons; and secure cleaning chemicals).

23. Establish policies and procedures to link the level of surveillance of the client to the treatment team's risk and lethality assessments (e.g., consistent one-to-one observation for clients who are symptomatic of severe levels of depression and/or psychosis; consistent group observation for clients who are responding to medical and or therapy interventions; intermittent observation prior to discharge).

24. Establish rules for visitation of the client (e.g., evaluate the benefit of certain visitors to the adjustment of the client; respond to his/her wishes for denial of

certain visitor privileges; in order to prevent smuggling onto the unit, request identification of all visitors, and, in certain clinically defined and ordered circumstances, monitor visits).

12. Accept feedback gathered from all sources and the treatment plan developed from the evaluation process. (25)

25. Summarize and give feedback to the client, and, if available and appropriate, caregivers regarding the risk factors found in the evaluation process; outline the treatment plan for him/her and incorporate his/her participation in this effort.

13. Identify current stressors and resultant symptoms that trigger the need to engage in suicidal behavior. (26, 27)

26. Assist the client in listing his/her most prominent stressors (e.g., recent loss of a relationship, employment, health, or financial security; victimization by spouse abuse; posttraumatic stress disorder; or unbearable depression symptoms).

27. Explore emotional reactions or symptoms (e.g., despair, hopelessness, fear, psychic turmoil, or pain) produced by the client's stressors and how those symptoms are currently dysfunctionally managed (e.g., suicide ideation, self-mutilation, or substance abuse).

14. Implement coping and management skills for identified stressors and symptoms other than suicide. (28, 29, 30, 31)

28. Establish a therapeutic alliance with the client that includes attending to the most disruptive and painful symptoms for immediate attention; encourage him/her to accept that there are other coping strategies available to him/her than suicide; acknowledge the therapy alliance goal of finding other solutions to his/her stressors and symptoms; encourage the

participation of the outpatient therapist, if appropriate and available.

29. Teach the client problem-solving skills (e.g., define the problem completely, explore alternative solutions, list the positives and negatives of each solution, select and implement a plan of action, evaluate the outcome, and adjust skills as necessary).

30. Formulate an appropriate view of the function of the client's suicide intent: It stems from his/her need to solve a seemingly unsolvable problem; it is fueled by hopelessness, self-directed rage, helplessness; and the antidote to this risk is to develop healthy coping strategies for these stressors and symptoms.

31. Assign the client a treatment journal; encourage him/her to continue the use of the journal in postdischarge outpatient therapy; encourage the client to track his/her daily stressors, the resultant symptoms, maladaptive coping patterns (e.g., substance abuse) and experiences with newly acquired problem-solving alternatives (e.g., anger management strategies or remaining on medication).

15. Identify triggers to suicide relapse and verbalize a crisis intervention plan designed to cope with trigger situations. (32)

32. Assist the client in identifying his/her triggers to relapse into suicidal risk (e.g., self-devaluation after a failure experience, inability to access emotions, or return of depressed mood) and educate him/her in using a crisis plan that

includes calling the outpatient therapist or local mental health help line to discuss emotional reactions to these events and, if needed, access emergency services.

16. Give permission for disclosure of treatment and assessment information to the outpatient therapist. (33, 34)

33. Communicate with the post-discharge treatment provider verbally and in writing (e.g., sending excerpts from the client's medical chart) and confirm with the client his/her initial appointment with the outpatient therapist.

34. Complete a predischarge suicide risk assessment that documents the client's relief from symptoms of initially reported risk factors and warning signs, involvement in group and individual therapy, identified triggers to relapse, and consideration of chronic suicide risk (e.g., borderline personality disorder); communicate this assessment to the outpatient therapist after obtaining the client's disclosure permission.

17. Verbalize an understanding of the need for the medication regimen. (35)

35. Educate the client and caregivers on the issues of prescribed medication(s) (e.g., needed laboratory tests, side effects, medical appointments, or diet concerns).

18. Communicate any sudden mood change to peace or euphoria. (36)

36. Assess the client for any signs of rapid relief from psychiatric and psychological turmoil; examine rapid reversal of symptoms because it may indicate he/she has calmly decided to complete suicide postdischarge; do not discharge the client under these

circumstances but seek a second
opinion on his/her suicide risk
potential.

—. _____   —. _____
    _____   _____
—. _____   —. _____
    _____   _____
—. _____   —. _____
    _____   _____

DIAGNOSTIC SUGGESTIONS:

Axis I:

296.xx	Major Depressive Disorder
296.2x	Major Depressive Disorder, Single Episode
296.3x	Major Depressive Disorder, Recurrent
296.34	Major Depressive Disorder, Recurrent, Severe with Psychotic Features
296.89	Bipolar II Disorder
296.xx	Bipolar I Disorder
295.xx	Schizophrenia
295.30	Schizophrenia, Paranoid Type
298.8	Brief Psychotic Disorder
297.1	Delusional Disorder
V62.82	Bereavement
309.81	Posttraumatic Stress Disorder
305.00	Alcohol Abuse
304.80	Polysubstance Dependence
300.02	Generalized Anxiety Disorder
V62.89	Phase of Life Problem

_____   _____

Axis II:

301.6	Dependent Personality Disorder
301.81	Narcissistic Personality Disorder
301.83	Borderline Personality Disorder
301.7	Antisocial Personality Disorder

_____   _____

_____   _____

SCHIZOPHRENIC

BEHAVIORAL DEFINITIONS

1. Indicates verbally a wish to die.
2. Demonstrates active delusions of guilt, deserved punishment, worthlessness, and/or persecution.
3. Demonstrates active delusions of bodily disease, damage, and malfunction.
4. Verbalizes anger and frustration at diminished cognitive capacity.
5. Demonstrates extreme withdrawal from social relationships.
6. Meets the criteria for a major depressive episode (e.g., sleep disturbance, lack of appetite, feelings of guilt, loss of energy, depressed mood, or flat affect).
7. Presents with history of suicide attempts where the activity was accidentally, inadvertently interrupted.
8. Verbalizes anger, fear, and sadness at lowered achievement levels, diminished expectations for the future, unwelcome feelings of isolation, and loss.
9. Verbalizes fears of mental illness (e.g., further deterioration, unwanted dependency on family, or life-long institutionalization) immediately after an inpatient episode or early in an inpatient episode.
10. Verbalizes a strong sense of hopelessness in dealing with life stressors, especially the loss of a significant relationship.
11. Demonstrates a complex diagnostic picture, comprised of significant occupational and social impairment, comorbid conditions (e.g., substance abuse or dependence, physical ailments, personality disorders, or depression), aggressiveness/hostility with paranoid features, and a steadily increasing debilitation because of mental illness.

—. _____
_____
_____
—. _____
_____
_____
—. _____
_____

LONG-TERM GOALS

1. Develop an engaging attitude toward life so that the suicidal impulse is ended.
2. Provide immediate and continued management of threatening depressive and psychotic symptomatology.
3. Develop a personal understanding and respect for his/her experience of mental illness.
4. Develop a respect for self as a mentally ill person.
5. Develop a sense of self in a social context.
6. Develop a sense of competence in an occupational context.
7. Develop a healthy sense of futuristic thinking.

—. _____
_____
_____
—. _____
_____
_____
—. _____
_____

SHORT-TERM OBJECTIVES

1. Identify facts and feelings associated with premorbid functioning. (1)

THERAPEUTIC INTERVENTIONS

1. Explore the client's social, academic, familial, and occupational functioning prior to the diagnosis of schizophrenia or the onset of the illness; encourage the client to characterize his/her premorbid functioning as highly satisfying, acceptable, or disappointing.

2. Identify life hopes and expectations prior to the diagnosis of schizophrenia or the onset of the illness. (2)

2. Explore the client's vocational, academic, professional, personal, and social hopes and aspirations prior to the diagnosis of schizophrenia or the onset of the illness; examine his/her feelings about how mental illness affects these hopes and aspirations, noting whether severe hopelessness is a factor in the risk assessment.

3. Client and family members, if available and agreeable to the client, provide appropriate symptom information for diagnostic formulation, risk assessment, and treatment strategies. (3, 4, 5)

3. Assist the client in identifying his/her symptoms (e.g., hearing voices, anxiety) most disruptive to social, occupational, and familial functioning and those symptoms most closely related to an elevated suicide risk (e.g., social withdrawal, depression, increased hopelessness for the future, fear of dependence on others, frustration over frequent exacerbations and remissions, anxiety around severe occupational and/or academic deterioration, and fear connected to increased aggressiveness).

4. Meet with family members and/or caregivers to gather information about the presence of high-risk schizophrenic suicide markers in the client's history (e.g., age of illness onset, social withdrawal, depression, increased hopelessness for the future, fear of dependence on others, frustration over frequent exacerbations and remissions, anxiety around severe occupational and/or academic deterioration, and fear connected to increased aggressiveness).

5. Discuss the nature of the client's illness with family members and caregivers, its connection to suicide risk, and high-risk factors and engage them, if possible, in a risk-management plan.

4. Provide complete information on current mood, affect, and thought process in a psychiatric evaluation, taking psychotropic medication as prescribed. (6, 7)

6. Refer the client for a psychiatric evaluation to determine the need for psychotropic medication and to validate any at-risk diagnoses (e.g., overlying major depression or schizophrenia, paranoid type).

7. Monitor the client's compliance with the psychotropic medication; chart the client's subjective and objective behavioral changes, and monitor his/her side effects.

5. Provide information on personal experiences with high-risk *behavioral* markers for suicide in schizophrenics. (8, 9, 10)

8. Assess the client for the high-risk schizophrenic suicide marker of substance abuse by administering a thorough evaluation (e.g., age of onset, choice of substances, place of use, effectiveness in calming psychotic symptoms, or effects on social network).

9. Assess the client for the high-risk schizophrenic suicide marker of incidents of aggressiveness because of paranoid features in thinking (e.g., elevated suspicions and distrust of others that leads to fearing their intentions or aggressive acting out motivated by self-protection needs).

10. Assess the client for history of previous suicide activity (e.g., motivation for suicide or

whether it was calculated for rescue, occurred during psychosis, accidentally interrupted, or the client is glad about the lack of success and to still be alive).

6. Provide information on personal experiences with high-risk *emotional* markers for suicide in schizophrenics. (11, 12)

11. Assess the client for the high-risk schizophrenic suicide marker of depression (e.g., depth of hopelessness, low energy level, lack of interest or pleasure in activities, social withdrawal, low self-esteem, or sleep disturbance).

12. Assess the client for the high-risk schizophrenic suicide marker of underlying personality disorder (e.g., borderline, antisocial, narcissistic, or schizoid).

7. Provide information on personal experiences with high-risk *social* markers for suicide in schizophrenics. (13, 14)

13. Assess the client for the high-risk schizophrenic suicide marker of recent rejection (e.g., family rejection, peer group rejection, feelings of isolation, or current social network).

14. Assess the client for the high-risk schizophrenic suicide marker of occupational impairment (e.g., number of jobs held since onset of illness, reason for termination of employment, current job status and level of satisfaction, dignity felt in current job, relationship with fellow workers, or sense that job meets skills level).

8. Provide specific information on the nature of the current suicide ideation/intent. (15, 16, 17, 18)

15. Assess whether the client can state a goal for his/her intended suicide act (e.g., to escape the fear of the future, fear of

dependency on others, anger at dashed hopes, or depression because of current functioning level).

16. Assess the level of planning the client is devoting to his/her intended suicide (e.g., time and place chosen, will written, or lethal means obtained).

17. Examine any decrease in agitation or experience of calm with the client since the planning for suicide started (e.g., a sense of peace is a high-risk factor).

18. Explore any doubts about the intended suicide with the client (e.g., fear of emotional impact on survivors, social stigma of suicide, or any existing ambivalence); such doubts may ameliorate the urge for suicide.

9. The client and, if available and agreeable to the client, the caregivers accept feedback gathered from all sources and the resulting treatment plan. (19)

10. Comply with placement in a more protective and restrictive therapeutic setting, if the assessments reveal high-risk suicide markers. (20, 21)

19. Summarize and give feedback to the client and, if possible and available, his/her caregivers on high-risk markers found in the evaluation process and outline the treatment plan.

20. If at any time in the therapy process the client demonstrates an increase in symptoms associated with high-risk for suicide, arrange for immediate placement in a protective therapeutic setting that will provide all necessary supervision to guard him/her from suicide impulse, decrease perturbation, remove him/her from environmental stress, decrease his/her isolation, and result in a close monitoring of

medical and psychological treatment effectiveness.

21. Develop a treatment plan that attends to all comorbid conditions, calls for caution if there is rapid clinical improvement, and addresses social support needs in discharge planning in consultation with the inpatient treatment team.

11. Affirm a safety plan that allows for a return to the community. (22)

22. Discharge planning should include monitoring of medications, case management services, occupational mainstreaming, and education on schizophrenia; obtain the client's affirmation of this plan.

12. Agree to a crisis response plan for dealing with situations when suicidal urges become strong. (23, 24)

23. Develop a crisis intervention plan to be implemented during trigger stressors and symptoms that includes the following: contacting therapist, using a local help line, and accessing emergency services in a responsible fashion; provide telephone numbers in writing to the client.

24. Ask the client to agree, as a verbal contract of the therapy relationship, to call someone on the emergency phone list in case he/she experiences strong suicide urges.

13. Verbalize statements of hope that problems have resolutions other than suicide. (25, 26)

25. Formulate an appropriate view of suicide for the client: It stems from a desire to solve a seemingly unsolvable problem; it is fueled by elements of hopelessness and helplessness; and the antidote is to acquire safe, simple coping and problem-solving skills over

identified stressors and symptoms; this can be done with the therapist's help.

26. Assign the client a treatment journal to track daily stressors, the resulting symptoms, maladaptive coping patterns, and experiences with newly acquired coping strategies; assign homework targeting symptom management; stress to the client that the goal of therapy is healthy symptom management and *not* symptom elimination.

14. Implement problem-solving skills to discover solutions to personal problems or life stresses that do not involve suicide. (27, 28, 29, 30)

27. Monitor the client's suicide risk at appropriate intervals through a risk-assessment interview and by administering, if possible, standardized suicide risk assessment instruments (e.g., Beck Scale for Suicide Ideation, Beck Depression Inventory, or Suicide Probability Scale).

28. Examine alternate solutions to problems with the client, challenging the perspective that suicide is the only solution.

29. Develop details of acceptable compromise solutions to those situations that are seen as irreversible, assisting the client in seeing that in any crisis an opportunity presents itself.

30. Use role-play, modeling, and behavior rehearsal to teach the client problem-solving skills (e.g., define the problem, explore alternative solutions, list the pros and cons of each solution, discuss the problem and solutions with trusted others

to get their input, select and implement a plan of action, evaluate the outcome, and adjust as necessary).

15. Identify the personal biological, social, and emotional vulnerabilities that contribute to the suicidal condition. (31)

31. Explore the client's personal vulnerabilities that contributed to the suicidal crisis (e.g., difficulty expressing emotions, tendency for feelings of extreme self-blame, a need to be perfect, or feelings of isolation); encourage the client to acknowledge the existence and influence of these personality factors (e.g., need to be perfect leads to denial of illness that leads to irregular compliance with medication program that leads to frequent exacerbation of illness).

16. Increase the frequency of statements that communicate pride in accomplishments and improved self-confidence. (32, 33)

32. Assist the client in enhancing his/her self-image by encouraging self-reports on recent incidents of improved coping and problem solving.

33. Enhance the client's self-esteem by validating examples of growth, accomplishments, improved coping, and appropriate independent behaviors (e.g., going to school or job regularly, medication compliance, feeling pride in a job well done, remaining in a social context).

17. List the benefits of sharing thoughts, feelings, and activities with friends. (34, 35)

34. Teach the client the value of verbalizing emotions in the context of personal relationships (e.g., sharing feelings promotes empathy from others, sharing their burden reduces their intensity, and sharing allows others to give their perspective

on your problems and to offer solutions).

35. Encourage the client to see himself/herself in a social context by emphasizing the benefits of participation in friendships and group activities.

18. List healthy ways to manage and express anger and frustration. (36, 37)

36. Assist the client in listing ways that self-directed anger can be replaced with alternate, constructive methods of managing frustration (e.g., acknowledging that anger is healthy, engaging in physical activity and exercise, or talking it out with a safe third party).

37. Use role-play and modeling to teach the client healthy ways to manage and express anger (e.g., acknowledging that anger is healthy, engaging in physical activity and exercise, or talking it out with a safe third party).

19. Affirm a decision about the necessity of long-term care. (38)

38. Engage in consultation with caregivers, primary care provider, and professional colleagues about a decision to continue or discontinue therapy, consider factors (e.g., chronicity of suicidal behavior, Axis I and Axis II comorbidity, current growth in therapy, and response to both medication and psychotherapy).

20. Verbalize agreement with a written suicide prevention plan. (27, 39, 40)

27. Monitor the client's suicide risk at appropriate intervals through a risk-assessment interview and by administering, if possible, standardized suicide risk assessment instruments

(e.g., Beck Scale for Suicide Ideation, Beck Depression Inventory, or Suicide Probability Scale).

39. Educate the client on preventing relapse into suicidal behavior (e.g., be aware of strategies to coping with trigger events and feelings, implement calming techniques, rely on trusted others, validate his/her own success without discounting them, avoid isolation and maintain social network, remain on medication program, avoid substance abuse, follow through with suggested psychological treatment, and remain engaged in occupational/vocational endeavors).

40. Assist the client in writing a personal suicide prevention plan that lists actions that will be taken in the future to avoid suicide; list such items as specific strategies for coping with trigger events, how and when calming techniques will be implemented, what trusted individuals will be relied on, what self-talk statements will be used to validate success, what social activities will be engaged in and with whom, when and what medication will be taken, what substances will be avoided, when counseling will be held, and what occupational activities will be maintained.

___. _____   ___. _____
      _____   _____

___. _____   ___. _____
      _____   _____

___. _____   ___. _____
      _____   _____

DIAGNOSTIC SUGGESTIONS:

Axis I: 295.30   Schizophrenia, Paranoid Type
                  295.10   Schizophrenia, Disorganized Type
                  295.20   Schizophrenia, Catatonic Type
                  295.90   Schizophrenia, Undifferentiated Type
                  295.60   Schizophrenia, Residual Type
                  295.70   Schizoaffective Disorder
                  297.1   Delusional Disorder
                  303.90   Alcohol Dependence

                  _____ _____
                  _____ _____

Axis II: 301.20   Schizoid Personality Disorder
                  301.7   Antisocial Personality Disorder
                  301.83   Borderline Personality Disorder
                  301.6   Dependent Personality Disorder

                  _____ _____
                  _____ _____

SUICIDAL/HOMICIDAL POPULATIONS

BEHAVIORAL DEFINITIONS

1. The elderly male experiences a sense of helplessness and hopelessness during a chronic or acute illness of an intimate partner or spouse.
2. The elderly male feels unable to manage strong emotions and has overwhelming feelings of hopelessness and difficulty adjusting to the role reversal caused by his spouse's illness.
3. The elderly male's primary intent is suicide, and the homicide is believed to be an act of altruism.
4. The elderly male demonstrates behaviors correlated to the diagnosis of major depressive disorder (e.g., chronic fatigue, anhedonia, dysphoria, increased irritability, hopelessness, melancholic despair) and substance abuse is used as a coping strategy.
5. The elderly male demonstrates lifetime patterns of emotional constriction, poor problem-solving skills, dependency, and performance anxiety.
6. The adult female believes her suicidal/homicidal action will save her children or loved ones from real or imagined abuse and terror.
7. The adult female's fears for her children's safety, which challenges her coping capacity and problem-solving skills, creates issues of shame, guilt, and remorse.
8. The adult female's primary intent is suicide, and the homicide of the children or loved ones is believed to be an act of rescue and escape.
9. The adult female demonstrates behaviors correlated to major depressive disorder (e.g., anhedonia, social isolation and withdrawal, dysphoria, or suicide ideation) and has been victimized in an abusive relationship.
10. The adult female demonstrates lifetime patterns of isolation, social withdrawal, poor self-esteem, PTSD, chronic suicide ideation, and poor problem-solving skills.

11. Motivated to commit the suicidal/homicidal act, in part, by a psychotic condition (e.g., unrealistic paranoia, major depression with psychosis, substance related psychotic condition, or postpartum depression with psychotic conditions).

—. _____
   _____

—. _____
   _____

—. _____
   _____

LONG-TERM GOALS

1. Abandon plan for suicide and homicide.
2. Develop effective, adaptive coping strategies and problem-solving skills.
3. Enhance access to emotions.
4. Develop realistic future time perspective that is fueled by hope.
5. Develop ability to assertively meet individual environmental, social, and psychological needs.
6. Enhance personal resiliency, flexibility, and capacity to manage crisis and failures.
7. Develop a supportive social network and an ability to engage in intimate relationships.

—. _____
   _____

—. _____
   _____

—. _____
   _____

SHORT-TERM OBJECTIVES	THERAPEUTIC INTERVENTIONS
1. Identify the nature and specifics of the goal and degree of planning related to the current suicide intent. (1, 2)	1. Explore in full detail the intended goal of the suicide intent (e.g., in the elderly male, evaluate issues of hopelessness,

helplessness, anger, and a sense of incompetence centered on the spouse's chronic or acute illness; in the adult female, evaluate issues of hopelessness, helplessness, fear, shame, and guilt centered on victimization by domestic violence) with the client.

2. Explore the amount of time and energy the client spends in planning the suicide event (e.g., has a lethal means or weapon been obtained; has a date and/or a place been assigned; does the plan include, or has the client considered, the homicide of children, spouse, or loved ones prior to his/her suicide).

2. Describe the intent of the planned homicide. (3, 4)

3. Explore the intended goal of the homicide of the loved ones (e.g., for the elderly male, evaluate issues of alleviating the spouse's chronic pain and/or deteriorating quality of life; for the adult female, evaluate issues of rescue, safety ["They would be better off in heaven"], or caring for the abused and terrorized children) with the client.

4. Explore whether a suicide/ homicide pact or an informal agreement has been established among the client and the loved ones.

3. Identify feelings associated with reaching a decision to complete a suicidal/homicidal plan. (5, 6)

5. Explore any issues of ambivalence about the suicidal/ homicidal intent (e.g., being open to explore other options of resolving their current crisis) with the client and/or any barriers to the suicidal/homicidal

plan (e.g., fear of impact on the survivors).

6. Examine whether the client has experienced an easing or relief from intense feelings of anxiety and/or depression since the planning for the suicide/homicide started or concluded.

4. Identify the nature and specifics of any and all previous suicide activity. (7)

7. Explore his/her history of suicide activity (e.g., activities where there was a clear intent to die, but the activity resulted in a nonfatal injury because of a rescue that was accidental and against the client's wishes; a history of chronic suicide ideation; a history of suicide gesturing that was calculated for rescue with no clear intent to die) with the client.

5. Cooperate with psychological testing designed to evaluate suicide ideation and/or intent and faulty problem-solving ability. (8)

8. Administer testing most commonly used to reveal and evaluate suicide ideation and intent levels and faulty problem-solving capacity (e.g., Scale for Suicide Ideation, Beck Depression Inventory, Beck Hopelessness Scale, or The Means-Ends Problem-Solving Procedure).

6. Acknowledge presence of and basis for cognitive rigidity, dichotomous thinking patterns, and poor problem-solving skills. (9, 10)

9. Examine the client for psychiatric states that appear to have a high correlation to cognitive rigidity and black-or-white thinking (e.g., depressive disorders, acute stress disorder, borderline personality, posttraumatic stress disorder, and obsessive-compulsive personality disorder).

10. Explore psychological/emotional conditions with the

client that appear to have a high correlation to impaired problem-solving capacity (e.g., overprotected childhood, delayed adolescent autonomy, an emotionally constricted family environment, or a verbally demeaning family environment).

7. Identify characteristics that are related to high-risk factors for suicidal/homicidal ideators. (11, 12)

11. Explore issues that are commonly correlated to the suicidal/homicidal perpetrator (e.g., an inability to accept an almost complete role reversal where the former nurturing spouse now requires full-time care from the client, the client has deteriorating health that makes caring for the spouse problematic, or the client exhibits extreme depression and hopelessness) with the elderly male.

12. Explore issues that are commonly correlated to the suicidal/homicidal perpetrator (e.g., chronic, severe victimization by an abusive partner; the partner displays pathological possessiveness; the client's children are victimized emotionally and/or physically; the client sees no escape or protection for herself or her loved ones) with the adult female.

8. Provide complete information on current mood, affect, and thought process in a psychiatric evaluation and take psychotropic medications as prescribed. (13, 14)

13. Refer the client for a psychiatric evaluation to determine his/her need for psychotropic medication and to validate any at risk diagnosis (e.g., borderline personality, depressive disorder, acute stress disorder,

9. Medical personnel provide relevant current information on the client's and the family's general health issues. (15)

10. Provide information on personal experiences with high-risk *behavioral* markers related to suicidal/homicidal ideators. (16, 17)

11. Provide information on personal experiences with high-risk *emotional* markers related to suicidal/homicidal ideators. (18)

12. Provide information on personal experiences with high-risk *social* markers related to suicidal/homicidal ideators. (19)

posttraumatic stress disorder, psychotic conditions related to affect, or mood disorders).

14. Monitor the client's compliance with and side effects of the psychotropic medication prescription; chart his/her subjective and objective behavioral changes.

15. After obtaining appropriate confidentiality and privacy releases, contact the client's medical provider for a report on current medical issues pertaining to him/her and involved loved ones.

16. Assess the client for the high-risk suicide marker of substance abuse (e.g., whether substance is used to cope with chronic feelings of hopelessness).

17. Assess the client for the high-risk suicide marker of loss of financial stability (e.g., the cause of the financial stress is due to medical expenses or, in the adult female, the result of the abusive partner preventing autonomous employment).

18. Assess the client for the high-risk suicide marker of chronic impulse control problems (e.g., any linkage to antisocial or borderline personality traits or issues of posttraumatic stress disorder).

19. Assess the client for the high-risk suicide marker of social isolation (e.g., whether the abusive partner is preventing access to the female's supportive social network; inability to

access supportive community resources; or lack of knowledge of helpful resources for the elderly male).

13. Accept feedback gathered from all sources and the treatment plan developed from the evaluation process. (20)

20. Summarize and give feedback to the client on high-risk markers found in the evaluation process; outline the treatment plan for the client and incorporate his/her participation in this effort.

14. Comply with placement in a more protective and, possibly, restrictive environment. (21, 22)

21. If at any time during the treatment process the client displays an increase in risk factors (e.g., despair, hopelessness, or anxiety) and demonstrates specific warning signs correlated to completed suicide (e.g., obtaining a lethal weapon), he/she should be placed in a structured, therapeutic setting that will protect him/her from the suicidal/homicidal impulse and remove him/her from environmental stress.

22. At the time of the client's inpatient stay, ensure the care and safety of the loved ones who may be under increased risk of harm (e.g., referral to caring relatives, social service agencies, or protective service agencies); the client should be informed of this action.

15. Affirm a discharge plan that allows a safe return to the community and family. (23)

23. Review the inpatient team's discharge plans with the client that includes knowledge of helping services and support systems (e.g., hospice, visiting nurses, protective service agencies, women's shelters, or support groups), individual psychotherapy appointments,

medication program, and activities of daily living.

16. Agree to a crisis response plan for dealing with situations when the risk of the suicidal/homicidal ideation and/or intent is strong. (24, 25, 26)

24. Develop a crisis intervention plan to be implemented by the client during trigger events (e.g., exacerbation of spouse's medical condition or incidents of physical abuse) and the resultant feelings (e.g., despair, anger, hopelessness, self-devaluation, or fear) that includes the alternatives of contacting the therapist, a trusted friend or family member, or a local help line to discuss the emotions and how to manage them.

25. Ask the client to agree, as a verbal contract of therapy, to call someone on the phone list in situations of strong suicidal/homicidal intent.

26. Consult with a local recipients' rights agency (e.g., local community mental health program) to determine the need to notify the potential homicide targets, local law enforcement agencies, and/or protective social service agencies about the client's suicidal/homicidal intent; notify the client of this obligation and the duty to warn and document all actions taken.

17. Identify current stressors and resultant symptoms that trigger the wish to die by suicide and include the need to kill family and loved ones. (27, 28)

27. Assist the client in making a list of his/her most prominent stressors (e.g., spouse's medical condition, medically related financial concerns, living in an abusive home, or observing the abuse of children); explore emotional reactions or symptoms

(e.g., anger, despair, help-lessness, fear, terror, or hopelessness) produced by those stressors.

28. Assist the client in developing a complete symptom inventory that includes identifying the symptoms that cause the most disruption in functioning; how these symptoms are currently dysfunctionally managed (e.g., substance abuse or suicidal/homicidal ideation) and whether these symptoms cause other reactions (e.g., neglecting the needs of the spouse or loved ones) that eventually overwhelm him/her.

18. Identify own biological, social, and psychological vulnerabilities and traits that hinder adaptive problem-solving strategies and contribute to the risk of a suicide plan that includes killing family members. (29, 30)

29. Explore the client's personal vulnerabilities and traits that contribute to problem-solving deficiencies and the suicide/homicide crisis (e.g., emotional constriction, black-and-white thinking, insecurities, or lack of assertiveness); help him/her to acknowledge the existence of these traits, understand their source, and track their influence on problem solving.

30. Assist the client in developing strategies to manage the influence of the traits that contribute to the suicide/homicide crisis (e.g., develop access to emotions, expand problem-solving alternatives, or learn assertiveness skills) to diminish their influence on the suicidal/homicidal intent.

19. Increase verbalized statements of hope that symptoms can be managed continuously in

31. Assure the client of the therapist's help in targeting the most serious symptoms for

ways other than suicide.
(31, 32, 33, 34)

31. immediate attention (e.g.,
solution-oriented therapies,
medications, or protective
inpatient services).

32. Teach the client problem-solving
skills (e.g., define the problem,
explore alternative solutions, list
the positives and negatives of
each solution, select and
implement a plan of action,
evaluate the outcome, and adjust
skills as necessary).

33. Formulate an appropriate view
of the function of suicide with
the client: It stems from a need
to solve a seemingly unsolvable
problem, it is fueled by a sense
of hopelessness and helplessness, and the antidote to the
suicide risk is to develop healthy
coping strategies for these
seemingly unsolvable stressors
and symptoms.

34. Assign the client a treatment
journal to track daily stressors,
the resultant symptoms,
maladaptive coping patterns
(e.g., suicidal/homicidal
ideation), and experiences with
newly acquired problem-solving
alternatives (e.g., relying on
helping services to assist with an
ailing spouse or removing loved
ones to the safety of a domestic
assault shelter); assign
homework targeting symptom
management.

20. Identify strategies to develop
personal resiliency; flexibility
in problem-solving strategies;
and calm, assertive responses
in crisis. (35, 36, 37, 38)

35. Examine the relationship among
cognitive rigidity, difficulty in
generating solutions to
problems, and his/her current
suicidal/homicidal urge (e.g.,
when faced with a severe

emotional problem, they may turn to suicide as the only available solution); assist the client in understanding that his/her own life history may offer detailed examples from which to develop problem-solving strategies.

36. Ask the client to write an autobiography focusing on times of crisis, stress, or unmanageable conditions; ask him/her to focus on behaviors they implemented during those times that may have calmed, managed, or resolved the problem.

37. Identify strategies, formed partly from the autobiographical recall, that may be applied to the problem-solving effort for the current crisis; use this problem-solving approach to address areas of coping where the client is deficient and provide him/her with skills that will prevent feelings of hopelessness from escalating into a suicide/homicide tragedy.

38. Assist the client in enhancing his/her personal resiliency and flexibility by encouraging self-reports from the treatment journal and homework assignments on recent incidents of improved coping, symptom management, and problem-solving skills (e.g., taking a respite from caring for an ailing spouse and allowing others to take charge for awhile or breaking all ties with the abusive partner).

21. Develop strategies to obtain community assistance in coping with personal crisis. (39, 40)

39. Assist the adult female on accessing community services such as domestic violence shelters, victim counseling, and support groups; alleviate any existing emotional impediments to accessing those services (e.g., embarrassment, fear, or lack of transportation).

40. Assist the elderly male on accessing community services (e.g., helpful social networks, medical and financial safety nets, and social services designed to improve the overall quality of life for seniors); alleviate any existing emotional impediments to accessing those services (e.g., embarrassment, lack of transportation, or characteristic difficulty in asking for help).

22. Develop a suicide prevention plan that incorporates the treatment journal's homework assignments. (41)

41. Assist the client in writing a personal suicide prevention plan that lists actions he/she will take to avoid the risk of impulse to suicide/homicide (e.g., be aware of lessons from the treatment journal, homework assignments, and autobiography on appropriate problem solving; rely on supportive social network; and remain on any prescribed medications).

—. _____

_____

—. _____

_____

—. _____

_____

—. _____

_____

—. _____

_____

—. _____

_____

DIAGNOSTIC SUGGESTIONS:

Axis I:

296.xx	Major Depressive Disorder
296.34	Major Depressive Disorder, Recurrent, Severe with Psychotic Features
311	Depressive Disorder NOS
295.xx	Schizophrenia
298.9	Psychotic Disorder NOS
305.00	Alcohol Abuse
303.9	Alcohol Dependence
296.90	Mood Disorder NOS
300.3	Obsessive-Compulsive Disorder
309.81	Posttraumatic Stress Disorder
308.3	Acute Stress Disorder
300.02	Generalized Anxiety Disorder
300.00	Anxiety Disorder NOS
300.15	Dissociative Disorder NOS
312.30	Impulse-Control Disorder NOS
309.xx	Adjustment Disorder
293.xx	Psychotic Disorder Due to General Medical Condition
293.83	Mood Disorder Due to General Medical Condition
_____	_____
_____	_____

Axis II:

301.7	Antisocial Personality Disorder
301.6	Dependent Personality Disorder
301.81	Narcissistic Personality Disorder
301.83	Borderline Personality Disorder
_____	_____
_____	_____

SUICIDE SURVIVOR

BEHAVIORAL DEFINITIONS

1. Verbalizes suicide intent after being overwhelmed by the suicidal death of a loved one.
2. Expresses irreconcilable feelings of frustration, hurt, and anger toward a loved one who committed suicide.
3. Displays an overwhelming obsession with the need to find out why the loved one chose suicide.
4. Expresses intense, often exaggerated and global, feelings of guilt and responsibility for the suicidal death of the significant other.
5. Overwhelmed by feelings of stigma and shame related to a loved one's suicide because of religious, social, and cultural norms, which lead to isolation from supportive resources.
6. Expresses feelings of distrust and insecurity toward all relationships, leading to further isolation.
7. Experiences intense feelings of anger toward the decedent that are repressed because of a belief that they are unacceptable.
8. Experiences intense feelings of rage toward others for their perceived roles in the loved one's suicidal death, leading to disruption in family social cohesion and increased isolation.
9. A child survivor demonstrates a significant increase in anxiety (e.g., night traumas) and a significant fracture in hope for the future as well as the loss of security in relationships.
10. A therapist survivor experiences a career threatening self-doubt centered on competency and self-esteem.

—. _____
_____
—. _____
_____
—. _____
_____

LONG-TERM GOALS

1. Manage the bereavement process that allows a healthy psychosocial adjustment and a desire to live.
2. Accept and reconcile the intense feelings of anger directed toward the decedent.
3. Forgive the decedent and any others perceived for their role in the suicidal death.
4. Increase engagement with a social network to reduce isolation.
5. Accept the mystery and unknowns of the decedent's suicide.
6. Integrate a sense of guilt where it is appropriate and allow a sense of forgiveness of self.

—. _____
_____
—. _____
_____
—. _____
_____

SHORT-TERM OBJECTIVES

1. Describe the specific grieving responses to the suicidal death. (1, 2, 3, 4, 5)

THERAPEUTIC INTERVENTIONS

1. Explore the client's problematic grieving responses as the survivor of a loved one's suicide (e.g., a preoccupation with finding the "Why?" of the suicide, exaggerated feelings of guilt, isolative behaviors because of a sense of stigma

from society, extreme social isolation because of diminished trust in the safety of relationships, or extreme rage that is repressed toward the decedent).

2. Explore the client's historical patterns of coping during times of stress and/or tragedy (e.g., emotional reactions to previous traumatic losses or coping strategies developed to deal with grief).

3. Explore the client's reaction to the loved one's suicidal death (e.g., was the death expected because of the chronic, unendurable psychological and physical pain experienced by the victim; has the death been experienced with a sense of relief because of the chronic abusive and malevolent behavior of the victim; or was the death sudden, with no warning, rendering the death a tragedy that the survivor is not equipped to grieve).

4. Explore the impact of the suicide on the client's family interaction patterns (e.g., were there preexisting dysfunctional family interaction patterns prior to the suicide or has the suicide event contributed to current depression among surviving members, created a distance among members, a distortion in communication patterns, isolation in their social network, or heightened risk for suicide in other family members).

5. Explore the nature of the client's common grief reactions

(e.g., somatic symptoms, depressive reactions, loneliness, or abandonment) and those grief reactions that are seen as specific to grieving a death by suicide (e.g., feeling embarrassed about the mode of death, concealing the mode of death from family and others, or assuming severe feelings of rejection by the decedent).

2. Identify the nature of current suicidal ideation, planning, and/or intent. (6, 7, 8)

6. Explore the client's goal of the intended suicide act (e.g., cessation of intolerable psychological pain, motivation to reunite with the lost loved one, or punishment for extreme levels of self-hate and guilt related to a perceived role in the suicidal death).

7. Explore whether any impediments to the plan exist (e.g., fear of bringing the same emotional pain he/she feels to other survivors) with the client.

8. Explore how much energy and planning has gone into the suicide intent (e.g., has a lethal means been chosen and obtained, has a date been assigned, has the client communicated the intent with anyone) with the client.

3. Identify the nature of any previous episodes of suicidal ideation, intent, and/or activity. (9)

9. Explore any previous suicide activities (e.g., ideation, gestures, or attempts) with the client and explore closely those acts when the client was accidentally, against his/her wishes, rescued from a potentially lethal suicide attempt; examine the circumstances of previous

suicide activity (e.g., significant loss, inability to cope with powerful emotions, or experiences of extreme self-hate) and how they compare to the current situation.

4. Cooperate with psychological testing designed to evaluate conditions related to suicide risk in the suicide survivor. (10)

10. Administer testing used to reveal and evaluate suicidal ideation and intent levels in the survivor of suicide (e.g., Grief Experience Questionnaire, Purpose-in-Life Test, Reasons for Living Inventory, or Beck Depression Inventory).

5. Provide information on personal experiences with high-risk *behavioral* markers for suicide in suicide survivors. (11, 12, 13)

11. Assess the client for the high-risk survivor's suicide marker of a preoccupation with finding the reason for the suicide (e.g., display of an obsessional inability to replace the search with other, less stressful, activities; mourning is put aside for the endless drive to uncover the one clue that will make the suicide understandable and, perhaps, bearable; and strives to deny or discount the suicide).

12. Assess the client for the high-risk survivor's suicide marker of distorted communications (e.g., refusal to discuss the decedent in social settings, telling family the death was due to some other mode besides suicide, and blaming others for their perceived role in the suicide).

13. Assess the client for the high-risk survivor's suicide marker of PTSD symptoms, especially if the death was sudden and unexpected and especially

violent (e.g., experience of night traumas; in children, dangerous play patterns where the suicide is acted out in fantasy; intrusive thoughts; or social isolation patterns).

6. Provide information on personal experiences with high-risk *emotional* markers for suicide in suicide survivors. (14, 15, 16, 17)

14. Assess the client for the high-risk survivor's suicide marker of guilt (e.g., feelings of inadequacy, self-hate, incompetence, unworthiness, or doubts of self as a good parent/spouse/child/friend).

15. Assess the client for the high-risk survivor's suicide marker of distorted mourning (e.g., feelings of shame, social stigma, embarrassment that disrupts the normal grieving process and may lead to feelings of isolation).

16. Assess the client for the high-risk survivor's suicide marker of depression (e.g., depth of sadness, increase in irritability, sleep disturbances, change in eating habits, anhedonia, or dysphoria).

17. Assess the client for the high-risk survivor's suicide marker of intense, excessive rage (e.g., toward the decedent may be caused by feelings of rejection and abandonment, especially note repressed anger toward the decedent; toward mental health agencies and/or professionals, and toward medical institutions and/or professionals for perceived incompetence resulting in the death of the decedent).

7. Provide information on personal experiences with high-risk *social* markers for suicide in suicide survivors. (18, 19)

8. Medical personnel, especially the primary care physician, provide relevant, current information on general health issues. (20)

9. Provide complete information on current mood, affect, and thought process in a psychiatric evaluation, taking psychotropic medication as prescribed. (21, 22)

10. Accept feedback on the assessments and the treatment plan developed from the evaluation process. (23)

18. Assess the client for the high-risk survivor's suicide marker of social isolation (e.g., avoiding friends who would be comforting and supportive).

19. Assess the client for the high-risk survivor's suicide marker of disruption of family cohesion (e.g., examine patterns of scapegoating, blaming, isolating, and distancing from family members for their perceived role in the decedent's death).

20. After obtaining appropriate confidentiality releases, contact the client's primary care physician for a medical report and evaluation, paying particular attention to recent somatic complaints, anxiety attacks, and depressive episodes and symptoms.

21. Refer the client for a psychiatric evaluation to determine the need for psychotropic medication and to validate any at-risk diagnoses; encourage him/her to take medication as prescribed.

22. Monitor the client's compliance with the prescribed medication, chart the subjective and objective behavioral changes and monitor side effects, and share observations with his/her psychiatrist.

23. Summarize and give feedback to the client and, if available and appropriate, caregivers about the high-risk survivor's suicide markers found in the evaluation process; formulate

his/her treatment plan and include the family system if the evaluations reveal severe disruption in that unit; engage caregivers in the treatment plan to provide support for the client.

11. Comply with placement in a more protective and, possibly, a more restrictive environment. (24, 25)

24. Monitor the client's suicide risk at appropriate intervals in the therapy process through interview for high-risk suicide markers and by administering standardized suicide risk assessment (e.g., Suicide Probability Scale).

25. If assessments reveal high-risk survivor's suicide markers that significantly challenge the client's coping capacity (e.g., increase in comments of self-blame, profound symptoms of depression, or extreme behaviors of isolation), place the client in a therapeutic setting that will protect him/her from suicidal impulse, decrease perturbation, decrease isolation, and monitor treatment effectiveness.

12. Affirm a plan that allows for a safe return to the community. (26, 27)

26. As an adjunct to psychotherapy engage the client in a Survivor of Suicide support group that will provide him/her with supportive relationships, help normalize the specific grieving of a survivor of suicide, and assist in verbalizing his/her repressed feelings.

27. Engage the client's family in the therapy process to mend the harm done in that system and to provide needed support for healthy psychosocial adjustment.

13. Agree to a written plan for dealing with situations when suicidal urges become strong. (28)

28. Develop a written crisis intervention plan to be implemented during times when the client experiences trigger events and feelings (e.g., shame, guilt, rage, stigma, or isolation) that includes calling a member of the Suicide Survivor support group, the therapist, or a trusted friend and discussing the impact of these emotions; have the client agree, as a verbal contract in the therapy relationship, to call someone on the list.

14. Identify current stressors and resultant symptoms that trigger the wish to die. (29, 30, 31)

29. Assist the client in making a list of his/her most prominent stressors (e.g., coming in contact with close friends of the deceased, living in the house where the suicide occurred, intrusive memories of the deceased, a sense that "the world goes on" without acknowledging his/her loss) and emotional reactions or symptoms (e.g., unbearable grief, abandonment, anger at the deceased, or stigma) produced by those stressors.

30. Assist the client in producing a complete symptom inventory that includes identifying the most disruptive symptoms (e.g., shame, guilt, or rage at the deceased), how these symptoms are currently dysfunctionally managed (e.g., social isolation, blaming others, repressing anger, or suicidal ideation), and the results of these symptoms (e.g., loss of cohesion in family and social network).

31. Assure the client of help in targeting the most serious symptoms for immediate attention, while not prematurely rescuing him/her from experiences of unbearable emotions.

15. Verbalize statements of hope that symptoms may be managed in ways other than suicide. (32, 33, 34, 35, 36)

32. Formulate an appropriate view of suicide for the client: It stems from a desire to solve a temporarily unsolvable problem; it is fueled by elements of hopelessness and helplessness; and the antidote is to acquire safe, simple coping and problem-solving skills with identified stressors and symptoms.

33. Educate the client about the phenomena of suicide, eliminating myths and stressing the facts and complexities of this human tragedy; encourage him/her to acquire a view that suicide is never caused by an isolated incident in a person's life but results from the untimely convergence of multiple factors for which the decedent had no management skills.

34. Assign the client a treatment journal to track daily stressors, the resulting symptoms, maladaptive coping patterns, and experiences with newly acquired coping strategies; assign homework targeting symptom management. Stress to the client that the goal of therapy is healthy symptom management and *not* symptom elimination.

35. Ask the client to note in his/her treatment journal a detailed plan with specific instructions on responding to and managing the perturbation associated with his/her immediate symptoms (e.g., when feeling shame remember not to judge the decedent or when feeling guilt remember the loving acts done for the decedent); these responses should be structured to assist the client during emotional upset.

36. Use role-play, modeling, and behavioral rehearsal to teach the client to implement the symptom management skills noted in his/her treatment journal.

16. Increase sharing the grieving process with others. (37, 38)

37. Provide sensitive guidance to the client so that his/her emotions do not disrupt functioning (e.g., allow the client to feel guilt; guide him/her in appropriate guilt but not to globalize this emotion and to forgive himself/herself; allow the client to feel anger at the decedent but also love, respect, and honor); remain alert not to dismiss these emotions too quickly or protect the client from these feelings but process these emotions deliberately.

38. Teach the client the value of verbalizing emotions in this and other safe, supportive settings (e.g., sharing feelings promotes empathy from others, sharing of the emotion lessens its burden, and sharing allows others to give their perspective on the subject so that the client gains further insight into his/her grieving process).

17. Verbalize a sense of confidence in the future as a survivor of suicide. (39)

39. Assist the client in integrating the identity of a suicide survivor, listing ways that his/her bereavement tasks can be safely integrated in a productive, healthy, fulfilling life (e.g., marking special anniversaries in the decedent's life with memorials).

18. Develop a suicide prevention plan that incorporates the treatment journal and all completed homework assignments. (40)

40. Educate the client about preventing relapse into suicidal behavior (e.g., rely on the treatment journal for reminders of strategies for coping with trigger events, feelings, and symptoms; maintain membership in Survivors of Suicide support network; avoid isolation; continuously respect identity as survivor of suicide; and maintain futuristic thinking).

__. _____   __. _____
    _____   _____
__. _____   __. _____
    _____   _____
__. _____   __. _____
    _____   _____

DIAGNOSTIC SUGGESTIONS:

Axis I:	296.2x	Major Depressive Disorder, Single Episode
	296.3x	Major Depressive Disorder, Recurrent
	296.xx	Bipolar I Disorder
	300.4	Dysthymic Disorder
	309.0	Adjustment Disorder with Depressed Mood
	V62.82	Bereavement
	_____	_____
	_____	_____

II. ASSAULTIVE/HOMICIDAL POPULATIONS

ASSAULTIVE/HOMICIDAL MALE

BEHAVIORAL DEFINITIONS

1. Has a history of violent behavior.
2. Demonstrates behaviors (e.g., distrust, projection, defensive anger, or persecutory delusions) correlated to a paranoid condition (e.g., paranoid schizophrenia, paranoid personality disorder, or drug induced paranoid condition).
3. Has significant anger management problems (e.g., frequent outbursts, highly intensive rage episodes, and lack of internal control capacity).
4. Has a life-long pattern of faulty problem-solving skills.
5. Has a history of substance abuse/dependency that leads to impulse control problems and violent behavior.
6. Demonstrates behaviors (e.g., projection of blame, impulsivity, disregard for rules, lack of empathy, or emotionally labile) positively correlated to violence-prone personality disorders (e.g., antisocial, borderline, narcissistic, schizoid, or histrionic).
7. Has a history of childhood pathology (e.g., fire-setting, cruelty to animals, ADHD, or attachment disorder).
8. Associates with a violence-prone peer group and shows extreme interest in violence-prone entertainment.
9. Prefers isolative leisure activities.
10. Has a history of central nervous system (CNS) trauma (e.g., closed head injury, traumatic brain injury, or seizure disorder) and presents with symptoms (e.g., dizziness, blackouts, amnesia, visual or olfactory hallucinations in the absence of a diagnosed mental illness, or severe headaches with nausea).
11. Presents with symptoms correlated to posttraumatic stress (e.g., intense need for chaos, violence, and risk-taking behaviors).

—. _____
   _____
—. _____
   _____
—. _____
   _____

LONG-TERM GOALS

1. Terminate the use of violence to meet social, psychological, and environmental needs.
2. Enhance access to emotions and a capacity for empathy toward the needs, feelings, and desires of others.
3. Develop effective, adaptive coping strategies and problem-solving skills.
4. Enhance personal resiliency, flexibility, and a capacity to manage crises and failures.
5. Develop a supportive social network and the ability to engage in intimate relationships based on mutuality.
6. Develop an honest sense of self-acceptance and the capacity for self-affirmation.

—. _____

_____

—. _____

_____

—. _____

_____

SHORT-TERM OBJECTIVES

1. Provide information on personal experiences with high-risk *behavioral* markers related to assaultive/homicidal males. (1, 2, 3, 4, 5)

THERAPEUTIC INTERVENTIONS

1. Assess the client for the high-risk assaultive/homicidal male marker of a history of violent behavior (e.g., age of onset, feeling states at the time of violence, frequency and intensity of the violence, role of drugs and/or alcohol, subsequent remorse, ability to assume responsibility for behaviors, or tendency to project blame and use denial when faced with faults).

2. Assess the client for the high-risk assaultive/homicidal male marker of predatory selection of victims (e.g., profile of victims,

specific themes in victim selection, stimulations to violence, or locations of violent behaviors).

3. Assess the client for the high-risk assaultive/homicidal male marker of isolative leisure activities (e.g., elements of paranoid or schizoid personality disorders, or activities that are focused on violence and killing).

4. Assess the client for the high-risk assaultive/homicidal male marker of job instability (e.g., feelings of loss of power when not employed or reaction to a lowered socioeconomic status because of unemployment).

5. Assess the client for the high-risk assaultive/homicidal male marker of extreme interest in lethal weapons (e.g., increased animation and/or excitability when talking about weapons).

2. Provide information on personal experiences with high-risk *emotional* markers related to assaultive/homicidal males. (6, 7, 8, 9, 10)

6. Assess the client for the high-risk assaultive/homicidal male marker of paranoid conditions (e.g., an unusually high, unrealistic level of guardedness; suspicion; or distrust of the therapist, his social network, or society at large).

7. Assess the client for the high-risk assaultive/homicidal male marker of childhood pathology (e.g., childhood attachment disorder; caregiver identity, constancy, and numbers; incidents of fire-setting; cruelty to animals; authority conflicts; stealing; lying; or history of legal involvement).

8. Assess the client for the high-risk assaultive/homicidal male marker of posttraumatic stress disorder (e.g., addiction to chaos and violence; level of physiological excitement when discussing violent experiences; and correlation of addiction to unresolved issues of previous trauma).

9. Assess the client for the high-risk assaultive/homicidal male marker of violence-prone personality disorders (e.g., behavioral correlates to borderline, antisocial, schizoid, histrionic, or narcissistic conditions).

10. Assess the client for the high-risk assaultive/homicidal male marker of a history of CNS trauma (e.g., incidents of brain trauma, closed head injury, traumatic brain injury; or symptoms of blackouts, recurrent headaches, seizures, loss of consciousness, or olfactory hallucinations).

3. Provide information on personal experiences with high-risk *social* markers related to assaultive/homicidal males. (11, 12)

11. Assess the client for the high-risk assaultive/homicidal male marker of a history of violence as a mode of communication in the family of origin (e.g., linkage to emotional constriction, use of rage to express *all* emotions, and lack of insight into the unacceptable nature of his violence).

12. Assess the client for the high-risk assaultive/homicidal male marker of current involvement with a violence-prone peer group (e.g., social cohesion

needs, or violence and rage validation needs).

4. Cooperate with psychological testing designed to evaluate conditions related to violent behavior and faulty problem-solving ability. (13, 14)

13. Administer tests most commonly used to reveal and evaluate violent tendencies and faulty problem-solving capacity (e.g., WAIS-3, MMPI, Millon Clinical Multiaxial Inventory, or The Means-Ends Problem-Solving Procedure).

14. Examine sources of violence for the mentally retarded/ developmentally disabled population (e.g., evaluate those with significantly below average intelligence with professional caution and respect since they are not predatory as a rule; frustration in areas of decision making, working through a crisis, solving relationship dilemmas, or accomplishing tasks that are required in their activities of daily living).

5. Provide complete information on current mood, affect, and thought process in a psychiatric evaluation, taking psychotropic medications as prescribed. (15, 16)

15. Refer the client for a psychiatric evaluation to determine his need for psychotropic medication and to validate any at-risk diagnoses (e.g., acutely psychotic paranoid schizophrenia with an active delusional or hallucinatory system; note whether a specifically identified individual is incorporated into his delusional system).

16. Monitor the client's compliance with the psychotropic medication prescription; chart his subjective changes and objective behavioral changes and monitor medication side effects.

6. Medical personnel provide relevant, current information pertaining to the client's general health. (17)

7. Identify sources of cognitive rigidity and poor problem-solving strategies. (18, 19)

8. Identify the emotion that motivates assaultive/homicidal behavior. (20, 21, 22, 23)

17. After obtaining appropriate confidentiality and privacy releases, contact the client's medical provider for a report on his current health issues (e.g., history of CNS trauma, closed head injuries, or seizure disorder).

18. Explore the client's psychological conditions that have a high correlation to impaired problem-solving capacity (e.g., delayed adolescent autonomy, over-protective childhood, an emotionally constricted family environment, or a verbally demeaning family environment).

19. Examine the client for psychiatric states that have a high correlation to impaired problem-solving capacity (e.g., depressive disorders, acute stress disorder, posttraumatic stress disorder, and obsessive-compulsive personality disorder).

20. Explore the emotion that fuels the paranoid client's assaultive/homicide intent (e.g., unrealistic elements of fear, guardedness, suspicion, and distrust that motivate assaultive behaviors for the purpose of self-protection).

21. Examine the client with post-traumatic stress conditions for the emotion that fuels his assaultive/homicide intent (e.g., the need for chaos, thrill-seeking, confrontation, violence, and high risk-taking behaviors that fulfill his addiction to action and excitement).

22. Examine the client with a life-long pattern of faulty problem-solving skills and an inability to delay gratification for the emotion that fuels his assaultive/homicide intent (e.g., history of using temper tantrums, intimidation, and rage to coerce immediate compliance with his wishes).

23. Examine the client with a history of childhood pathology and a displayed lack of empathy for the rights of others for the emotion that fuels the assaultive/homicide intent (e.g., his sense of privilege to vent his rage with no regard to social constraints or consequences).

9. Comply with placement in a more protective and, possibly, restrictive environment. (24, 25)

24. If at any time during the treatment process the client displays an exacerbation of acute delusional and/or hallucinatory episodes produced by paranoid schizophrenia, he should be placed, either voluntarily or involuntarily, in a structured therapeutic setting that will protect him from the assaultive/homicide impulse.

25. If the client has identified a specific individual incorporated into his delusional system, consult with the local Recipient's Rights officer to determine whether there is a duty to warn the identified person.

10. Affirm a discharge plan that allows for a safe return to the community. (26)

26. Review the inpatient team's treatment plan with the client that includes referral to case management services for the severely mentally ill (e.g., paranoid schizophrenic),

individual psychotherapy appointments, an activities of daily living program, and a medication regimen.

11. Accept feedback gathered from all sources and the treatment plan developed from the evaluation process. (27)

27. Summarize and give feedback to the client about high-risk markers found in the evaluation process; outline the treatment plan for him and incorporate his participation in this effort.

12. Identify current stressors and resultant symptoms that trigger the need to engage in assaultive/homicidal behaviors. (28, 29)

28. Assist the client in listing his most prominent stressors (e.g., intense feelings that people are plotting against him, intense need for excitement and/or risk-taking behaviors, intense need to have immediate gratification and have things go his way, and inability to accept society's constraints on his sense of privilege).

29. Explore emotional reactions or symptoms produced by those stressors (e.g., unbearable fears, agitation and feelings| of frenzy, frustration and anger, and controlled rage) with the client and how these symptoms are currently dysfunctionally managed (e.g., substance abuse, self-mutilation, death-defying risk-taking activities, violent acting out toward property, or violent assaults toward people).

13. Implement coping and management skills for the identified stressors and symptoms, resulting in termination of violence toward others. (30, 31, 32, 33)

30. Establish a therapeutic alliance with the client that includes providing empathy within the context of healthy boundaries, teaching problem-solving skills, helping him to access and regulate emotions, assisting in the development of pain

tolerance, and teaching interpersonal skills.

31. Teach the client problem-solving skills (e.g., define the problem completely, explore alternative solutions, list positives and negatives of each solution, select and implement a plan of action, and evaluate and adjust skills as necessary) and anger management strategies (e.g., mediational or self-control techniques).

32. Formulate an appropriate view of the function of his assaultive/homicidal intent with the client: It stems from his need to meet significant social, psychological, environmental needs; it is fueled by either feelings of fear, addictive excitement, immediate gratification, or unrelenting rage; and the antidote to this is to develop healthy coping strategies for these seemingly overwhelming feelings.

33. Assign the client a treatment journal to track daily stressors (e.g., feeling that someone is going to hurt him, craving for excitement, forced to delay gratification, or provocation), the resulting symptoms (e.g., fear, agitation, frustration, or rage), maladaptive coping patterns (e.g., assaultive behavior), and experiences with newly acquired problem-solving alternatives (e.g., anger management or problem-solving skills).

14. Identify strategies to develop personal resiliency and

34. Identify strategies for the client with a paranoid condition, which

flexibility in problem solving. (34, 35, 36, 37)

will be applied to his problem solving efforts (e.g., for the paranoid schizophrenic, monitor medication and case management program; for the paranoid personality, enhance a sense of trust; for the drug induced paranoid psychotic, engage in substance abuse treatment).

35. Identify strategies for the client with a posttraumatic stress condition, which will be applied to his problem-solving efforts (e.g., educate him on the nature of his condition and its linkage to thrill-seeking and violent behaviors and teach him safer and more socially accepted methods of meeting his need for excitement).

36. Identify strategies for the client who uses violence to achieve immediate gratification, which will be applied to his problem-solving efforts (e.g., in the therapy relationship, teach him mutuality, reciprocity, compromise, and respect and encourage him to engage in supportive social networks and track this experience in his treatment journal).

37. Identify strategies for the client with a deficit in emotional regulation, which will be applied to his problem-solving efforts (e.g., provide a consistent therapeutic atmosphere of empathic responses to his emotional expressions; engage him in sessions where mutual respect for emotional expression is the foundation; and inform him of the consequences of violence toward the therapist).

15. Agree to a crisis response plan for dealing with situations when the risk of assaultive behavior is strong. (38, 39)

38. Develop a crisis intervention plan to be implemented by the client during trigger events (e.g., feelings of paranoia, agitation for excitement, frustration with unmet needs, or impulse to hurt someone) and the resultant feelings (e.g., fear, extreme anxiety, frustration, or rage) that includes alternatives of contacting the therapist or a local mental health help line to discuss these emotions and how to manage them.

39. Consult with a local Recipient's Rights agency to determine the need to notify local law enforcement agencies and/or protective social service agencies about the client's assaultive/homicidal intent; notify him of this obligation and the duty to warn and document all actions taken.

16. Write an individual and personal violence prevention plan that incorporates the treatment journal's homework assignments. (40)

40. Assist the client in writing a personal prevention plan that lists actions he will take to avoid the risk of violent behavior (e.g., remain aware of lessons from the treatment journal and homework assignments; if appropriate, remain on medication; and remain alert to and respectful of the fueling emotions that contribute to his violent acting out).

__. _____

_____

__. _____

_____

__. _____

_____

__. _____

_____

__. _____

_____

__. _____

_____

DIAGNOSTIC SUGGESTIONS:

Axis I:

296.xx	Major Depressive Disorder
300.02	Generalized Anxiety Disorder
295.30	Schizophrenia, Paranoid Type
295.xx	Schizophrenia
305.00	Alcohol Abuse
304.80	Polysubstance Dependence
300.4	Dysthymic Disorder
312.34	Intermittent Explosive Disorder
297.1	Delusional Disorder
300.3	Obsessive-Compulsive Disorder
309.81	Posttraumatic Stress Disorder

_____ _____

_____ _____

Axis II:

301.81	Narcissistic Personality Disorder
301.83	Borderline Personality Disorder
301.7	Antisocial Personality Disorder
301.6	Dependent Personality Disorder

_____ _____

_____ _____

HOMICIDAL/SUICIDAL MALE

BEHAVIORAL DEFINITIONS

1. Demonstrates an impulse to homicide/suicide because of a disruption (e.g., divorce, rejection, or abandonment) of an intimate relationship in which he uses coercive means (e.g., physical violence, or emotional intimidation) to control the partner.
2. Experiences a disruption in his intimate relationship that challenges his need to control, his possessiveness, and narcissism.
3. Intends homicide of the love object as the primary act, and the suicide is designed to avoid legal consequences and incarceration or to alleviate emotionally unbearable reactions of remorse.
4. Demonstrates behaviors correlated to a paranoid condition (e.g., paranoid schizophrenia, paranoid personality disorder, and substance induced psychosis with paranoid features).
5. Demonstrates lifetime patterns of insecurity, antisocial traits, impulse control problems, possessiveness in relationships, use of violence for need gratification, limited access to emotions, and an overall sense of inadequacy.
6. Has a history of childhood pathology (e.g., fire-setting, cruelty to people or animals, authority conflicts, assault, lying, bedwetting, stealing, attachment pathology, and, in some instances, ADHD).
7. Has a history of family violence (e.g., violence used as a mode of communication, child physical abuse, or child verbal abuse).
8. Has a history of job instability (e.g., moves from job to job or fired from jobs because of an inability to respond to workplace regulations).
9. Involved currently in a violence-prone peer group.
10. Displays extreme interest in skill with and possession of weapons.
11. Involved in solitary leisure activities (e.g., usually described as a loner).
12. Has a history of polysubstance dependence/abuse.
13. Demonstrates predatory behaviors (e.g., usually avoids mutual relationships and seeks out partners who display potential for submissiveness) and is enraged if the partner tries to leave him.

—. _____
_____
—. _____
_____
—. _____
_____

LONG-TERM GOALS

1. Resolve impulse for homicide and suicide.
2. Enhance an access to emotions and a capacity for empathy toward others needs, feelings, and desires.
3. Develop effective, adaptive coping strategies and problem-solving skills.
4. Enhance personal resiliency, flexibility, and a capacity to manage crisis and failures.
5. Develop a supportive social network and the ability to engage in intimate relationships based on mutuality.
6. Develop an honest sense of self-acceptance and a capacity for self-affirmation.

—. _____
_____
—. _____
_____
—. _____
_____

SHORT-TERM OBJECTIVES	THERAPEUTIC INTERVENTIONS
1. Provide information on personal experiences with high-risk *behavioral* markers related to homicide/suicide ideators. (1, 2, 3, 4, 5)	1. Assess the client for the high-risk homicide/suicide male marker of a history of violence (e.g., evaluate the age of onset of this behavior, feeling states at the time of violence, frequency and intensity of violence, the role of drugs and/or alcohol,

stimulating events, or subsequent remorse).

2. Assess the client for the high-
risk homicide/suicide male
marker of substance abuse (e.g.,
polysubstance abuse patterns or
subjective reaction to alcohol
and/or drugs).

3. Assess the client for the high-
risk homicide/suicide male
marker of isolative leisure
activities (e.g., elements of the
paranoid personality disorder or
activities that are focused on
violence and killing).

4. Assess the client for the high-
risk homicide/suicide male
marker of job instability (e.g.,
feelings of loss of power when
not employed or lowered
socioeconomic status because
of unemployment).

5. Assess the client for the high-
risk homicide/suicide male
marker of an extreme interest in
possession of and skill with
weapons (e.g., increased
animation and/or excitability
when talking about weapons).

2. Provide information on
personal experiences with
high-risk *emotional* markers
related to homicide/suicide
ideators. (6, 7, 8, 9)

6. Assess the client for the high-
risk homicide/suicide male
marker of paranoid conditions
(e.g., paranoid schizophrenic
condition, paranoid personality
disorder, or drug-induced
paranoia).

7. Assess the client for the high-
risk homicide/suicide male
marker of attachment pathology
(e.g., childhood attachment
history, who raised the client,
how many caregivers the client

had, whether caregivers left and never returned).

8. Assess the client for the high-risk homicide/suicide male marker of childhood pathology (e.g., fire-setting, cruelty to people or animals, authority conflicts, stealing, lying, bed-wetting, assault, history of ADHD; or history of conduct disorder and current antisocial traits).

9. Assess the client for the high-risk homicide/suicide male marker of a history of central nervous system trauma (e.g., incidents of brain trauma, closed head injury, traumatic brain injury or symptoms of black-outs, recurrent headaches, seizures, loss of consciousness, or olfactory hallucinations).

3. Provide information on personal experiences with high-risk *social* markers related to homicide/suicide ideators. (10, 11, 12)

10. Assess the client for the high-risk homicide/suicide male marker of a history of violence as a mode of communication in the family of origin (e.g., patterns of child physical abuse or reported behaviors correlated to PTSD).

11. Assess the client for the high-risk homicide/suicide male marker of current involvement with a violence-prone peer group.

12. Assess the client for the high-risk homicide/suicide male marker of predatory patterns in relationships (e.g., no capacity for bonding or mutuality in a relationship; needs to be in control and will choose partners

that fulfill that requirement; no capacity for ownership or responsibility for behavior; or consistently projects blame and uses denial when faced with faults).

4. Cooperate with psychological testing designed to evaluate conditions related to violent behavior and faulty problem-solving ability. (13)

13. Administer tests most commonly used to reveal and evaluate violent tendencies, co-occurring suicide intent, and faulty problem-solving capacity (e.g., MMPI, Millon Clinical Multiaxial Inventory, Reasons for Living Inventory, or The Means-Ends Problem-Solving Procedure).

5. Provide complete information on current mood, affect, and thought process in a psychiatric evaluation, take psychotropic medications as prescribed. (14, 15)

14. Refer the client for a psychiatric evaluation to determine his need for psychotropic medication and to validate any at-risk diagnoses (e.g., acutely psychotic paranoid schizophrenia with an active delusional, hallucinatory system; be alert to incorporation of a specifically identified individual into the client's delusional system).

15. Monitor the client's compliance with the psychotropic medication prescription; chart his subjective and objective behavioral changes and monitor the side effects.

6. Identify the nature and specifics of previous experiences with suicide ideation and/or activities. (16)

16. Explore the client's history of suicide activity (e.g., activities where there was a clear intent to die but the activity resulted in a nonfatal injury because of an accidental rescue that was against the perpetrator's wishes; a lifetime pattern of suicide ideation; a history of suicide gesturing, with no clear intent to

7. Medical personnel provide relevant, current information on the client's general health. (17)

8. Identify the sources of cognitive rigidity and poor problem-solving strategies. (18, 19)

9. Identify the nature and specifics of the current impulse to homicide. (20)

10. Accept feedback gathered from all sources and the treatment plan developed from the evaluation process. (21)

die, that was used as a control strategy in relationships).

17. After obtaining appropriate confidentiality and privacy releases, contact the client's medical provider for a report on current health issues (e.g., history of head trauma, closed head injuries, seizure disorder).

18. Explore the client's psychological/emotional conditions that appear to have a high correlation to impaired problem-solving capacity (e.g., delayed adolescent autonomy, overprotected childhood, an emotionally constricted family environment, or a verbally demeaning family environment).

19. Examine the client for psychiatric states that appear to have a high correlation to impaired problem-solving capacity (e.g., depressive disorders, acute stress disorder, posttraumatic stress disorder, and obsessive-compulsive personality disorder).

20. Explore the client's emotions that fuel the homicide/suicide intent (e.g., damage to narcissistic needs, an if-I-can't-have-her-no-one-will attitude of pathological possessiveness, or elements of paranoia).

21. Summarize and give feedback to the client on high-risk markers found in the evaluation process; outline the treatment plan for him and incorporate his participation in this effort.

11. Comply with placement in a more protective and, possibly, restrictive environment. (22, 23)

22. If at any time during the treatment process the client displays an exacerbation of acute delusional and/or hallucinatory episodes produced by paranoid schizophrenia, he should be placed, either voluntarily or involuntarily, in a structured therapeutic setting that will protect him from the homicide/suicide impulse and monitor medical management.

23. If the client has identified a specific individual incorporated into his delusional system, consult with the local Recipient's Rights office will determine whether there exists a duty to warn that identified person.

12. Affirm a discharge plan that allows a safe return to the community. (24)

24. Review the inpatient team's treatment plan with the client that includes referral to case management services for the severely mentally ill, individual psychotherapy appointments, an activities of daily living program, and a medication program.

13. Agree to a crisis response plan for dealing with situations when the risk for homicide/suicide ideation and/or intent is strong. (25, 26)

25. Develop a crisis intervention plan to be implemented by the client during trigger events (e.g., abandonment issues or disruption of pathological control and possessiveness behaviors) and the resultant feelings (e.g., rage, revenge, panic, need for ultimate control, or homicidal urges) that includes alternatives of contacting the therapist or a local help line to discuss emotions and how to manage them.

26. Consult with a local Recipient Rights agency to determine the need to notify local law enforcement agencies and/or protective social service agencies about the client's homicide/suicide intent; notify him of this obligation and the duty to warn and document all actions taken.

14. Identify own biological, social, and psychological traits and vulnerabilities that hinder adaptive problem-solving strategies and contribute to the risk of the homicide/suicide intent. (27, 28)

27. Explore the client's personal vulnerabilities and traits that contribute to problem-solving deficiencies and the homicide/ suicide crisis (e.g., faulty emotional regulation, poor access to emotions, lack of empathy to the needs of others, cognitive rigidity, or feelings of insecurity and inadequacy).

28. Help the client to acknowledge the existence of his traits that contribute to the homicide/ suicide crisis, understand their source, and track their influence on problem-solving and resultant homicidal/suicidal ideation.

15. Identify current stressors and resultant symptoms that trigger the wish to murder and die by suicide. (29, 30)

29. Assist the client in listing his most prominent stressors (e.g., abandoned in a relationship in which he used physical/ emotional abuse to control, fired from a job, charged with a crime, held accountable for dysfunctional behaviors, and incidents of narcissistic injury).

30. Explore emotional reactions or symptoms produced by those stressors (e.g., uncontrollable rage, revenge, denial, or projection of blame) and how those symptoms are currently dys-

16. Identify coping and management skills for stressors and symptoms that can be done continuously in ways other than violence toward others and self. (31, 32, 33, 34)

functionally managed (e.g., homicide/suicide ideation, substance abuse, self-mutilation, or violent assault toward others).

31. Establish a therapeutic alliance with the client that includes providing empathy within the context of healthy boundaries, teaching problem-solving skills, helping the client to access and regulate emotions, assisting in the development of pain tolerance, and teaching interpersonal skills.

32. Teach the client problem-solving skills (e.g., define the problem completely, explore alternative solutions, list the positives and negatives of each solution, select and implement a plan of action, and evaluate the outcome and adjust skills as necessary).

33. Formulate an appropriate view of the function of his homicide/suicide intent with the client: It stems from his need to solve a seemingly unsolvable problem; it is fueled by hopelessness, unregulated rage, and helplessness; and the antidote to this risk is to develop healthy coping strategies for these seemingly unsolvable stressors and symptoms.

34. Assign the client a treatment journal to track his daily stressors, the resultant symptoms, maladaptive coping patterns (e.g., substance abuse or homicide/suicide ideation), and experiences with newly acquired problem-solving alternatives (e.g., using anger management techniques or expressing

difficult emotions to the empathic therapist); assign homework targeting symptom management.

17. Identify strategies to develop personal resiliency and flexibility in problem solving. (35, 36, 37)

35. Ask the client to write an auto-biography focusing on times of crisis; have him focus on behaviors he produced during those times that may have calmed or resolved the problem.

36. Identify strategies, formed partly from the autobiographical recall, which may be applied to the problem-solving effort for the current crisis; use this problem-solving approach to address areas of coping where he is deficient and will prevent feelings of rage and hopeless-ness from escalating into a homicide/suicide tragedy.

37. Encourage the client to give reports from the treatment journal and homework assign-ments of recent incidents on improved problem solving (e.g., a sense of relief felt when owning responsibility for problematic behavior; a sense of pride felt when exercising an anger management tactic; or refusing substance abuse when in emotional turmoil).

18. Identify strategies to enhance access to emotions and a capacity for empathy. (38)

38. Provide a consistent atmosphere of an empathic response to the client's emotional expression; engage him in sessions where mutual respect for emotional expression and understanding is the foundation.

19. Identify strategies to develop a positive, nurturing social

39. Encourage the client to engage in supportive social networks

network and the ability to engage in relationships based on mutual respect. (39)

and to track this experience in his treatment journal; along with the issue of mutuality, stress the client's need for using active listening skills and consider the use of role-play and/or behavioral rehearsal to resolve this social deficit.

20. Develop a violence prevention plan that incorporates the treatment journal's homework assignments. (40)

40. Assist the client in writing a personal prevention plan that lists actions he will take to avoid the risk of homicide/ suicide intent (e.g., remain aware of lessons from the treatment journal, homework assignments, and autobiography on appropriate problem-solving; continue to define self in a social context; and if appropriate, remain on medication).

__. _____   __. _____
     _____   _____
__. _____   __. _____
     _____   _____
__. _____   __. _____
     _____   _____

DIAGNOSTIC SUGGESTIONS:

Axis I:

296.24	Major Depressive Disorder, Single Episode, Severe with Psychotic Features
296.xx	Major Depressive Disorder
300.4	Dysthymic Disorder
295.xx	Schizophrenia
295.30	Schizophrenia, Paranoid Type
297.1	Delusional Disorder
312.34	Intermittent Explosive Disorder
305.00	Alcohol Abuse
304.80	Polysubstance Dependence

300.3	Obsessive-Compulsive Disorder
309.81	Posttraumatic Stress Disorder
300.02	Generalized Anxiety Disorder
321.30	Impulse-Control Disorder

———— ————————————————————

———— ————————————————————

Axis II:

301.7	Antisocial Personality Disorder
301.6	Dependent Personality Disorder
301.81	Narcissistic Personality Disorder
301.83	Borderline Personality Disorder

———— ————————————————————

———— ————————————————————

Appendix A

BIBLIOTHERAPY SUGGESTIONS

Ackerman, R. (1990). *Perfect Daughters*. New York: Simon & Schuster.

Ackerman, R. (1993). *Silent Sons*. New York: Simon & Schuster.

Alberti, R., and Emmons, M. (2001). *Your Perfect Right: Assertiveness and Equality in Your Life and Relationships*. San Luis Obispo, CA: Impact Publishers.

Benson, H. (1975). *The Relaxation Response*. New York: William Morrow & Company.

Black, C. (1982). *It Will Never Happen to Me*. Denver: MAC Printing and Publishing.

Black, J., and Enns, G. (1998). *Better Boundaries: Owning and Treasuring Your Life*. Oakland, CA: New Harbinger Publications.

Bolton, I. (1983). *My Son . . . My Son . . . A Guide to Healing After Death, Loss, or Suicide*. Atlanta, GA: Bolton Press.

Bower, S., and Bower, G. (1991). *Asserting Yourself: A Practical Guide for Positive Change*. Cambridge, MA: Perseus Publishing.

Branden, N. (1994). *The Six Pillars of Self-Esteem*. New York: Bantam Books.

Burns, D. (1980). *Feeling Good: The New Mood Therapy*. New York: Signet.

Burns, D. (1989). *The Feeling Good Handbook*. New York: Blume.

Burns, D. (1993). *Ten Days to Self-Esteem!* New York: William Morrow & Company.

Butler, P. (1991). *Talking to Yourself: Learning the Language of Self-Affirmation*. New York: Perigee.

Carlson, T. (1995). *Suicide Survivors Handbook: A Guide for the Bereaved and Those Who Wish to Help Them*. Duluth, MN: Benline Press.

Chance, S. (1992). *Stronger Than Death*. New York: W.W. Norton & Company.

Colgrove, M. (1991). *How to Survive the Loss of a Love*. Los Angeles: Prelude Press.

Cudney, M., and Handy, R. (1993). *Self-Defeating Behaviors*. San Francisco: HarperSanFrancisco.

Davis, M., Eshelman, E., and McKay, M. (1988). *The Relaxation and Stress Reduction Workbook*. Oakland, CA: New Harbinger Publications.

Drews, T. R. (1980). *Getting Them Sober: A Guide for Those Living with Alcoholism*. South Plainfield, NJ: Bridge Publishing.

Eichberg, R. (1991). *Coming Out: An Act of Love*. New York: Penguin.

Flannery, R. (1995). *Post-Traumatic Stress Disorder: The Victim's Guide to Healing and Recovery*. New York: Crossroad Publishing.

Frankl, V. (1959). *Man's Search for Meaning*. New York: Simon & Schuster.

Geisel, T. (1990). *Oh, The Places You'll Go*. New York: Random House.

Gil, E. (1984). *Outgrowing the Pain: A Book for and About Adults Abused as Children*. New York: Dell Publishing.

Gorski, T. (1989/1992). *The Staying Sober Workbook*. Independence, MO: Herald House Publishing.

Gorski, T., and Miller, M. (1986). *Staying Sober: A Guide to Relapse Prevention*. Independence, MO: Herald House Publishing.

Hallinan, P. K. (1976). *One Day at a Time*. Minneapolis, MN: CompCare.

Hazelden Staff. (1991). *Each Day a New Beginning*. Center City, MN: Hazelden Publishing.

Heckler, R. A. (1994). *Waking Up Alive: The Descent, the Suicide Attempt, and the Return to Life*. New York: G.P. Putnam's Sons of the Putnam Berkley Group.

Helmstetter, S. (1986). *What to Say When You Talk to Yourself*. New York: Fine Communications.

Hutschnecker, A. (1951). *The Will to Live*. New York: Cornerstone Library.

Jamison, K. R. (1995). *An Unquiet Mind: A Memoir of Moods and Madness*. New York: Alfred A. Knopf.

Johnson, V. (1980). *I'll Quit Tomorrow*. New York: Harper & Row.

Katherine, A. (1993). *Boundaries: Where You End and I Begin*. New York: Fireside Books.

Katz, J. (1996). *The Invention of Heterosexuality*. New York: Plume.

Kindlon, D., and Thompson, W. (1992). *Raising Cain*. Royal Oak, MI: Self-Esteem Workshop.

Knauth, P. (1977). *A Season in Hell*. New York: Pocket Books.

Kushner, H. (1981). *When Bad Things Happen to Good People*. New York: Schocken Books.

Leith, L. (1998). *Exercising Your Way to Better Mental Health*. Morgantown, WV: Fitness Information Technology.

Lewis, C. S. (1961). *A Grief Observed*. New York: Seabury Press.

McKay, M., and Fanning, P. (1987). *Self-Esteem*. Oakland, CA: New Harbinger Publications.

McKay, M., Rogers, P., and McKay, J. (1989). *When Anger Hurts*. Oakland, CA: New Harbinger Publications.

Marcus, E. (1993). *Is It a Choice? Answers to 300 of the Most Frequently Asked Questions About Gays and Lesbians*. San Francisco: HarperSanFrancisco.

Matsakis, A. (1992). *I Can't Get Over It: A Handbook for Trauma Survivors*. Oakland, CA: New Harbinger Publications.

Mellonie, B., and Ingpen, R. (1983). *Lifetimes*. New York: Bantam Books.

Miller, A. (1984). *For Your Own Good*. New York: Farrar, Straus and Giroux.

Peurito, R. (1997). *Overcoming Anxiety*. New York: Henry Holt and Company.

Pipher, M. (1993). *Reviving Ophelia*. New York: Henry Holt and Company.

Pollack, W. (1998). *Real Boys*. New York: Henry Holt and Company.

Powell, J. (1969). *Why I'm Afraid to Tell You Who I Am*. Allen, TX: Argus Communications.

Quinnett, P. G. (1987). *Suicide: The Forever Decision*. New York: Continuum.

Quinnett, P. G. (1992). *Suicide: Intervention and Therapy: Undoing the Forever Decision*. Spokane, WA: Classic Publishing.

Rando, T. (1991). *How to Go on Living When Someone You Love Dies*. New York: Bantam Books.

Rosellini, G., and Worden, M. (1986). *Of Course You're Angry*. San Francisco: HarperSanFrancisco.

Ross, J. (1994). *Triumph Over Fear*. New York: Bantam Books.

Rubin, T. I. (1969). *The Angry Book*. New York: Macmillan.

Schiff, N. (1977). *The Bereaved Parent*. New York: Crown Publication.

Seligman, M. (1990). *Learned Optimism: The Skill to Conquer Life's Obstacles, Large and Small*. New York: Pocket Books.

Shapiro, L. (1993). *Building Blocks to Self-Esteem*. King of Prussia, PA: Center for Applied Psychology.

Signorile, M. (1996). *Outing Yourself: How to Come Out as Lesbian or Gay to Your Family, Friends, and Coworkers*. New York: Fireside Books.

Silber, S. (1981). *The Male*. New York: C. Scribner's Sons.

Simon, S., and Simon, S. (1990). *Forgiving: How to Make Peace with Your Past and Get on with Your Life*. New York: Warner Books.

Smedes, L. (1982). *How Can It Be All Right When Everything Is All Wrong*. San Francisco: HarperSanFrancisco.

Smedes, L. (1991). *Forgive and Forget: Healing the Hurts We Don't Deserve*. San Francisco: HarperSanFrancisco.

Smolin, A., and Guinan, J. (1993). *Healing After the Suicide of a Loved One*. New York: Simon & Schuster.

Styron, W. (1990). *Darkness Visible*. New York: Random House.

Tavris, C. (1989). *Anger: The Misunderstood Emotion*. New York: Touchstone Books.

Thompson, M. (1999). *Raising Cain*. New York: Guilford Press.

Torrey, M. D., and Fuller, E. (1988). *Surviving Schizophrenia: A Family Manual*. New York: Harper & Row.

Underland-Rosow, V. (1995). *Shame: Spiritual Suicide—We Have Faced the Shame and in Facing the Shame We Have Set Ourselves Free*. Waterford Publishing.

Weisinger, H. (1985). *Dr. Weisinger's Anger Work Out Book*. New York: Quill.

Weisman, A. D. (1984). *The Coping Capacity: On the Nature of Being Mortal*. New York: Human Sciences Press.

Westberg, G. (1962). *Good Grief*. Philadelphia: Augsburg Fortress Press.

Whitfield, C. (1987). *Healing the Child Within*. Deerfield Beach, FL: Health Communications.

Williams, R., and Williams, V. (1993). *Anger Kills*. New York: Time Books.

Wolterstorff, N. (1987). *Lament for a Son*. Grand Rapids, MI: Eerdmans.

Zonnebelt-Smeenge, S., and DeVries, R. (1998). *Getting to the Other Side of Grief: Overcoming the Loss of a Spouse*. Grand Rapids, MI: Baker.

Appendix B

PROFESSIONAL BIBLIOGRAPHY

SUICIDAL POPULATIONS

Adolescent—Caucasian Female

Rich, A. R., (1992). Gender Differences in the Psycho-Social Correlates of Suicide Ideation Among Adolescents. *Suicide and Life Threatening Behavior, 23,* 46–54.

Robbins, D. R., and Alessi, N. E. (1985). Depressive Symptoms and Suicidal Behavior in Adolescents. *American Journal of Psychiatry, 142,* 588–592.

Topol, P. (1982). Perceived Peer and Family Relationships, Hopelessness, and Locus of Control as Factors in Adolescent Suicide Attempts. *Suicide and Life Threatening Behavior, 12,* 141–150.

Adolescent—Caucasian Male

Brent, D. A. (1993). Psychiatric Risk Factors for Adolescent Suicide: A Case Controlled Study. *Journal of the American Academy of Child and Adolescent Psychiatry, 32,* 521–529.

Cole, D. A. (1989). Psychopathology of Adolescent Suicide: Hopelessness, Coping Beliefs, and Depression. *Journal of Abnormal Psychology, 98,* 248–255.

Fremouw, W. (1993). Adolescent Suicide Risk: Psychological, Problem-S, and Environmental Factors. *Suicide and Life Threatening Behavior, 22,* 364–373.

Adult—Caucasian Female

Jacobs, D. G. (1999). *Guide to Suicide Assessment and Intervention.* San Francisco: Jossey-Bass.

Linehan, M. M., Camper, P., Chiles, J. A., Strosahl, K., and Shearin, E. (1987). Interpersonal Problem-Solving and Parasuicide. *Cognitive Therapy and Research, 11,* 1–12.

MacLeod, A. K., Williams, J. M. G., and Linehan, M. M. (1992). New Developments in the Understanding and Treatment of Suicidal Behavior. *Behavioral Psychotherapy, 20,* 193–218.

Maris, S. (1981). *Pathways to Suicide: A Survey of Self-Destructive Behaviors.* Baltimore: Johns Hopkins University Press.

Adult—Caucasian Male

Rudd, M. D., Joiner, T. E., and Rajav, M. H. (1995). Help Negation After Acute Suicidal Crisis. *Journal of Consulting Clinical Psychology, 63,* 499–503.

Rutz, W. (1995). Prevention of Male Suicide: Lessons from the Gotland Study. *Lancet, 345* (8948), 524.

Wise, M. L. (1989). Adult Self-Injury as a Survival Response in Victim-Survivors of Childhood Abuse. *Journal of Chemical Dependency Treatment, 3,* 185–201.

Adult—Native American Male

American Indian/Alaska Native Suicide Task Force. (1996). *American Indian/Alaska Native Suicide Task Force Report.* Alexandria, VA: Council on Social Work Education.

Berlin, I. N. (1987). Suicide Among American Indian Adolescents: An Overview. *Suicide and Life Threatening Behavior. 17,* 218–232.

Duclos, C. W., and Manson, S. M. (Eds.). (1994). *Calling from the Rim: Suicidal Behavior Among American Indian and Alaska Native Adolescents* (Vol. 4). Boulder, CO: University of Colorado Press.

May, P. A. (1987). Suicide and Self-Destruction Among American Indian Youths. *American Indian and Alaska Native Mental Health Research, 1*(1), 52–69.

African American Male

Davis, R. A. (1979). Suicide Among Blacks: Trends and Perspectives. *Phylon, 43,* 223–229.

Early, K. E. (1992). *Religion and Suicide in the African-American Community.* Westport, CT: Greenwood Press.

Gibbs, J. T. (1997). African-American Suicide: A Cultural Paradox. Suicide and Life Threatening Behavior, 27, 68–79.

Asian American Male

Bettes, B. A., and Walker, E. (1986). Symptoms Associated with Suicidal Behavior in Childhood and Adolescence. *Journal of Abnormal Child Psychology, 14,* 591–604.

Marks, P. A., and Haller, D. L. (1977). Now I Lay Me Down for Keeps: A Study of Adolescent Suicide Attempts. *Journal of Clinical Psychology, 33,* 390–400.

Pfeffer, C. R. (1986). *The Suicidal Child.* New York: Guilford Press.

Porcidano, M., and Heller, K. (1983). Measures of Perceived Social Support from Friends and Family: Three Validation Studies. *American Journal of Community Psychology, 11,* 1–24.

Bipolar

Angst, J., Angst, F., and Stassen, H. H. (1999). Suicide Risk in Patients with Major Depressive Disorder. *Journal of Clinical Psychiatry, 60,* 57–62.
Palmer, A. G. (1995). CBT in a Group Format for Bipolar Affective Disorder. *Behavioral and Cognitive Psychotherapy, 23,* 153–168.
Winther, G. (1994). Psychotherapy with Manic-Depressives: Problems in Interaction between Patient and Therapist. *Group Analysis, 27,* 467–474.
Yalom, I. D. (1985). *The Theory and Practice of Group Psychotherapy* (3rd ed.). New York: Basic Books.

Borderline Personality Disorder

Adler, G., and Buie, D. (1979). Aloneness and Borderline Psychopathology: The Possible Relevance of Child Development Issues. *International Journal of Psychopathology, 60,* 83–96.
Linehan, M. (1993). *Cognitive-Behavioral Treatment of the Borderline Personality Disorder*. New York: Guilford Press.
Maris, S. (1981). *Pathways to Suicide: A Survey of Self-Destructive Behaviors*. Baltimore: Johns Hopkins University Press.
Masterson, J. (1976). *Psychotherapy of the Borderline Adult*. New York: Brunner/Mazel.

Chemically Dependent

Davidson, F. (1978). Suicide and the Abuse of Drugs. *Aspects of Suicide in Modern Civilization* (pp. 220–227). Jerusalem: Academic Press.
Haberman, P. (1979). Cause of Death in Alcoholics. *Proceedings in the 10th Annual Conference for Suicide Prevention* (pp. 108–115). Vienna: International Association for the Prevention of Suicide.
Lester, D. (1988). *The Biochemical Basis of Suicide*. Springfield, IL: Charles C Thomas.
Saxon, S. (1980). Self-Destructive Behavior Patterns in Male and Female Drug Abusers. *American Journal of Drug Abuse, 7*(1), 19–29.
Ward, N. (1980). Factors Associated with Suicide Behavior in Poly Drug Abusers. *Journal of Clinical Psychiatry, 41,* 379–385.

Child

Carlson, G. A., and Cantwell, D. P. (1982). Suicidal Behavior and Depression in Children and Adolescents. *Journal of the American Academy of Child Psychiatry, 21,* 361–368.

Corder, B. F., and Haizlip, T. M. (1983). Recognizing Suicidal Behavior in Children. *Resident and Staff Physician, 29,* 18–23.

Jacobziner, H. (1960). Attempted Suicides in Children. *Journal of Pediatrics, 56,* 519–525.

Pfeffer, C. R. (1981). The Family System of Suicidal Children. *American Journal of Psychotherapy, 35,* 330–341.

Pfeffer, C. R. (1981). Suicidal Behavior of Children: A Review with Implications for Research and Practice. *American Journal of Psychiatry, 138,* 154–159.

Sabbath, J. C. (1969). The Suicidal Adolescent: The Expendable Child. *Journal of the American Academy of Child Psychiatry, 8,* 272–289.

Chronic Medical Illness

Bennett, D. S. (1994). Depression Among Children with Chronic Medical Problems: A Meta-Analysis. *Journal of Pediatric Psychology, 19*(2), 149–169.

Cassem, E. (1990). Depression and Anxiety Secondary to Medical Illness. *The Psychiatric Clinics of North America, 13*(4), 597–612.

Cassem, E. (1995). Depressive Disorders in the Medically Ill: An Overview. *Psychosomatics, 36,* S2–S10.

Maris, R., Berman, A., Maltsberger, J., and Yufit, R. (Eds.). (1992). *Assessment and Prediction of Suicide.* New York: Guilford Press.

College Student

Dean, P. J., and Range, L. M. (1996). The Escape Theory of Suicide and Perfectionism. *Death Studies, 20,* 415–424.

Hewitt, P., and Dyck, D. (1986). Perfectionism, Stress, and Vulnerability to Depression. *Cognitive Therapy and Research, 10,* 137–142.

Hewitt, P. L., and Flett, G. L., (1992). Perfectionism and Suicide Potential. *British Journal of Clinical Psychology, 31,* 181–190.

Rudd, M. D. (1990). An Integrative Model of Suicidal Ideation. *Suicide and Life Threatening Behavior, 20,* 16–31.

Elderly

DeLeo, D., and Diekstra, R. (1990). *Depression and Suicide in Late Life.* Bern: Hogrefe and Huber Publishers.

Miller, M. (1979). *Suicide After Sixty: The Final Alternative.* New York: Springer.

Moore, T., and Tanney, B. (1991). *Suicide in Older Adults: Selected Readings*. Calgary: SEIC Publishing.

Osgood, N. (1985). *Suicide in the Elderly: A Practitioner's Guide to Diagnosis and Mental Health Interventions*. Rockville, MD: Aspen Press.

Gay/Lesbian/Bisexual

Bagley, C., and Tremblay, P. (1997). Suicidal Behavior in Homosexual and Bisexual Males. *Crisis, 18,* 24–34.

Ferguson, D. M., Horwood, J., and Beautrais, A. L. (1999). Is Sexual Orientation Related to Mental Health Problems and Suicidality in Young People? *Archives of General Psychiatry, 56,* 876–880.

Remafedi, G. (1999). Suicide and Sexual Orientation: Nearing the End of Controversy? *Archives of General Psychiatry, 56,* 885–886.

Hispanic Male

Farris, B. E., and Glenn, N. D. (1976). Fatalism and Familism Among Anglos and Mexican-Americans in San Antonio. *Sociology and Social Research, 60,* 393–402.

Hovey, J. D., and King, C. A. (1996). Acculturative Stress, Depression, and Suicidal Ideation Among Immigrant and Second Generation Latino Adolescents. *Journal of the American Academy of Child and Adolescent Psychiatry 35*(9), 1183–1192.

Johnson, G. R., Krug, E. G., and Potter, L. B. (2000). Suicide Among Adolescents and Young Adults: A Cross-National Comparison of 34 Countries. *Suicide and Life-Threatening Behavior, 30,* 74–82.

Smith, J. C., Mercey, J. A., and Warren, C. W. (1985). Comparison of Suicides Among Anglos and Hispanics in Five Southwestern States. *Suicide and Life-Threatening Behavior, 15*(1), 14–26.

Homeless Male

Blumenthal, S. K., and Kupfer, D. (Eds.). (1990). *Suicide Over the Life Cycle: Risk Factors, Assessment, and Treatment of Suicidal Patients*. Washington, DC: American Psychiatric Press.

Caldwell, C., and Gottesman, I. (1989). Schizophrenia: A High-Risk Factor for Suicide—Clues to Risk Reduction. *Suicide and Life-Threatening Behavior, 42,* 479–493.

Isometsa, E. (1996). Suicide Among Subjects with Personality Disorders. *American Journal of Psychiatry, 153,* 667.

Murphy, G., and Wetzel, R. (1992). The Lifetime Risk of Suicide in Alcoholism. *Archives of General Psychiatry, 47,* 383–392.

Incarcerated Male

Bonner, R. L., and Rich, A. R. (1990). Psychosocial Vulnerability, Life Stress, and Suicide Ideation in a Jail Population. *Suicide and Life-Threatening Behavior, 20,* 213–224.

Dear, G. E., Thomson, D. M., Hall, G. J., and Howells, K. (1998). Self-Inflicted Injury and Coping Behaviors in Prison. *Suicide Prevention: The Global Context* (pp. 189–199). New York: Plenum Press.

Liebling, A. (1992). *Suicides in Prison.* London: Routledge.

Yufit, R. I., and Bongar, B. (1992). Suicide, Stress, and Coping with Life Cycle Events. *Assessment and Prediction of Suicide* (pp. 398–419). New York: Guilford Press.

Law Enforcement Officer

Dash, J., and Reiser, M. (1978). Suicide Among Police in Urban Law Enforcement Agencies. *Journal of Police Science and Administration, 3,* 267–273.

Janik, J., and Kravitz, H. (1994). Linking Work and Domestic Problems with Police Suicides. *Suicide and Life Threatening Behavior, 24,* 267–274.

Violanti, J. M. (1995). The Mystery Within: Understanding Police Suicide. *FBI Law Enforcement Bulletin, 2,* 19–23.

Violanti, J. M. (1996). *Police Suicide: Epidemic in Blue.* Springfield, IL: Thomas Books.

Pathological Gambler

Frank, M. L., Lester, D., and Wexler, A. (1991). Suicidal Behavior Among Members of Gambler's Anonymous. *Journal of Gambling Studies, 7,* 249–254.

Newman, S. C., and Thompson, A. H. (2003). A Population-Based Study of the Association between Pathological Gambling and Attempted Suicide. *Suicide and Life-Threatening Behavior, 33,* 80–87.

Phillips, D. P., Welty, W. R., and Smith, M. M. (1997). Elevated Suicide Levels Associated with Legalized Gambling. *Suicide and Life-Threatening Behavior, 27,* 373–378.

Physician

Ross, K. D., and Rosow, I. (1973). Physicians Who Kill Themselves. *Archives of General Psychiatry, 29,* 800–805.

Simpson, L. A., and Grant, L. (1991). Sources and Magnitude of Job Stress Among Physicians. *Journal of Behavioral Medicine, 14*(1), 27–42.

Vaillant, G. E., Sobowale, N. C., and McArthur, C. (1972). Some Psychological Vulnerabilities of Physicians. *New England Journal of Medicine, 287,* 372–375.

Wilhelm, K., Diamond, M., and Williams, A. (1997). Prevention and Treatment of Impairment in Doctors. *Advances in Psychiatric Treatment, 3,* 267–274.

Psychiatric Inpatient

Goldacre, M., Seagroatt, V., and Hawton, K. (1993). Suicide After Discharge from Psychiatric Inpatient Care. *Lancet, 342,* 283–286.

Lewis, G., Hawton, K., and Jones, P. (1997). Strategies for Preventing Suicide. *British Journal of Psychiatry, 171,* 351–354.

Roy, A. (1982). Risk Factors for Suicide in Psychiatric Patients. *Archives of General Psychiatry, 39,* 1089–1095.

Pokorny, A. D. (1983). Prediction of Suicide in Psychiatric Patients. *Archives of General Psychiatry, 40,* 249–257.

Schizophrenic

Jacobs, D. G. (1999). *Guide to Suicide Assessment and Intervention.* San Francisco: Jossey-Bass.

Rudd, M. D. (2001). *Treating Suicidal Behavior.* New York: Guilford Press.

Shneidman, E. (1993). *Suicide as Psychache: A Clinical Approach to Self-Destructive Behavior.* Northvale, NJ: Jason Aronson.

Shneidman, E. (1996). *The Suicidal Mind.* New York: Oxford University Press.

Suicide/Homicide Populations

Allen, N. H. (1983). Homicide Followed by Suicide. *Suicide and Life Threatening Behavior 13,* 155–165.

Berman, A. L. (1979). Dyadic Death: Murder-Suicide. *Suicide and Life-Threatening Behavior, 9,* 15–23.

Cooper, M., and Eaves, D. (1996). Suicide Following Homicide in the Family. *Violence and Victims, 11,* 99–112.

Santoro, J. P., Dawood, A. W., and Ayral, G. (1989). The Murder-Suicide: A Study of Postaggressional Suicide. *The American Journal of Forensic Medicine and Pathology, 6,* 222–225.

Suicide Survivor

Calhoun, L. G., and Allen, B. G. (1991). Social Reactions to the Survivor of a Suicide in the Family: A Review of the Literature. *Omega, 32,* 95–107.

Clark, S., and Goldney, R. D. (1995). Grief Reactions and Recovery in a Support Group for People Bereaved by Suicide. *Crisis, 16,* 27–33.

Hauser, M. J. (1987). Special Aspects of Grief after a Suicide. *Suicide and Its Aftermath: Understanding and Counseling the Survivors* (pp. 57–72). New York: W.W. Norton & Company.

Kniepper, A. (1999). The Suicide Survivor's Grief and Recovery. *Suicide and Life-Threatening Behavior, 29,* 353–364.

ASSAULTIVE/HOMICIDAL POPULATIONS

Assaultive/Homicidal Male

Brizer, D., and Crowner, M. (1989). *Current Approaches to the Prediction of Violence.* Washington, DC: American Psychiatric Press.

Durie, F., and Foust, C. (1987). *The Prediction of Violence.* Springfield, IL: Charles C Thomas.

Howells, K., and Hollin, C. (1989). *Clinical Approaches to Violence.* New York: John Wiley & Sons.

Reiss, A., and Roth, J. (1993). *Understanding and Preventing Violence.* Washington, DC: National Academy Press.

Homicidal/Suicidal Adult Male

Allen, N. H. (1983). Homicide Followed by Suicide. *Suicide and Life Threatening Behavior 13,* 155–165.

Rosenbaum, M. (1990). The Role of Depression in Couples Involved in Murder-Suicide and Homicide. *American Journal of Psychiatry, 147,* 1036–1039.

Stack, S. (1997). Homicide Followed by Suicide: An Analysis of Chicago Data. *Criminology, 35,* 435–453.

West, D. J. (1966). *Murder Followed by Suicide.* Cambridge, MA: Harvard University Press.

Appendix C

INDEX OF *DSM-IV-TR* CODES ASSOCIATED WITH PRESENTING PROBLEMS

Major Depressive Disorder, Single Episode, Severe 296.23
Elderly
Gay/Lesbian/Bisexual

Major Depressive Disorder, Single Episode, Severe with Psychotic Features 296.24
Homicidal/Suicidal Male

Major Depressive Disorder, Recurrent 296.3x
African American Male
Caucasian Female—Adolescent
Caucasian Male—Adolescent
Chemically Dependent
Homeless Male
Psychiatric Inpatient
Suicide Survivor

Major Depressive Disorder, Recurrent, Severe, with Psychotic Features 296.34
Caucasian Male—Adolescent
Homeless Male
Homicidal/Suicidal Male
Psychiatric Inpatient
Schizophrenic
Suicidal/Homicidal Populations

Mood Disorder NOS 296.90
Caucasian Male—Adult
College Student
Elderly
Gay/Lesbian/Bisexual
Incarcerated Male
Physician
Suicidal/Homicidal Populations

Mood Disorder Due to . . . [Indicate the General Medical Illness] 293.83
Suicidal/Homicidal Populations

Narcissistic Personality Disorder 301.81
Assaultive/Homicidal Male
Borderline Personality Disorder
Caucasian Male—Adult
Chemically Dependent
Elderly

Homicidal/Suicidal Male
Psychiatric Inpatient
Suicidal/Homicidal Populations

Nightmare Disorder 307.47
Child

No Diagnosis or Illness V71.09
Caucasian Male—Adolescent

Noncompliance with Treatment V15.81
Homeless Male

Obsessive-Compulsive Disorder 300.3
Assaultive/Homicidal Male
Elderly
Homicidal/Suicidal Male
Pathological Gambler
Physician
Suicidal/Homicidal Populations

Obsessive-Compulsive Personality Disorder 301.4
Caucasian Male—Adult
College Student
Elderly
Pathological Gambler

Occupational Problem V62.2
Hispanic Male
Law Enforcement Officer
Native American Male
Physician

Opioid Abuse 305.50
Chemically Dependent

Opioid Dependence 304.0
Chemically Dependent

Oppositional Defiant Disorder 313.81
Child

Pain Disorder Associated with Psychological Factors 307.80
Elderly

Schizophrenia, Catatonic Type   295.20
  Schizophrenic

Schizophrenia, Disorganized Type   295.10
  Homeless Male
  Schizophrenic

Schizophrenia, Paranoid Type   295.30
  Assaultive/Homicidal Male
  Homeless Male
  Homicidal/Suicidal Male
  Psychiatric Inpatient
  Schizophrenic

Schizophrenia, Residual Type   295.60
  Homeless Male
  Schizophrenic

Schizophrenia, Undifferentiated Type   295.90
  Homeless Male
  Schizophrenic

Schizoid Personality, Disorder   301.20
  Homeless Male
  Schizophrenic

Sedative, Hypnotic, or Anxioltyic Abuse   305.40
  Chemically Dependent

Sedative, Hypnotic. or Anxioltyic Dependence   304.10
  Chemically Dependent

Separation Anxiety Disorder   309.21
  Caucasian Female—Adolescent
  Caucasian Female—Adult
  Child

Sexual Abuse of Child (Victim)   995.53
  Child

Social Phobia   300.23
  Child

Somatization Disorder   300.81
  College Student
  Elderly

Tourette's Disorder   307.23
  Caucasian Male—Adolescent